THE VALUE OF ACADEMIC LIBRARIES

A Comprehensive Research Review and Report

Prepared by Dr. Megan Oakleaf, Syracuse University
for the Association of College and Research Libraries

Value of Academic Libraries: A Comprehensive Research Review and Report

Megan Oakleaf for the Association of College and Research Libraries (ACRL)

ISBN: 978-0-8389-8568-7

September 2010

Association of College and Research Libraries
A Division of the American Library Association
50 E. Huron St.
Chicago, IL 60611

Citation:
Association of College and Research Libraries. *Value of Academic Libraries: A Comprehensive Research Review and Report*. Researched by Megan Oakleaf. Chicago: Association of College and Research Libraries, 2010.

Published online at www.acrl.ala.org/value

Value of Academic Libraries:
A Comprehensive Research Review and Report

Prepared by Megan Oakleaf
for the Association of College and Research Libraries

Advisory Committee: Debra Gilchrist, Bruce Kingma, Martha Kyrillidou, George Kuh
Assistant Researchers: Patricia L. Owen, Leah Sopchak, Anna Dahlstein, Tamika Barnes

Table of Contents

Librarians are increasingly called upon to document and articulate the value of academic and research libraries and their contribution to institutional mission and goals. ACRL's Value of Academic Libraries Initiative responds to these demands and positions academic librarians as contributors to campus conversations on accountability and impact. Quality of higher education continues to be a focus for national debate. For example, in early September *The Chronicle of Higher Education* launched a series, called the "Measuring Stick," to explore the quality of higher education; in it the editors "hope to foster a conversation about how to assess colleges' quality—and how not to." Clearly calls for accountability will continue to influence the landscape of higher education. To understand ACRL's stake in this conversation, we start by looking at this issue in the higher education perspective. We will then share with you ACRL's plans to help librarians address the many questions about value and accountability.

The National Conversation on Assessment, Accountability, and Value
Since the 1970s, higher education has adopted an increasingly managerial orientation in response to external calls for accountability. In 2006, under the Bush administration, the focus of the Spellings commission sent a strong message to higher education that the sector was being scrutinized. Some in academia feared that standards-based education reform similar to the K-12 No Child Left Behind Act would be legislated for higher education. While many had hoped this climate would change under the Obama administration, four years later the pressure on higher education remains steady (Lederman, 2010a). Government interest in the effectiveness of higher education seems to be increasing as the role of knowledge workers becomes more valuable in contributing to economic growth and national competitiveness. If policymakers in the United States emulate the Bologna process, with student learning as the primary measure of quality, it is likely that government regulation and calls for accountability will only increase (Lederman, 2010b).

Like any issue of national importance, there are a variety of perspectives through which higher education assessment, accountability, and value can be viewed. Many assessment measures central to the accountability movement have been imported from the private sector and some in the academy feel that they do not work well with the mission of higher education and academic libraries. Attempting to transfer corporate management theory to colleges and universities (such as TQM, benchmarking, balanced scorecard, management for results, and other techniques adopted from business) could readily offend some in a collegial culture who may meet them with profound skepticism and even hostility (Bergquist and Pawlak, 2008). While profit is a measurement one can quantify, understanding student learning, faculty scholarly work, and institutional quality require a much more nuanced approach, as some aspects may be ineffable.

Those critical of the assessment movement say there is danger in adopting marketplace standards, rather than intellectual standards. Some point to the homogenizing effects of speedy and clear-cut measures of performance, believing it need not be inevitable that higher education adopt these corporate values and practices (Currie and Newson,

1998). Some go so far as to advocate that academics not even engage in designing appropriate performance indicators, as that would be tacit endorsement, but instead use their analytical and rhetorical skills to create counter narratives to these calls for accountability or call for alternative approaches to demonstrating value (Polster and Newson, 1998).

While we appreciate this critical perspective, such an approach seems impractical, given the realities we face today in our institutions. Moreover, we believe that, for libraries and the institutions they serve, setting high standards and seeking to attain them is not the same as standardization. As an association representing multiple types of academic libraries, ACRL recognizes individual institutions have defined their values, and they must set goals, define outcomes, and assess them as is appropriate for local contexts.

Other scholars point to the internal paradox between assessment to improve academic programs and assessment for external audiences designed to answer calls for accountability from policymakers and the public. Assessing for internal improvement depends on local context, while assessing to meet an external perspective focuses on facts that are standardized and can be compared across institutions. Both have value, but conflating them leads to unintended consequences and perverse incentives (Borden, 2010). Such scholars would say that policymakers seeking unambiguous, concise, and quick accountability measures should refrain from an excessive focus on state guidelines to assess student learning; instead they should delegate that hard work to the campuses, as it is already a faculty priority (Shulock, 2003).

The "twin pillars" of twentieth-century higher education—collegial culture on the one hand and managerial culture on the other (Bergquist and Pawlak, 2008)—influence the ways academic librarians approach their work. Librarians seek to protect the life of the mind and defend knowledge for knowledge's sake. At the same time, we strive to create effective and efficient operations that are responsive to the needs of our faculty and students.

While we are aware of these larger national conversations swirling through the higher education and public policy sectors, this report is not intended to take sides in such debates. Consequently, this report takes a pragmatic approach; it lays out multiple assessment perspectives and invites librarians to adapt them to their local circumstances. In the face of the evidence we see in today's external policy and funding climate, we believe academic libraries, and the colleges and universities they serve, are now and will continue to be compelled to participate in these conversations and find appropriate ways to show their value.

ACRL's Intention in Issuing this Report

Increasing recognition of the value of libraries and librarians by leaders in higher education, information technology, funding agencies, and campus decision making is one of ACRL's six strategic priorities. ACRL has been listening to this national conversation on assessment, accountability, and value. Recognizing the sense of urgency around this issue, ACRL created the Value of Academic Libraries Initiative to help academic librarians participate in the conversation and to identify resources to support them in demonstrating the value of academic libraries in clear, measurable ways.

ACRL has long been interested in accountability and assessment. In the early 1980s, ACRL created an Ad Hoc Committee on Performance Measures that issued an RFP and selected Dr. Nancy Van House to develop a manual on assessment. ACRL sought to "stimulate librarians' interest in performance measures and to provide practical assistance so that librarians could conduct meaningful measurements of effectiveness with minimum expense and difficulty." While the resulting *Measuring Academic Library Performance: A Practical Approach* developed measures designed primarily for "internal library decision-making, performance assessment, and resource allocation [–] a secondary purpose is to demonstrate library performance in a meaningful way to university and other parent organizations."

So with this long-held interest in performance assessment, and the discussions in the current environment, the ACRL Board in spring 2009 created a working group to consider an initiative on the value of academic libraries. This group explored several possible paths forward and convened an invitational meeting of subject experts in July 2009. Based on the recommendations of that group, ACRL determined it had a vital role developing research that will support advocacy efforts for libraries with decision-makers and funders in higher education. ACRL's first step was to issue a request for proposal for a comprehensive review of the quantitative and qualitative literature, methodologies, and best practices currently in place for demonstrating the value of academic libraries. Subsequently, we selected Dr. Megan Oakleaf to carry out this work. We are pleased now to offer her report. We believe it will empower academic libraries and influence the association going forward.

What ACRL Plans to Do Next
As part of the ACRL initiative on the value of academic libraries, we look forward to the upcoming release of the toolkit, developed by the ACRL Assessment Committee, to provide academic librarians with tools and examples they can emulate. We will begin creating more professional development opportunities so that academic librarians can develop the assessment and research skills needed. We will look at securing funds to help further the research agenda within this report and will seek out partners as appropriate.

How We Hope You Use the Report
We encourage you to use this document to start a conversation with your chief academic officer, provost, president, or your library's advisory committee. At our request, Dr. Oakleaf wrote the executive summary with an external audience in mind. It is, we hope, a document that can stand alone, so that you can share it with administrators on campus in order to promote dialogue on the value of the academic library in higher education.

We hope that LIS researchers and practicing librarians alike will find that the research agenda (pg. 102-140) provides fodder for thought as you plan your next research projects.

We see this report as a starting point to assist you in thinking about what kind of evidence would help you tell the story of your library and how best to gather that evidence. You will find within it many useful suggestions as you consider how you can gather data locally in your library.

Mary Ellen K. Davis
ACRL Executive Director
mdavis@ala.org

Lisa Janicke Hinchliffe
ACRL President
Associate Professor
University of Illinois at Urbana-
Champaign
ljanicke@illinois.edu

References

Bergquist, W. H., K. Pawlak, and W. H. Bergquist. *Engaging the Six Cultures of the Academy* (2nd ed.). San Francisco: Jossey-Bass, 2008.

Borden, Victor M. H. "The Accountability/Improvement Paradox." *Inside Higher Ed.* 2010. http://insidehighered.com/layout/set/print/views/2010/04/30/borden.

Currie, J. and J. Newson. *Universities and Globalization: Critical Perspectives.* Thousand Oaks, CA: Sage Publications, 1998.

Lederman, Doug. "No Letup From Washington." *Inside Higher Ed.* 2010. http://www.insidehighered.com/news/2010/04/13/hlc.

Lederman, Doug. "Slipping (Further) Off the Pedestal." *Inside Higher Ed.* 2010. http://www.insidehighered.com/news/2010/02/17/squeeze.

Polster, Claire and Janice Newson. "Don't Count Your Blessings: The Social Accomplishments of Performance Indicators." In *Universities and globalization: Critical perspectives*, by J. Currie and J. Newson, 173-191. Thousand Oaks, CA: Sage Publications, 1998.

Shulock, Nancy. "A Fundamentally New Approach to Accountability: Putting State Policy Issues First." Association for the Study of Higher Education's Forum on Public Policy in Higher Education. 2003. http://www.csus.edu/ihe/PDFs/ASHE%20paper%202003%20FINAL.pdf.

Van House, Nancy A., Beth T. Weil, and Charles R. McClure. *Measuring Academic Library Performance: A Practical Approach.* Chicago: American Library Association, 1990.

Academic libraries have long enjoyed their status as the "heart of the university." However, in recent decades, higher education environments have changed. Government officials see higher education as a national resource. Employers view higher education institutions as producers of a commodity—student learning. Top academic faculty expect higher education institutions to support and promote cutting-edge research. Parents and students expect higher education to enhance students' collegiate experience, as well as propel their career placement and earning potential. Not only do stakeholders count on higher education institutions to achieve these goals, they also require them to *demonstrate evidence* that they have achieved them. The same is true for academic libraries; they too can provide evidence of their value. Community college, college, and university librarians no longer can rely on their stakeholders' belief in their importance. Rather, they must demonstrate their value.

Purpose—The following review and report is intended to provide Association of College and Research Libraries (ACRL) leaders and the academic community with 1) a clear view of the current state of the literature on value of libraries within an institutional context, 2) suggestions for immediate "Next Steps" in the demonstration of academic library value, and 3) a "Research Agenda" for articulating academic library value. It strives to help librarians understand, based on professional literature, the current answer to the question, "How does the library advance the missions of the institution?" The report is also of interest to higher educational professionals external to libraries, including senior leaders, administrators, faculty, and student affairs professionals.

Scope—This report is intended to describe the current state of the research on community college, college, and university library value and suggest focus areas for future research. The report emphasizes library value *within the context of overarching institutions*. It has been said, "few libraries exist in a vacuum, accountable only to themselves. There is always a larger context for assessing library quality, that is, what and how well does the library contribute to achieving the overall goals of the parent constituencies?" (Pritchard, Determining Quality in Academic Libraries 1996). In recognition of this fact, this report includes significant research from other library types: school, public, and special (e.g., corporate, medical, law) libraries. The literature of school, public, and special libraries offers examples of numerous library value approaches and lessons learned from each. Academic libraries in universities, colleges, and community colleges would do well to learn from those experiences. Furthermore, because this report is focused on the articulation of library value to external audiences, this report does not emphasize measures of internal library processes such as input and output measures, external perceptions of quality, and satisfaction with library services. Internal, service quality, and satisfaction measures are of great utility to librarians who seek to manage library services and resources, but they may not resonate with institutional leaders as well as outcomes-based approaches.

Next Steps—A selection of recommendations for university, college, and community college librarians who wish to demonstrate value is included below. Additional details are available in the "Next Steps" section of this report.

⇒ **Define outcomes.** Libraries cannot demonstrate institutional value to maximum effect until they define outcomes of institutional relevance and then measure the degree to which they attain them (Kaufman and Watstein 2008, 227). Librarians in universities, colleges, and community colleges can establish, assess, and link academic library outcomes to institutional outcomes related to the following areas: student enrollment, student retention and graduation rates, student success, student achievement, student learning, student engagement, faculty research productivity, faculty teaching, service, and overarching institutional quality.

⇒ **Create or adopt systems for assessment management.** Assessment management systems help higher education educators, including librarians, manage their outcomes, record and maintain data on each outcome, facilitate connections to similar outcomes throughout an institution, and generate reports. Assessment management systems are helpful for documenting progress toward strategic/organizational goals, but their real strength lies in managing learning outcomes assessments. Individual librarians have assessed student learning for decades. However, such assessment efforts are typically "one-shot" and tend to capture limited amounts of information, e.g., only one librarian's class, one group of students, or one assessment method. In contrast, assessment management systems allow multiple librarians to enter assessment data, focus on different student groups (or the same groups over time), and use different assessment methods. Because they aggregate data by outcomes, they generate reports that demonstrate how well the library is achieving its outcomes as well as contributing to the mission of its overarching institution (Oakleaf, Are They Learning? 2011). Ideally, assessment management systems are used by an entire institution, but libraries can take the lead and pioneer their use at individual institutions. These systems can be developed by individual libraries or institutions; several assessment management systems are available for purchase, as well.

⇒ **Determine what libraries enable students, faculty, student affairs professionals, administrators, and staff to do.** Librarians may wish to conduct "help" studies that collect information about the impact libraries have on their target audiences. Librarians can also explore existing products, like MINES for Libraries, that enable libraries to collect information from users (e.g., how they use library resources). Results from these investigations will demonstrate library value and provide essential information for continuing improvements to library services and resources.

⇒ **Develop systems to collect data on individual library user behavior, while maintaining privacy.** In order to determine the impact of library interactions on users, libraries can collect data on how individual users engage with library resources and services. Currently, most libraries do not maintain records on individual users' behavior; consequently, they cannot easily correlate behaviors with the outcomes of those behaviors. For example, they do not track data that would provide evidence that students who engage in more library instruction are more likely to graduate on time, that faculty who use library services are more likely to be tenured, or that student affairs professionals that integrate library services into their work activities are more likely to be promoted. Of course, any such data systems need to protect the privacy of individuals by following appropriate and ethical practices in the maintenance of such records.

⇒ **Record and increase library impact on student enrollment.** Institutions of higher education want to admit the strongest possible students at both the undergraduate and graduate levels. Entering student class characteristics are major predictors of institutional rank, prestige, graduation, alumni donations, and other positive markers. According to the Association of Higher Education Facilities Officers (2006), libraries are an important consideration when students select a university or college, and, as a result, academic libraries can help institutional admissions boost enrollment (Simmel 2007, 88). Specifically, the library ranked second in terms of facilities important in the selection decision process; only facilities for students' majors ranked higher. Libraries were ranked ahead of technology facilities, the student union center, and even recreational facilities (Michigan Academic Library Council 2007, 2). It is clear that libraries can help their institutions attract the best possible prospective students, as well as matriculate the best possible admitted students, in a variety of ways depending on the institution type, size, profile, etc. Typically, librarians take part in campus-wide recruiting and orientation efforts. In the future, libraries can play a more prominent role in reaching key prospective student groups and communicating the ways in which librarians can help students attain academic success. One can imagine assigning incoming students to librarians as "research advisors" and envision librarians innovating ways to provide just-in-time and just-for-you assistance based on students' enrollment records or individual characteristics. Ideally, librarians will send individual students instructional content relevant to their newly assigned projects proactively, rather than waiting passively to be asked to help (Eisenberg 2010; Shupe 2007, 53). Such service could target both students of great need and of great potential.

⇒ **Link libraries to improved student retention and graduation rates.** Most retention and graduation rate studies have focused on explanations for student persistence or departure, either due to personal characteristics or institutional practices (Bailey 2006, 10). Because most librarians are not in positions that enable them to influence students' personal traits, they should focus on creating institutional environments that foster retention and eventual graduation. To this end, librarians can integrate library services and resources into high-impact educational practices (Kuh, High-Impact Educational Practices 2008) and embrace "proactive early warning and intervention strategies for students with academic deficiencies" (Ewell and Wellman 2007, 9). High-impact practices include: first-year seminars and experiences, common intellectual experiences, learning communities, writing-intensive courses, collaborative assignments and projects, undergraduate research, diversity/global learning, service learning/community-based learning, internships, capstone courses and projects (Kuh, High-Impact Educational Practices 2008, 9-11). Note: In many cases, data exists that can link libraries to retention and graduation rates, but these correlations are not easily investigated. For example, National Center for Educational Statistics (NCES) institutional data and academic library data are currently maintained in different databases with separate searching capabilities. However, combining the Academic Libraries Survey with Integrated Postsecondary Educational Data System (IPEDS) information can facilitate meaningful exploration of connections between community college, college, and university libraries and institutional outcomes. When examining IPEDS data, librarians can begin by investigating retention, graduation, completion, and transfer rates. Librarians can also investigate the utility of similar data in the National Student Clearinghouse (NSC). Integrating library data with institutional data is critical; without joined data, joint analysis is difficult.

⇒ **Enhance library contribution to student job success.** Libraries support students' ability to do well in internships, secure job placements, earn salaries, gain acceptance to graduate/professional schools, and obtain marketable skills. Although it may be difficult to make direct and clear connections between academic libraries and students' educational and professional futures, these outcomes are of critical importance to institutions and their stakeholders. Consequently, librarians can investigate the linkages between academic libraries and student job success, and—if no linkages currently exist—librarians can form them. For example, many institutions place emphasis on students' job placements immediately after college and most invite employers to campus to interview students. Librarians can help students prepare for these interviews by sharing resources, such as company profiles, market analyses, etc., with career resources units on campus and with students directly.

⇒ **Track library influences on increased student achievement.** Libraries support student achievement in the form of GPA and professional/educational test scores. In order to demonstrate this impact, librarians can investigate correlations between student library interactions and their GPA well as conduct test item audits of major professional/educational tests to determine correlations between library services or resources and specific test items.

⇒ **Demonstrate and develop library impact on student learning.** Although librarians have long taught and assessed information literacy, most of the published evidence of the impact of libraries on student learning is sporadic, disconnected, and focused on limited case studies. To effectively establish the role of libraries in student learning, systematic, coherent, and connected evidence is required. The best learning assessments are authentic, integrated, performance assessments focused on campus learning outcomes including information literacy. Capturing such assessments in assessment management systems provides the structure critical to establishing a clear picture of academic library contributions to student learning.

⇒ **Review course content, readings, reserves, and assignments.** Librarians can use course information to identify students who have had substantial library exposure and compare them to those who have not; track the integration of library resources into the teaching and learning processes of their institution; and answer questions such as: What percent of readings used in courses or co-curricular activities are available and accessed through the library? How much do these materials save students? What contributions do they make to student learning? How many assignments do students complete that require use of information skills? What do library services and resources enable students to do or do better? Are faculty assessing these skills in their own ways, and if so, what have they learned about student skill levels?

⇒ **Document and augment library advancement of student experiences, attitudes, and perceptions of quality.** National student experience studies tend to focus on the entire student experience and often do not include questions directly related to libraries. However, there are questions that are at least tangentially related to information behaviors, and these questions may reveal information about the impact of the community college, college, or university library on student experiences. In addition, librarians can continue to work to develop library-related questions for these national surveys as well as local institutional surveys, especially those aimed at seniors and alumni.

⇒ **Track and increase library contributions to faculty research productivity.** Librarians contribute to faculty research productivity in a number of ways. To some degree, librarians have investigated the impact of library resources on faculty productivity, but librarians can explore the linkages between library services and faculty research productivity. How do librarians serve faculty who are preparing publications, presentations, or patent applications? How do librarians help faculty prepare their tenure and promotion packages? Fortunately, surrogates for faculty research productivity are well established; the challenge for librarians is to collect data on those surrogates for individual faculty and correlate them to faculty behavior and library characteristics.

⇒ **Continue to investigate library impact on faculty grant proposals and funding, a means of generating institutional income.** Librarians contribute to faculty grant proposals in a number of ways. Recent studies have documented the contribution of library resources to citations in grant applications (P. T. Kaufman, Library as Strategic Investment 2008). In addition, academic librarians can investigate other ways in which libraries contribute to the preparation of grant proposals, both funded and unfunded.

⇒ **Demonstrate and improve library support of faculty teaching.** Librarians contribute to faculty teaching in a variety of ways. Librarians provide guest lectures, online tutorials, and LibGuides. They integrate library resources into course materials on a massive scale. They collaborate with faculty on curriculum, assignment, and assessment design. They also provide resources that cover the scholarship of teaching and learning; some libraries also partner in campus-wide teaching and learning support centers. Librarians clearly support teaching; now librarians can also collect the data and communicate the value of that support.

⇒ **Record library contributions to overall institutional reputation and prestige.** Academic libraries can augment their institution's reputation and prestige in four ways. First, they can help department chairs to recruit faculty (Simmel 2007, 88) or retain them (Tenopir, Investment in the Library: What's the Return? 2010). Traditionally, libraries contribute to faculty recruitment by building collections that support faculty activities. In the future, librarians have opportunities to be more proactive in this area, by actively engaging in dialogue with "star" faculty recruits prior to their hiring. Second, strong libraries, especially those that win awards or other distinctions, may also impact their institutional rank by bringing attention to the institution and therefore potentially influencing the peer assessments that make up a large portion of well-known ranking entities. Third, library special collections can bring significant prestige to their institutions (Webster and Flowers 2009, 306). Finally, library services and resources support institutional engagement in service to their communities locally, nationally, and globally, thus contributing to their institution's reputation and prestige through service.

⇒ **Participate in higher education assessment initiatives.** Librarians can familiarize themselves with national movements such as the Voluntary System of Accountability (VSA), the Voluntary Framework of Accountability (VFA), the University and College Accountability Network (U-CAN), and the National Institute for Learning Outcomes Assessment (NILOA), as well as international efforts such as Assessment of Higher Education Learning Outcomes (AHELO). They can participate in these activities whenever possible; for example, they might participate in the Rubric Assessment of Information Literacy Skills (RAILS) project, funded by the Institute of Museum and Library Services (IMLS), which seeks to integrate the new Association of American Colleges and Universities (AAC&U) Valid Assessment of Learning in Undergraduate Education (VALUE) information literacy rubric into their institutional assessment processes. Librarians can also be involved in Tuning USA's effort to develop common postsecondary learning standards in disciplinary areas; they can be aware of the new national "College and Career Readiness" standards, as well.

⇒ **Engage in higher education accreditation processes.** Librarians can prepare for and participate in institutional accreditation efforts in their own institutions. They may also engage in accreditation processes at a higher level, perhaps working to increase the integration of information literacy concepts into regional accreditation guidelines (Gratch-Lindauer, Comparing the Regional Accreditation Standards 2001; Rader 2004).

⇒ **Appoint liaison librarians to support senior institutional leadership and/or offices of assessment or institutional research.** Providing top-notch information services to key decision makers can help overarching institutions achieve a culture of assessment and evidence.

⇒ **Create library assessment plans.** Librarians can develop detailed plans that organize assessment efforts, keep them on track, and record assessment results and lessons learned. These assessment plans can be integrated into library budget, strategic planning, and reward systems.

⇒ **Promote and participate in professional development.** Librarians learning to demonstrate their value require training and support to acquire new skills (Oakleaf, Are They Learning? 2011). Their attendance at existing assessment professional development opportunities, such as the Association of Research Libraries (ARL) Library Assessment Conference, the ACRL Assessment Immersion program, the Indiana University-Purdue University Indianapolis (IUPUI) Assessment Institute, or other higher education assessment venues, can be encouraged and supported. In some cases, inviting consultants, participating in webinars, and establishing assessment resource collections are required to update librarian skills.

⇒ **Mobilize library administrators.** Library administrators can help their libraries demonstrate value by taking a number of actions: communicating assessment needs and results to library stakeholders; using evidence-based decision making; creating confidence in library assessment efforts; dedicating assessment personnel and training (Blankenship 2008, 321-322); fostering environments that encourage creativity and risk taking (Stoffle, Guskin and Boisse 1984, 9); integrating library assessment within library planning, budget (Hoyt 2009, 10), and reward structures (Dow 1998, 279); and ensuring that assessment efforts have requisite resources.

⇒ **Leverage library professional associations.** Major library professional associations can play a crucial organizing role in the effort to demonstrate library value. First, they can create online support resources and communities to serve as a nexus of value demonstration activities. Second, they can serve a "pulse taking" role, learning how member libraries are showing value and communicating this information to the membership. Third, they can orchestrate an "all hands on deck" approach to assessment, helping librarians determine which part of the Research Agenda might be best suited to their institutions and ensuring that the agenda is covered. Fourth, they can encourage library-centric publications and conferences to index their work in library and education literature databases. Finally, they can identify expert researchers and grant-funding opportunities that can partner with librarians to take on the most challenging aspects of the Research Agenda.

Research Agenda—The Research Agenda lays out 10 specific areas of library value within the context of an institutional mission and/or outcomes: student enrollment, student retention and graduation, student success, student achievement, student learning, student experience, faculty research productivity, faculty grants, faculty teaching, and institutional reputation. For each area of library value, the Research Agenda also identifies potential surrogates (see Figure 1) as well as potential areas of correlation.

For example, student enrollment is one area of institutional value. Surrogates for library impact on student enrollment include the recruitment of prospective students, matriculation of admitted students, and willingness of current students to recommend the institution to others. In other words, libraries can demonstrate their value by providing evidence that they play a role in student recruitment, matriculation, and willingness to recommend. They can do that by participating in prospective student events or new student orientation, assigning librarians as student advisors, or offering services that positively impact student judgments of institutional quality. These surrogates may be correlated to library services and resources in other ways; potential correlations are listed in the Research Agenda section of this report.

Just as there are no "quick fixes" to the problem of demonstrating the value of higher education, there are no simple solutions to the challenge of articulating academic library value. A fact well known in higher education is that "the more valuable evaluative data is, the harder it is to arrive at them" (Gorman 2009, 3). However, there are a number of steps librarians can take to move forward in the effort. Academic librarians at universities, colleges, and community colleges all can take part in the quest to document the existing value of libraries and maximize their value in future years.

Student Enrollment
- Recruitment of prospective students
- Matriculation of admitted students
- Recommendation of current students

Student Retention & Graduation
- Fall-to-fall retention
- Graduation rates

Student Success
- Internship success
- Job placement
- Job salaries
- Professional/graduate school acceptance
- Marketable skills

Student Achievement
- GPA
- Professional/educational test scores

Student Learning
- Learning assessments
- Faculty judgments

Student Experience, Attitude, & Perception of Quality
- Self-report engagement studies
- Senior/alumni studies
- Help surveys
- Alumni donations

Faculty Research Productivity
- Number of publications, number of patents, value of technology transfer
- Tenure/promotion judgments

Faculty Grants
- Number of grant proposals (funded or unfunded)
- Value of grants funded

Faculty Teaching
- Integration of library resources and services into course syllabi, websites, lectures, labs, texts, reserve readings, etc.
- Faculty/librarian collaborations; cooperative curriculum, assignment, or assessment design

Institutional Reputation & Prestige
- Faculty recruitment
- Institutional rankings
- Community engagement

Figure 1. Areas of Library Value and Potential Surrogates

Value can be defined in a variety of ways and viewed from numerous perspectives (Zeithaml 1988), including use, return-on-investment, commodity production, impact, and alternative comparison.

Internal Focus

Use or utility is one popular way of defining value (Näslund, Olsson and Karlsson 2006, 302), especially from an efficiency-based perspective (Sánchez and Pérez Pérez 2001). Many library statistics, especially inputs and outputs, equate use with value, suggesting that the more books circulated or the more instruction sessions offered, the better the library. Certainly such statistics are helpful to library service and resource managers. However, use-based definitions of value are not compelling to many institutional decision makers and external stakeholders. Furthermore, use is not meaningful, unless that use can be connected to institutional outcomes (e.g., student learning and faculty productivity).

Another common definition of value, sometimes termed financial value, cost/benefit analysis, **return-on-investment**, or value for money, is based upon the following formula:

$$Library\ value = \frac{perceived\ benefits}{perceived\ costs}$$

To library users and stakeholders, perceived costs include price, time, and effort (Day 1994). Many librarians struggle to both deliver benefits to users and reduce costs associated with library services and resources (Dumond 2000). One method for examining this definition of value is to determine "purchase" or "exchange" value, that is, what a user is willing to pay for library services and resources in money, time, or effort (Machlup 1993). Return-on-investment works well in many environments, but can be difficult to use in academia. For example, return-on-investment usually captures the most that users are prepared to pay. This is further complicated by three factors: what individuals are willing to pay depends on their ability to pay (Whitehall 1995, 8), users will pay more of other people's money than their own (in one academic library study faculty were willing to pay six times as much with departmental funds than with their own) (Hawgood and Morley 1969), and students tend to undervalue immaterial goods (like information) as compared to material goods (Sakalaki and Kazi 2007, 324). Another method asks users to estimate an "alternative cost" or the price they would have to pay if the library ceased to exist (Whitehall 1995, 8). However, this method does not capture users who would not pursue their own information needs (Whitehall 1995, 8). Still more methods elicit how much time users spend or save using library services and resources. Typically, time spent or saved is translated into financial terms using user salaries, but this type of calculation does not fit student users (Whitehall 1995, 8; Poll and Payne, Impact Measures 2006, 554). Even contingent valuation methods are difficult to deploy in academic environments because "most library services have no equivalent on the common market and therefore no 'market prices' can be determined" (Poll and Payne, Impact Measures 2006, 554). Thus contingent valuation asks users "to financially rate services or institutions that they never thought of in terms of money" (Poll and Payne, Impact Measures 2006, 555).

Aside from methodological issues, some authors warn that financial values do not mesh easily with the values of higher education (Town, Value and Impact 2010). According to Lutz and Field, "the major purpose of the university is not profit, except in the ultimate sense of society profit. Success of universities should not be measured in dollars and cents" (1998, 416). Lewin states that the public believes that colleges act like businesses, "concerned more with their bottom line than with the educational experiences of students" (Lewin 2010). According to Streatfield, viewing library value through a financial lens can stifle creativity (attributed by Everest and Payne 2001) and is often perceived as "retrospective" in that it "looks back to what has already been done…is managerial rather than academic…is despite the rhetoric not functionally concerned with the quality of teaching and learning…but with…coming to some kind of a costs/benefits decision" (Biggs 2001, 222). Still, despite these concerns, few authors would disagree that libraries must demonstrate that they use financial resources effectively and responsibly (Matthews, Determining and Communicating 2003).

Value can also be defined as the **production of a commodity**. In higher education, the production of commodities can be calculated using the formula below (Kelly, McNicholl and McLellan, Towards the Estimation 2005, 27):

$$value = quantity\ of\ commodity\ produced \times price\ per\ unit\ of\ commodity$$

The "use," "return-on-investment," and "commodity production" definitions are traditional approaches to value creation. In these approaches, the emphasis is on value suppliers first, and how users perceive the value second (Gronroos 2000; Ulaga and Chacour 2001). In this way, these definitions can be perceived as "introspective" (Näslund, Olsson and Karlsson 2006, 302-303).

External Focus

Other definitions of value are based on the idea that value suppliers have to collaborate with their users to create value (Woodruff 1997; Chernatony, Harris and Dall'Olmo Riley 2000; Dumond 2000; Huber, Herrmann and Morgan 2001). For example, a fourth definition of value focuses on **library impact** on users. It asks, "What is the library trying to achieve? How can librarians tell if they have made a difference?" In universities, colleges, and community colleges, libraries impact learning, teaching, research, and service. A main method for measuring impact is to "observe what the [users] are actually doing and what they are producing as a result" (Everest and Payne 2001). However, direct measurement of impact is challenging, and librarians may avoid examining impact, despite a long professional tradition of measurement (Streatfield attributed by Everest and Payne 2001). In fact, one new survey indicates that impact assessment is a field in its infancy for research libraries (Li and Koltay 2010). Instead, librarians can measure surrogates of impact (Brophy attributed by Everest and Payne 2001). According to Everest and Payne (2001):

> Assessing impact is not easy and it is not an exact science. We are dealing with a changing environment where people, services, and needs are constantly evolving. Any research will inevitably provide a snapshot of what is happening at a particular point in time. It is very difficult to prove that the actions taken by library management have led to improvements in learning, teaching, and research. This is particularly the case as we deal with the extent of integration between our resources/services and learning, teaching, and research. As we achieve more integration, it is going to be intrinsically more difficult to identify our specific contribution to students' learning or to the research of a member or staff.

Despite the difficulty of measuring impact directly, this approach to library value is seen as "prospective" and "concerned with assuring that teaching and learning does now, and in the future will continue, to fit the purpose of the institution. It also encourages continuing upgrading and improvement of teaching through quality enhancement" (Biggs 2001, 222).

A fifth definition of value is based on user perceptions of the library in relation to **competing alternatives** (Butz and Goodstein 1996; Woodruff 1997). According to this definition, libraries need to develop bonds with their users and help users achieve their goals so that users perceive libraries to be more valuable than competitors (e.g., Google). A related definition is "desired value" or "what a [user] wants to have happen when interacting with a [library] and/or using a [library's] product or service" (Flint, Woodruff and Fisher Gardial 2002). Both "impact" and "competing alternatives" approaches to value require libraries to gain new understanding of their users' goals as well as the results of their interactions with academic libraries.

Academic Libraries Focus

Of the five ways of defining value, library stakeholders tend to focus on two: financial value and impact value (see Figure 2). To meet the needs of their stakeholders, academic librarians can pursue value studies in both areas. For some academic library stakeholders, financial realities take precedence. They recognize the business-like characteristics of higher education, and view money as the bottom line. They know that institutions that do not attend to their financial situation cannot survive long enough to achieve other goals. For those stakeholders, librarians must demonstrate that academic librarians manage their financial resources well and help bring money into their institutions. These stakeholders are most interested in a financial approach to library value. (Note: A good portion of library literature refers to this aspect as "return-on-investment" which, technically, is a particular form of financial value estimation. Alternatively, some authors refer to the financial aspect generically as "value"; others use more specific terms, usually related to the particular methodology used in a study such as "cost/benefit" or "valuation.")

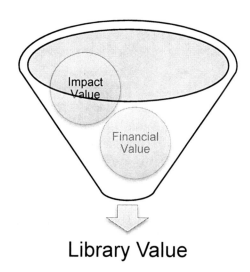

Library Value

Figure 2. Library Value

The other large group of academic library stakeholders focuses on the contribution of higher education to learning, research, and service. For these stakeholders, an impact-focused definition of value is more meaningful. To demonstrate value to these stakeholders, librarians can elicit information from users about what the library enables them to do. This second approach also may be more meaningful to librarians, since they are often less interested in establishing library value and more focused on what library users actually accomplish and how librarians can support their endeavors.

Increasingly, academic library value is linked to service, rather than products (P. T. Kaufman, Carpe Diem 2009, 2). Library literature reveals this shift in library emphasis from collections to experience, from resources to educational impact (Dow 1998, 279), from access to sense-making, from mediation to enabling (Lougee 2009, 612). The change is logical. Because information products are generally produced outside of libraries, library value is increasingly invested in service aspects and librarian expertise. In fact, academic provosts have a future library focus that is "less on the library qua institution and more on the people who work in libraries…less on the library and more on the librarian" (Webster and Flowers 2009, 306).

Thus, service delivery supported by librarian expertise is an important library value. However, librarian expertise alone is not a sufficient demonstration of library value; librarian expertise must be manifested in excellent service that results in a value for users. According to Saracevic and Kantor, this concept of value—one focused on the impact of library service—is known as "value as results" (or "value in use"). The value as results concept equates value with the "subsequent results from the [information] interaction…and their worth or benefits" (1997, 540). This conceptualization of value focuses on how library service helps people change in some way. According to IMLS, "we know this [change] happens; outcome measurement can help us prove it" (Institute of Museum and Library Services n.d., 22). Taking this approach to library value requires academic librarians to consider: 1) What did the user get out of the library service? 2) What did the user accomplish as a result? (Saracevic and Kantor 1997, 540). Whitehall agrees, stating "it is the use to which a piece of information is put which expresses its value" (Whitehall 1995, 8)

In this way, value as results helps academic libraries articulate what one might call library "value on investment" or VOI. Administrators want to know how libraries help, not just "what's the return" (Dukart 2007, 49). One author describes this notion particularly well: "You can spend a lot of time coming up with all kinds of calculations…we can come up with some kind of number….[but] some [value] is much more intangible. What you want is for people to start saying that we are doing this because we believe in the concept, rather than here is mathematically how it is all going to work" (Dukart 2007, 49). This position posits that academic library value is not primarily a financial concept; rather the value of information is its contribution to making improvements in users (Wilson, Stenson and Oppenheim 2000, 3-4).

The major challenge to demonstrating library "value on investment" is that "people have to be able to see clearly that the information that 'caused' benefit came from the service, and not from the client's own work or ideas" (D. J. Urquhart 1976). One fairly simple way to isolate library value is to "collect from individual [library users] specific examples of beneficial information that they know came to them with the aid of your service. They will tell you about the advantage to their work, and you will write it down" (Whitehall 1995, 8). There are numerous other methods to capturing this information; many do not require direct questioning of individual users. The "Next Steps" and "Research Agenda" sections of this report outline some of these methods, informed by the lessons learned by school, public, special, and academic librarians who have contributed their efforts to demonstrate library value to the literature of the profession.

This report was commissioned to provide ACRL leaders and the broader academic community with 1) a view of the current state of the literature on value of libraries within an institutional context, 2) suggestions for immediate "Next Steps" in the demonstration of academic library value, and 3) a "Research Agenda" for articulating academic library value. The report is intended to help librarians understand, based on professional literature, the current answer to the question, "How does the library advance the mission of the institution?"

Readers should note that this report focuses on library value *within the context of overarching institutions*. It does not attempt to address methods for assessing library value within a library context. Therefore, this report does not emphasize measures of internal library processes, such as inputs and outputs. Nor does it focus on satisfaction or and service quality approaches. These measures are of great utility to librarians who seek to manage library services and resources, but they may not resonate with institutional decision makers as well as outcomes-based, mission-focused approaches.

In order to cast a wide net, this report includes significant library value research in academic library literature as well as other library types: school, public, and special. To prepare this report, the author organized a team of researchers with expertise in a variety of library environments. The author and research team identified relevant library value literature, including monographs, scholarly and trade articles, Web sites, statistical sources, data sources, white papers, and gray literature. To identify unpublished efforts to demonstrate library value, the author also engaged in numerous conversations with academic librarians at universities, colleges, and community colleges; librarians in other library environments; and library vendors. The author and research team divided the identified literature by library type and evaluated each item for inclusion in the final report. (Evaluation criteria included: ability to contribute to the documentation of academic library value, depiction of models for best practices in evidence-based librarianship, articulation of library impact of goals of the larger institution, emphasis on student/patron learning or development, and an outcome-based perspective.) In addition, the author identified selected higher education resources in order to provide the desired institutional (rather than library-centric) context. Throughout the entire process, the role of academic libraries in contributing to institutional missions and outcomes was emphasized, in accordance with the goals of the report.

Based on the literature, the author extrapolated recommendations for how academic libraries should move forward in demonstrating their value, identified potential surrogates for library value, and suggested possible areas of correlation to collectable library data. These recommendations, surrogates, and correlations are outlined in the "Next Steps" and "Research Agenda" sections of this report.

Academic Library

It has been said that "there is a paucity of research on the value of academic libraries" (Snelson 2006, 490). That is true; much more investigation of academic library value is merited. However, future research should build on the work of librarians over the last several decades. The following review includes major contributions to the literature of academic library value.

Expectations of Higher Education

Academic librarians, like their colleagues throughout all of higher education, face increased external pressure for accountability, ongoing internal commitments to improvement (Keeling, et al. 2008, 1), and heightened demands for affordable and accessible postsecondary education (Simmons-Welburn, Donovan and Bender 2008, 130). In higher education, these demands have emerged from a variety of forces, including: growing criticisms of higher education, developing government concern, heightened competition among educational institutions, greater consumer savvy, and increased spotlight on rising institutional costs (Michael 2005, 368; Merisotis 2009). In general, higher education administrators have responded to demands for accountability, affordability, and accessibility with attempts to "hold the line" against pressures; they have focused on the production of accountability data rather than engaging in the transformative thinking necessary to improve learning, research, and service in higher education for all stakeholders (Simmons-Welburn, Donovan and Bender 2008, 130), including students, parents, faculty, student affairs professionals, administrators, professional staff, employers, accreditors, secondary schools, legislatures, funders, and donors. According to Guskin and Marcy, "while muddling through problems is a time-honored practice for dealing with recurring fiscal problems in higher education, [it] may actually undermine the nature of the academic profession." Indeed, "modifying or 'patching'" old programs and services often "promotes a false sense of movement and importance, and often costs more in the end" (Guskin and Marcy, Dealing with the Future NOW, 131). In the end, Barnett states, "higher education is being obliged to examine itself or be examined by others" (Improving Higher Education: Total Quality Care 1992, 16). While at first glance these external pressures may seem overwhelming, in fact they offer higher education administrators an exciting opportunity to engage in rigorous self-examination, an examination that can lead to the development of a new concept of higher education—one aligned with current stakeholder expectations.

According to Matarazzo and Prusak (1990), library value should be measured in user terms. Consequently, library value research "needs to address...stakeholders other than librarians" (Association of College and Research Libraries 2000). One stakeholder group not only expects, but demands greater accountability from higher education: state and national government. Government officials consider higher education an economic asset. In an information economy, an economy in which "ideas, and the ability to manipulate them, count for far more than the traditional factors of production—the university has come to look like an increasingly useful asset" (*The Economist* 1997). In fact, an educated workforce is a requirement of future economic growth (Alexander 2000, 412). In contrast, government often sees higher education as unresponsive to these economic demands (Alexander 2000, 414) and in recent years had determined that higher education is "too important to leave to the universities to themselves" (Alexander 2000, 415). Instead, government takes a more "utilitarian" view of higher education. From this viewpoint, "economic values are supreme and the quantification of fiscal resources is the true measure of value" (Alexander 2000, 427). According to the Spellings Commission, government officials need more comprehensive data to determine whether national investments in higher education are paying off (U.S. Department of Education 2006, 14). In response to these expectations, higher education must demonstrate success in economic terms. The government wants results. However, according to Kaufman, academics generally take a "trust us" approach (American Association of State Colleges and Universities 2006, 1) or, if pressed, focus exclusively on "means, resources, and activities," not results (R. Kaufman 2001, 1).

Other stakeholder groups—students, parents, communities, employers, and graduate/professional schools—expect higher education to make impacts in ways that are not primarily financial. They expect faculty to be good teachers and conduct important research. They expect students to engage in learning, gain skills, complete programs, and secure good jobs (Rhodes 2008, 62) or positions in strong graduate/professional programs. Employers in particular expect students to be prepared for the workplace, but only one in four believes that community colleges, colleges, and universities do a "good job" preparing students for the world of work (Hart Research Associates 2010, 1). (Interestingly, three of the areas employer stakeholders ask higher education to emphasize are related to the skills libraries have always taught: critical thinking and analytical thinking skills (81% of employers); ability to analyze and solve complex problems (75%); and ability to locate, organize, and evaluate information from multiple sources (68%) (Hart Research Associates 2010, 2).) Furthermore, these stakeholders expect institutions as whole entities to produce benefits for their communities—locally, nationally, and globally (Rhodes 2008, 62).

Finally, internal stakeholders also have expectations. Individual units within larger institutions need to understand the perceptions and desires of faculty and administrators. For libraries, this means investigating the mindset of colleagues and institutional leaders, knowing what metrics will resonate with them (Pike, Measuring Quality 2004), and taking proactive, rather than defensive approaches to communicating library value (Housewright, Themes of Change 2009, 268).

In sum, government entities, students, parents, communities, employers, graduate/professional schools, institutional faculty, and administrators all have expectations of higher education in general and academic libraries in particular. Librarians can surface and fulfill specific expectations by taking a variety of approaches, such as:

- "Proactively engaging stakeholders…in open communication to discover their definition(s) of success and the specific type(s) of data, evidence, or knowledge needed to determine the definition(s)" (Durrance and Fisher, How Libraries and Librarians Help 2005, 323).
- "Providing all stakeholders with the opportunity to participate in the assessment process" (Durrance and Fisher, How Libraries and Librarians Help 2005, 323).
- "Designing assessment processes that most specifically address and obtain the assessment information required by library leadership and stakeholders" (Durrance and Fisher, How Libraries and Librarians Help 2005, 326).
- "Using assessment practices, methods, and metrics that stakeholders approve of and can easily understand and appreciate" (Durrance and Fisher, How Libraries and Librarians Help 2005, 326).
- "Focusing on the results of assessment and its usage instead of focusing on how the process of assessment works" (Durrance and Fisher, How Libraries and Librarians Help 2005, 326).

Once known, stakeholder expectations can be used to tailor the services and resources that are considered valuable (Matthews, Determining and Communicating 2003), change the types of assessments that are perceived as credible evidence of quality (Upcraft and Schuh 2002, 16), and update traditional conceptions of higher education with a new emphasis on academic library contributions.

Reconceptualizing Academic Libraries

New conceptions of the nature of higher education must be accompanied by new conceptions of academic libraries. Although libraries have enjoyed an emotional "heart of the campus" status (Rothstein 1955) in the past, many individual libraries have not realized their full potential in support of institutional missions (Stoffle, Guskin and Boisse 1984, 3). Traditionally, librarians may have taken a passive role on campus, rather than an active one. This places librarians in a precarious position (Michalko, Malpas and Arcolio 2010), because this passive role leads to institutional administrators viewing libraries as "underutilized, expensive storehouses" and faculty seeing librarians as "keepers of the books" rather than instructional and research partners (Stoffle, Guskin and Boisse 1984, 3). According to Simmons-Welburn, Donovan, and Bender, "the transformed library seeks to fulfill the campus's goals, even endeavors that currently do not involve the library. This represents a significant turn from the time-honored practice of measuring success against peer libraries, in favor of judging ourselves by how libraries help their institutions succeed" (2008, 132). It asks people to move from a "what is" mindset to a "what should/could be" (R. Kaufman 2001, 2)—from a content view to a competency view (K. R. Smith 2007, 32). However, Kaufman asks, "Is there…an alternative to not linking what any organization does…to [the] external value added? Certainly data are not easy to come by, but how long can any culture insist that the absence of data is an excuse for not collecting it when it is vital for decision making? (R. Kaufman 2001, 2). He continues, "Satisfaction with the status quo in terms of the quality of any university is not ethical, responsible, or useful. If we're missing valid and useful data we should be able to make the pragmatic case for collecting and using it" (R. Kaufman 2001, 8), bearing in mind that accountability is not about "proving or justifying" but rather about improving (Keeling, et al. 2008, 28).

Although librarians acknowledge the need to reconceive the notion of academic library value, they might note that no one appears to be asking librarians to develop this new concept (other than fellow librarians). That is true; much of the higher education community views libraries as a support organization alone, rather than an instructional organization (Allen 1992, 63). According to Preer, experts and decision makers have not recognized the contributions libraries make to academia and have not included libraries in their research and reports (2001). Instead, librarians are often quietly omitted from the accountability and assessment conversation—so quietly in fact, that librarians themselves, who are busy with doing what they believe they need to do, sometimes fail to recognize what they are *not* being asked to do. Those who do notice, often engage in "hand-wringing and self-reproaches...[and] the faulting of experts" (Durrance and Fisher, How Libraries and Librarians Help 2005, 4). The unfortunate truth, according to Durrance and Fisher, "is that librarians have failed to explain to those outside the field what contributions they...make" (2005, 4). Like others in higher education, librarians find it hard to "embrace systematic change...[until] the stakes...[are] high enough to make radical reinvention imperative" (Deiss and Petrowski 2009, 3).

Viewed through a more positive lens, the current higher education environment offers librarians an opportunity to accelerate change (Rader 2004, 311). To capitalize on this great opportunity to update their role, librarians can reconceptualize their expertise, skills, and roles in the context of institutional mission, not traditional library functions alone (Simmons-Welburn, Donovan and Bender 2008, 132). They can be guided by the institutional mission, willing to release services or resources that do not contribute to the institutional mission, able to resist temptations to "stray" beyond the mission, and dedicated to assessing themselves according to the mission (Simmons-Welburn, Donovan and Bender 2008, 134). Embracing this transformational change is necessary so libraries can maintain their viability as a centerpiece of their institutions (Simmons-Welburn, Donovan and Bender 2008, 134) and develop an even higher profile (Walter 2000) within the context of institutional missions and outcomes.

Achieving Institutional Missions and Outcomes

Institutions of higher education want to recruit and retain students, faculty, and staff; support teaching and learning that results in high levels of student engagement, graduation rates, test scores, and job placement rates; encourage research of high value, utility, and citation; earn awards, prestige, honors, and grant funding (Poll and Payne, Impact Measures 2006, 550; Bosanquet 2007); and contribute through service to their communities. As an important part of higher education institutions, libraries "do not exist for themselves"; rather they exist to promote institutional missions (Goetsch 2009, 502; Lynch, et al. 2007, 227; L. S. Estabrook 2007). Thus, academic librarians must understand institutional missions and how they contribute to them (Bosanquet

2007); they must also share that information with others by clearly aligning library services and resources to institutional missions. Communicating that alignment is crucial for communicating library value in institutional terms (Bosanquet 2007; McRostie and Ruwoldt 2009, 5; Estabrook 2006).

Because institutional missions vary (Keeling, et al. 2008, 86; Fraser, McClure and Leahy 2002, 512), the methods by which academic libraries contribute value vary as well. According to Rodger, "A library is successful if it serves the needs and priorities of its host institution, whatever those may be" (2009). Consequently, each academic library must determine the unique ways in which they contribute to the mission of their institution and use that information to guide planning and decision making (Hernon and Altman, Assessing Service Quality 1998, 31). For example, the University of Minnesota Libraries has rewritten their mission and vision to increase alignment with their overarching institution's goals and emphasis on strategic engagement (Lougee 2009, 614).

Not only should academic libraries align themselves with the missions of their institutions, they should also allow institutional missions to guide library assessment. According to ACRL (1998), "the purpose of outcomes assessment of academic libraries is to measure their quality and effectiveness…and the contributions they make to accomplishing the purposes of the university or college of which it is a part." Library assessment plans should also reflect an institutional focus and answer questions related to institutional missions (Association of College and Research Libraries 2004), even though "this may require that decisions be made to stop certain types of data collection so that time and resources are available for new data collection. It…means that changes may be needed in the types of questions asked of users and in the unobtrusive ways that computerized systems can document use" (MacEachern 2001). It may also mean expecting librarians to expand their knowledge of strategic positioning and recommit to continuous improvement (Neal 2009). However, using institutionally focused, rather than library-centric, assessments can allow library administrators to demonstrate library value to institutional missions (Neal 2009, 465).

Assessment vs. Research

In community colleges, colleges, and universities, assessment is about defining the purpose of higher education and determining the nature of quality (Astin 1987). Academic libraries serve a number of purposes, often to the point of being overextended. According to Rogers (2009, 550):

> We know that we cannot be all things to all people and that we will have to make some tough choices about whose needs we can and will meet. What will we use to inform those choices about whose needs we can and will meet? What will we use to inform those choices that we know are crucial going forward?… It is clear that we are in desperate need of more hard data.

Through assessment, librarians can gain the hard data they need to make decisions about what purposes they can meet and how well they can meet them. In addition, assessment offers librarians the opportunity to gain the "internal and external credibility that stem[s] from a fundamental organizational transparency that links mission to practice; it sends the powerful message, 'This is who we are; these are the skills and competencies that we strive to instill in students; these programs and efforts are how we do that; and these data illustrate the sum of our efforts'" (Keeling, et al. 2008, 74). Not only does assessment give librarians a venue for communicating with stakeholders, it determines "the fit" between institutional mission and achieved outcomes (Maki, Developing an Assessment Plan 2002, 8), articulates effectiveness, fosters improvement, increases efficiency (Dougherty 2009, 418), and demonstrates accountability. Additionally assessment provides "an opportunity...for organizational reflection, critique, and learning" (Keeling, et al. 2008, 91) and a chance to engage in "institutional curiosity" (Maki, Developing an Assessment Plan 2002, 8). Although assessment is a "process that may or may not give rise to evidence of success" (Streatfield and Markless, What is Impact Assessment 2009, 140), assessment also gives librarians the "hard numbers and accurate intel" necessary to advocate for greater resource allocations (Rogers 2009, 550) or to facilitate improvement (Dow 1998, 279; Saunders, Regional Accreditation 2007, 325). And, as Kassel states, assessment is the next step "in the evolution of information professionalism" (Kassel 2002).

Some librarians have the resources to conduct rigorous research. In contrast, librarians who operate without the benefit of these resources can be stymied by a perceived inability to design projects of sufficient rigor. Assessment rigor is strongly influenced by the theories, practices, and standards of qualitative research and evaluation (Lincoln and Guba, 2003). Although there is a great need for rigorous research to demonstrate library value, there is an equal or greater need for practical, local, less arduous assessment. So, what is the difference between assessment and research? Assessment "strives to know...what is" and then uses that information to change the status quo (Keeling, et al. 2008, 28); in contrast, research is designed to test hypotheses (Keeling, et al. 2008, 28). Assessment focuses on observations of change; research is concerned with the degree of correlation or causation among variables (Keeling, et al. 2008, 35). Assessment "virtually always occurs in a political context," while research attempts to be apolitical" (Upcraft and Schuh 2002, 19). Assessment seeks to document observations, but research seeks to prove or disprove ideas. Assessors have to complete assessment projects, even when there are significant design flaws (e.g., resource limitations, time limitations, organizational contexts, design limitations, or political contexts); whereas researchers can start over (Upcraft and Schuh 2002, 19). Assessors cannot always attain "perfect" studies, but must make do with "good enough" (Upcraft and Schuh 2002, 18). Of course, assessments should be well planned, be based on clear outcomes (Gorman 2009, 9-10), and use appropriate methods (Keeling, et al. 2008, 39); but they "must be comfortable with saying 'after' as well as 'as a result of'...experiences" (Keeling, et al. 2008, 35). In other words, "assessment does not need to prove that a certain...experience alone produced a certain...outcome—only that [users] who completed [an] activity had, at the end of it, the desired [outcome]" (Keeling, et al. 2008, 35).

Although assessment may not be as rigorous as research, there are parameters within which it should operate. For example, assessors must acknowledge and communicate all limitations on their work so that a prospective audience can weigh them (Upcraft and Schuh 2002, 20), such as whether assessment results imply correlation or causation. If limitations are not clearly stated, assessors run the risk of producing results that are not credible and therefore useless (Keeling, et al. 2008, 34). In other words, assessors are often confronted with less than ideal circumstances for their efforts. Not engaging in assessment is not a good option; a "lack of assessment data can…lead to policies and practices based on intuition, prejudice, preconceived notions, or personal proclivities—none of them desirable bases for making decisions" (Upcraft and Schuh 2002, 20). The solution? Engage in assessment, make the best possible decisions, clearly state any and all limitations, and use multiple methods.

Librarians are "increasingly examining tools and techniques" for assessment (Town, SCONUL Value and Impact 2006, 114) as well as inventorying institutionally available data collection methods (MacEachern 2001). All assessment techniques have advantages and disadvantages (Oakleaf, Dangers and Opportunities 2008). No tools are perfectly valid or reliable (Kerby and Weber 2000; Oakleaf and Kaske, Guiding Questions 2009); none adequately represent entire libraries (Nicholson 2004, 174). In fact, sometimes there are no existing assessments and librarians must be creative and employ multiple measures (Kerby and Weber 2000). Two multiple measure approaches are most significant for library assessment: 1) triangulation "where multiple methods are used to find areas of convergence of data from different methods with an aim of overcoming the biases or limitations of data gathered from any one particular method" (Keeling, et al. 2008, 53) and 2) complementary mixed methods, which "seek to use data from multiple methods to build upon each other by clarifying, enhancing, or illuminating findings between or among methods" (Keeling, et al. 2008, 53).

Student Retention and Graduation Rates

Student retention and graduation rates are currently among the most discussed foci of institutional missions. According to Krupnick (2010), "graduation rates are likely to move to the forefront of national higher-education discussions this year." This is not a new phenomena—retention has been a major area of higher education interest for the last 30 years (Tinto and Pusser 2006, 4). There are a number of reasons for this: losing students prior to graduation hurts college rankings as well as the economic, educational, and emotional well-being of institutions (Bell, Keeping Them Enrolled 2008, 4). For example, lower retention rates can mean higher costs per degree conferred, a metric that some consider a measure of institutional productivity (Rampell 2009).

Despite decades of research on retention, authors generally agree that there are "no magic formulas" for retaining students (Bell, Keeping Them Enrolled 2008, 1). They acknowledge that many student characteristics that predict student dropout likelihood are not within institutional control (Tinto and Pusser 2006, 10). However, higher education institutions can control many environmental factors, factors that are key to Astin's, Tinto's, and Pascarella's theories of student development (Student

Development Theory Chart 2010). For example, "institutional commitments, the expectational climate established by members of the institution, the academic, social, and financial supports provided by the institution, the feedback that is provided to and about students by the institution, and the educational and social activities that shape student academic and social involvements and/or engagements within the classroom and with other members of the campus" are all within institutional control (Tinto and Pusser 2006, 10). Many of these areas are significant in student decisions to leave an institution, but the most important ones are related to student interactions with other people (Bell, Keeping Them Enrolled 2008, 1; Long 2006, 4): faculty, advisors, other students, or possibly librarians. These interactions are particularly impactful in the first year of study (CollegeBoard 2009, 9), even affecting student grades (Kuh, Cruce, et al. 2008, 555). In short, "many students don't develop a [personal] connection with their institution. And when they don't, they leave" (Gonzalez 2010).

Therefore, strategies for increasing retention, and ultimately graduation rates, center on helping students engage with other students and educators (Bell, Keeping Them Enrolled 2008, 2). According to Bell, "this includes...developing out-of-classroom learning experiences and improving teaching quality. These strategies focus on people—not physical resources" (Keeping Them Enrolled 2008, 2). Specific strategies include:

- curricular and behavioral integration (Ewell and Wellman 2007, 5)
- frequent contact with faculty (Ewell and Wellman 2007, 5)
- consistently accessible and responsible staff (Scott, et al. 2008, 14)
- prompt and effective management of student queries (Scott, et al. 2008, 14)
- efficient, convenient, and responsive libraries (Scott, et al. 2008, 14)

Additional strategies include "high-impact educational practices" such as first-year seminars and experiences, common intellectual experiences, learning communities, writing-intensive courses, collaborative assignments and projects, undergraduate research, diversity/global learning, service learning/community based learning, internships, capstone courses and projects (Kuh, High-Impact Educational Practices 2008, 9-11).

Recently, the Obama administration set ambitious goals for graduation rates of community college, college, and university students. To track these goals, government officials hope to compile student data files from preschool through adult education (Basken 2010). Currently, NCES and NSC collect data on graduation rates in higher education (P. T. Ewell, We Actually Have 2009, 13). Despite efforts to collect graduation data, there are many complicating factors, including the methods used to collect data. Currently, NCES graduation data focuses on first-year students who start in the fall and track whether they've graduated four or six years later. Transfers, especially out of state, are particular problematic. For example, it is estimated that including transfers will increase overall graduation rates for four-year degrees from 65% to 75% (P. T. Ewell,

We Actually Have 2009, 13). As tracking systems improve, they will be even more relevant to the assessment of retention and graduation rates.

Academic libraries can help higher education institutions retain and graduate students, a keystone part of institutional missions (Mezick 2007, 561), but the challenge lies in determining how libraries can contribute and then document their contribution (Bell, Keeping Them Enrolled 2008, 1). A variety of studies have attempted to do so (Breivik 1977; Knapp 1996; Hiscock 1986; Mallinckrodt and Sedlacek 1987; Lara 1981; Bean 2003; Rushing and Poole 2002). Early studies connected library use to retention (Kramer and Kramer 1968), but a more active paradigm now calls for librarians to make conscious efforts to increase their contact with students (Dow 1998, 280), especially individualized research assistance and personal attention (Bell, Keeping Them Enrolled 2008, 2; Mezick 2007, 565; Emmons and Wilkinson). Then librarians can conduct research that shows the impact of these interactions (Bell, Keeping Them Enrolled 2008, 4). According to Bell, higher education "administrators can help to involve the library by inviting and opening doors to librarian participation in campus social programs where more student-librarian interaction occurs" (Keeping Them Enrolled 2008, 2). Mezick states, "the more librarians interact with the university community, the greater their impact…on students' lives" (Mezick 2007, 565). Librarians can begin investigating potential impacts by creating local surveys. Bell suggests that surveys might ask, "How often do [students] come into contact with librarians? Have they received help from a librarian with research, and if so how has that helped their academic achievement? These surveys should target seniors and recent alumni to best ascertain in what ways the library contributed to their persistence to graduation" (Keeping Them Enrolled 2008, 3).

Librarians can also increase their contact with students by collaborating with student affairs offices to become a part of campus strategic enrollment and recruitment plans (National Conference on Student Recruitment, Marketing, and Retention 2010). One example is the admissions office. Retention research shows that new student orientations are a good starting point for integrating students into their institutions (CollegeBoard 2009, 8). Libraries have been included in orientation surveys with positive results (Tenofsky 2005, 291). Orientations also provide librarians opportunities to connect with parents to support student success; parents are "the perfect target for library outreach efforts…[and] academic librarians can be enlisted to be accessible to parents who expect their child to receive personalized assistance and support" (Bell, Keeping Them Enrolled 2008, 2-3).

Library instructional efforts are thought to impact student retention, but more research is needed in this area. For example one study showed "library orientations, workshops, or courses" to have a weak connection to student retention; however, the item that explored this connection was the penultimate answer choice (#81 of 82 items) and grouped under "additional activities" instead of "learning assistance/academic support" (Habley and McClanahan 2004, 16-17). Thus, it is possible that study design may have impacted the results; replication of a redesigned study may show different results.

Finally, traditional input studies show that institutions in all Carnegie Classifications with libraries that spend more on materials and have more staff are correlated to greater retention rates (Hamrick, Schuh and Shelley 2004; Mezick 2007, 565). Library expenditures (as a part of academic support expenditures) also may be related to higher graduation rates in many institutions (Gansemer-Topf and Schuh 2006, 632). Of course, these studies report correlations, which is not causation. Still, it is possible that cuts to library expenditures may have negative consequences for student retention and graduation (Hamrick, Schuh, and Shelley 2004); research indicates that institutions that have low graduation rates tend to spend less on library functions (Gilmore and To 1992, 43).

Student Engagement

In recent years, academic libraries have been transformed to provide "technology and content ubiquity" as well as individualized support (Neal 2009), and consequently they are well positioned to engage students curricular, co-curricular, and social experiences. The challenge is to document and articulate the value academic libraries bring to institutional student engagement efforts.

Several surveys elicit information on student engagement; examples include the National Survey of Student Engagement (NSSE), the Community College Survey of Student Engagement (CCSSE), Beginning College Survey of Student Engagement (BCSSE), and the Faculty Survey of Student Engagement (FSSE).

One of these surveys, the NSSE, focuses on "the extent to which students engage in good educational practices…[and it] measures student behaviors that are highly correlated with many desirable learning and personal development outcomes of college" (Gratch-Lindauer, College Student Engagement 2008, 102). It is considered the premier measure of student engagement, and it has been linked to the Information Literacy Competency Standards for Higher Education (Mark and Boruff-Jones 2003, 430; Gratch-Lindauer, College Student Engagement 2008, 109). In fact, two of the five NSSE benchmarks (Level of Academic Challenge and Active and Collaborative Learning) can be aligned with the Standards (Mark and Boruff-Jones 2003, 485-486). Consequently, NSSE can be used either as a whole to gain "a snapshot of information literacy at an institutional level" (Mark and Boruff-Jones 2003, 484) or as individual questions which can be combined with individual student records data (Gratch-Lindauer, College Student Engagement 2008, 112; National Survey of Student Engagement 2009, 10-11). The latter option appears to have significant potential. By tying NSSE to student records data, librarians can "identify sub-populations of interest" within the student body (e.g., students who took a particular course or first-generation college students) and look for potential correlations to other markers (e.g., GPA or post-graduation job placement) (National Survey of Student Engagement 2009, 4). Potential correlations might also help "determine whether improvement efforts are having the desired effect" (National Survey of Student Engagement 2009, 10).

NSSE items related to academic libraries have been identified (Gratch-Lindauer, Information Literacy-Related 2007, 433). Other items may also be revised to integrate academic libraries into the study. For example, NSSE questions students about the quality of their relationships with faculty and administrative personnel (National Survey of Student Engagement 2009, 7), but do not mention librarians. Although it can be arduous to change the core list of established questions, each campus can add local items; librarians can include library value questions as local items on national surveys.

Initial investigations have revealed connections between academic libraries and student NSSE responses. For example, senior students report engaging in library-related activities more often; so do some majors and demographic groups (Gratch-Lindauer, College Student Engagement 2008, 109-110). Laird and Kuh found that behaviors such as using the library Web site to find academic sources, asking librarians for help, and making judgments about Web sites all "go hand-in-hand" with student engagement in other areas (Laird and Kuh 2005). In addition, researchers found that institutional expenditures on academic support (including libraries) have strong positive correlations to student engagement (Pike, Smart, et al. 2006, 868). However, Gonyea points out that correlations do not imply causation and that it can be quite challenging to identify the impact of individual campus elements (Gonyea attributed in Gratch-Lindauer, Information Literacy-Related 2007, 443). Even so, according to Gratch-Lindauer, "even without better or more items related to information and library use behaviors…the current items…can supply evidence to help substantiate the need and resources for [library] program and service improvements" (College Student Engagement 2008, 113).

Certainly, NSSE is not the only survey of student engagement; other surveys also can be investigated to determine how they might demonstrate library value (Gratch-Lindauer, College Student Engagement 2008, 104-105). For example, Kuh and Gonyea (Role of the Academic Library 2003) investigated eighteen years of College Student Experiences Questionnaire (CSEQ) data and found that student contact with librarians has increased (Kuh and Gonyea, Role of the Academic Library 2003). According to Whitmire, the CSEQ shows that undergraduates at universities with greater library resources self-report higher gains in critical thinking (Academic Library Performance 2002, 124). In another study of CSEQ data, researchers learned that library use is related to "other important educationally valuable activities", that seniors more frequently make judgments about information quality than younger students, and that institutional academic challenge is related to library use (Kuh and Gonyea, Role of the Academic Library 2003). In sum, they state that their study indicates that libraries "play an important supporting role in helping the institution achieve its academic mission" (Kuh and Gonyea, Role of the Academic Library 2003).

It is important to note, like other assessment methods, there are potential pitfalls associated with student engagement surveys. Most pitfalls derive from the fact that engagement studies rely on indirect measures (National Survey of Student Engagement 2009, 4) in which students self-report their experiences (Gordon, Ludlum and Hoey 2008, 37). The difficulty is that students tend to over-report their engagement (Olsen and Kristensen 2002; Pike, Limitations of Using 1996, 111). In addition, Pike states that stakeholders can "forget that self-reports of learning and academic development are not precisely the same as more traditional measures of the same outcomes" (Pike, Limitations of Using 1996, 111). For example, NSSE benchmarks do not explain first-year retention, GPA, pursuit of graduate education, or job placements (Gordon, Ludlum and Hoey 2008, 19), although it is possible that individual items may do a better job of explaining student outcomes. Still other studies suggest that NSSE attributes do indeed correlate with learning outcomes (Jaschik 2009). Despite the conflicting information, "data from the college student engagement surveys are useful as a part of a librarian's assessment toolbox and for program planning and improvement" (Gratch-Lindauer, College Student Engagement 2008, 112). Perhaps the most important advice to remember regarding student engagement surveys is that "there is a distinction between participating in NSSE and using NSSE. In the end, what good is it if all you get is a report?" (Alexander McCormick attributed in Jaschik 2009). The goal is to gain insight into the relationship between engagement and library outcomes (Gordon, Ludlum and Hoey 2008, 20) and to translate that insight into action (National Survey of Student Engagement 2009, 29).

Student Learning

Clearly, a major goal of postsecondary education is learning (Marsh 2007). Therefore, to be successful contributors to their overarching institutions, academic libraries must maximize their contributions to student learning (K. R. Smith 2007, 36; Council on Library and Information Resources 2008, 3).

In the area of student learning, academic libraries are in the middle of a paradigm shift. In the past, academic libraries functioned primarily as information repositories; now they are becoming learning enterprises (Bennett 2009, 194). This shift requires academic librarians to embed library services and resources in the teaching and learning activities of their institutions (Lewis 2007). In the new paradigm, librarians focus on information skills, not information access (Bundy 2004, 3); they think like educators, not service providers (Bennett 2009, 194).

Also, in the new paradigm, academic librarians articulate student learning outcomes (American Association of State Colleges and Universities 2006, 11). According to IMLS, outcomes are "the benefits or changes for individuals or populations during or after participating in program activities, including new knowledge, increased skills, changed attitudes or values, modified behavior, improved condition, or altered status" (Kyrillidou, From Input to Output 2002). By articulating outcomes, academic librarians can state exactly what their instructional goals are, why they are teaching the way they are (Carter 2002, 41), and how they expect students to be impacted by instruction. The articulation of outcomes also moves libraries away from satisfaction measures and opinion surveys (Dow 1998, 278). Keeling states, "if outcomes are the priority, and outcomes are achieved, students (and parents and other constituents) will have abundant reasons to be satisfied. But if there are no clear student outcomes…or if those outcomes are not produced, ultimately no one will be satisfied" (R. P. Keeling 2006, 57). Smith concurs, "if we cannot demonstrate the results of learning or even define them very clearly, it is hard to convince anyone that the results achieved, whatever they may be, are worth the price" (D. N. Smith 2009, 6).

After academic librarians articulate student learning outcomes, they can "think…differently about day-to-day activities, renew…relationships with colleagues and students, and adopt…the assumptions and values of a culture of assessment" (R. P. Keeling 2006, 55). Knowing how to assess student learning outcomes is another challenge, but it is central to librarians' ability to teach effectively (Keeling, et al. 2008, 4). Because librarians, like other higher education professionals, have to be prepared to think and act in new ways, two steps are necessary. First, librarians require professional development "to increase their ability to write learning outcomes, create assessment plans, use assessment methods and tools, and prepare reports that document the work" (R. P. Keeling 2006, 55-56). Second, they need to change library "attitudes, perspectives, and working styles" in order to use assessment tools and techniques effectively (R. P. Keeling 2006, 55-56). Once adequately trained, librarians can not only articulate student learning outcomes, they can collect evidence, document successes, share results, and make improvements (Council for Higher Education Accreditation 2010). In sum, they can provide proof that libraries make differences in students' lives (Keeling, et al. 2008, 4).

For librarians, the main content area of student learning is information literacy; however, they are not alone in their interest in student information literacy skills (Oakleaf, Are They Learning? 2011). The Boyer Commission notes that students often lack "a coherent body of knowledge or any inkling as to how one sort of information might relate to another" (Boyer Commission on Educating Undergraduates in the Research University 1998). NCES named critical thinking skills (among them the ability to find and evaluate information) as a critical skill for college students to attain (E. Jones 1995). AAC&U includes information skills among key educational outcomes for college students (Association of American Colleges and Universities 2008). The ACT National Curriculum Survey shows that information literacy ranks in importance between 6th and 9th out of 26 21st century skills taught by postsecondary instructors, according to both high school teachers and college faculty (ACT 2009). Business communities also emphasize the need for critical thinking and analytical skills (Rockman 2002). And of course ALA believes that information literacy is "central to the practice of democracy" (American Library Association 1989).

Most academic library student learning outcomes focus on information literacy, a concept that has been described as the core literacy of the 21st century by some (Garner 2005, 68) and included as a key factor of other definitions of 21st century skills (Institute of Museum and Library Services 2009, 35). While there is no consensus on what general academic skills college students should learn (Ewell and Wellman 2007, 17), 74% of institutions say their general learning outcomes include critical thinking, 59% include information literacy, and 51% included research skills (Hart Research Associates 2009, 5). Students who learn the most information literacy skills come from institutions that communicate the importance of information literacy (Kuh, High-Impact Educational Practices 2008). Because students learn what assessments require of them

(Nimon 2001, 50), it is logical to believe that institutions that assess information literacy outcomes might also produce students with greater information literacy skills.

Information literacy outcomes assessment offers the potential to demonstrate the value of academic libraries to student learning. According to one study, "if librarians could demonstrate gains in student learning and improved knowledge as a direct outcome of their instruction, they would be able to justify their programs and open a dialogue with faculty" (Saunders, Future of Information Literacy 2009, 107). Many librarians have contributed to the voluminous body of literature on information literacy assessment. In fact, the "sheer quantity of examples in the literature…can make it hard…to find examples of best practice" (Walsh 2009, 19-20). Traditionally, information literacy assessment focused on satisfaction (Association of College and Research Libraries 2000) or self-report surveys, like the Research Practices Survey, rather than outcomes. More recent literature is outcomes-focused and emphasizes multiple choice tests like the Standardized Assessment of Information Literacy Skills (SAILS) as well as bibliography analysis (Walsh 2009, 21). However, most of the literature relates the details of case studies focused on one group of students, one class, or one semester (Matthews Evaluation p 243). In other words, most examples are "micro-level studies" (Streatfield and Markless, Evaluating the Impact 2008, 103) or "narrow and momentary glances" at impact of instructional efforts (Shupe 2007, 54), rather than the broader, more coherent demonstrations of value that librarians need to articulate the importance of information literacy learning in an institutional context. It is not that small scale local assessments are not valuable; indeed, useful assessments need not be large scale, and local results can be highly persuasive at individual institutions (Saunders, Future of Information Literacy 2009, 107). But, there are large gaps in the literature and a need for rigorous, larger-scale assessments that emphasize "changes in levels of student competence…changes in student behavior…effects of information literacy based changes in the curriculum…the comparative efficacy of different levels and types of information literacy interventions…[and] the overall value of library based information literacy work to the academic community" (Carrigan 1992, 104). Some literature gaps can be closed by using assessment management systems to compile small scale institutional assessments into larger, more systematic investigations; others can be filled by organized, cooperative studies.

Large scale studies can correlate surrogates of student learning such as grades (Jager 2002; Zhong and Alexander 2007; Julien and Boon 2004, 132) with library-related interactions (Dickenson 2006, vii, iv) and behaviors (Poll, Impact/Outcome Measures for Libraries 2003, 332; Poll and Payne, Impact Measures 2006, 552). They can also follow students over time. Longitudinal studies can assess the difference in learning outcome achievement between the time students begin college and graduation (Halpern 1987) and then link that learning to student collegiate experiences (Borden and Young 2008, 27). The best way to assess library value longitudinally is to assess the same students at the beginning and end of their college careers; however, it can be challenging to maintain connections with the same students for extended periods of time (Borden 2004). Many assessments "make do" with cross-sectional longitudinal studies in which first-year students and senior students are assessed at the same time. However, seniors represent a more select group than first-year students by virtue of their persistence through years of college (Flowers, et al. 2001, 565), and this influences results. In both scenarios, control groups of students who are not in college during the same years are typically not included (Flowers, et al. 2001, 565). Even among college-enrolled students, control group information literacy assessment studies are rare. At one community college, librarians investigated the impacts of an information literacy program, especially library workshops and courses. Using a control group design, they found that students who passed the course had higher GPAs, completed more semester hours, and were more likely to persist, even once self-selection bias was taken into account (Glendale Community College 2007, 13-14; Moore, et al. 2002). In the future, librarians can use similar study design to replicate or increase the scope of this study.

Because learning is somewhat intangible and difficult to simplify (Kantor, Library as an Information Utility 1976, 101), institutions have developed surrogates. Common tangible surrogates for student learning are found in Figure 3. Because there are so many different definitions, a variety of approaches are necessary to assess the degree to which institutions achieve student learning (Gordon, Ludlum and Hoey 2008, 20).

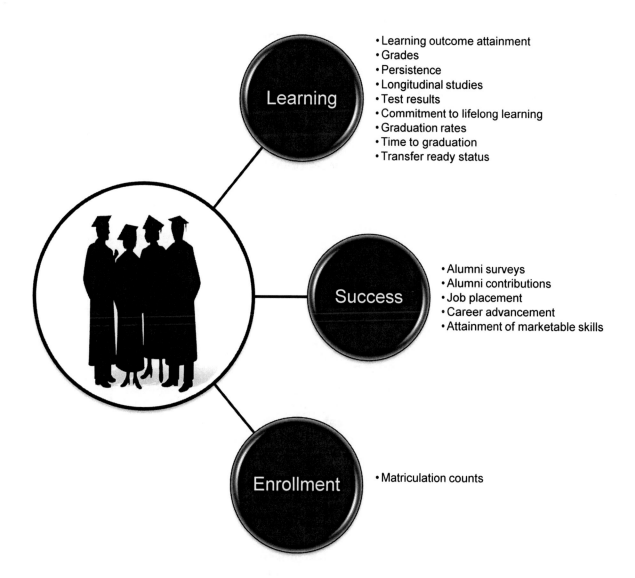

Figure 3. Surrogates for Student Learning (Gordon, Ludlum and Hoey 2008; Pascarella and Terenzini, How College Affects Students 2005; Pfeiffer 1998; Ewell and Wellman 2007; Wimmer 2009; Borden and Young 2008)

Several categories of measures are noticeably absent from the chart above: inputs and process measures; outputs, including use statistics; satisfaction feedback; and service quality data. Instead, the focus is on the answers to questions like, "So what? What difference does it all make? Was it worth it?" (Keeling, et al. 2008, 5). Although these measures have created a rich tradition of data collection in libraries, inputs and outputs no longer resonate with many higher education stakeholders. Input and output measures have enabled librarians to track detailed information and understand how library services function, but not what they produce in learners (Keeling, et al. 2008, 42). While satisfaction and service quality measures like LibQUAL+ demonstrate librarians' commitment to user feedback (Cook, et al. 2001, 268), they do not focus on the outcomes of interaction with library services and resources.

This mismatch between easily available data and data that is useful for measuring outcomes is not unique to libraries. According to Borden and Young (2008, 20), the mismatch between useable data and available data is attributable to the "sheer volume of data" as well as "the common practice of collecting data that are readily available without due consideration to what exactly we are measuring." Not only is much of easily collected data less useful, it also is not convincing when used as justification for funding decisions (Ackermann 2007, 6). Satisfaction measures, for instance, may show that everyone loves the idea of the library, but institutional satisfaction measures will probably show that everyone loves "other ideas better" (Ackermann 2007, 6). The best data for influencing funding decisions shows how libraries impact institutional outcomes and success (Ackermann 2007, 6).

Differences in assessment approaches are not insignificant, because metrics tend to drive conversations in higher education (P. T. Ewell, Power in Numbers 2005, 10). For example, "if we choose to primarily assess graduation and retention rates, then we identify clearly what is symbolically valued, to what the institution gives its attention, and by what criteria the institution seeks to be understood and evaluated" (Keeling, et al. 2008, 76). When selecting metrics, it is important to "look for evidence of learning, not just statistics" (Leskes and Wright 2005, 21), to look for attainment of outcomes, not just outputs (Hernon, Dugan and Schwartz, Revisiting Outcomes 2006, 373). In the case of graduation and retention, they are "at best described as partial indicators of student success—necessary, but scarcely sufficient. The college degree is meaningful, after all, only when it represents forms of learning that are both valued by society and empowering to the individual (Kuh, High-Impact Educational Practices 2008, 2). And the academic library is only meaningful, if it can prove its value to student learning (Pritchard, Determining Quality in Academic Libraries 1996).

Strategic Planning for Learning

To ensure that academic libraries contribute maximum value to the institutional outcome of student learning, community college, college, and university libraries can integrate information literacy learning into strategic planning processes and, if necessary, revise library missions, visions, outcomes, and activities to produce student learning (R. P. Keeling 2006, 53). Keeling advises, "rethink everything" and align everything with accountability for student outcomes. However Keeling acknowledges, "it is difficult to imagine how a department, division, or whole campus would reorient thought and action to address its accountability for educating and preparing the whole student without questioning existing organizational structures, the current allocation of resources, and established goals and priorities; and the process through which those questions are asked, answered, and linked to future commitments is exactly that of strategic planning" (R. P. Keeling 2006, 54). This approach presupposes that library leaders are "in fact committed to [student learning] purposes and willing to act on those commitments" (R. P. Keeling 2006, 55). If they are, then including student learning outcomes in library strategic planning processes is a good practice.

According to Kantor, the university library "exists to benefit the students of the educational institution as *individuals*" (Library as an Information Utility 1976, 101). In contrast, academic libraries tend to assess learning outcomes using groups of students; a position that merits possible reconsideration. According to Doran and Lockwood (2006, 205), "a basic truism of learning implies that an *individual* student, not a student *group*, has increased in knowledge and skills during a specific period of time. As such, analytical models concerned with student learning should reasonably reflect this basic principal and consider individual students as the unit of analysis with their growth trajectories employed as outcomes." If academic libraries collect data on students who participate in library instruction activities or demonstrate information literacy skills through classroom discussions, individual consultations, online tutorials, peer group discussions, artistic performances, project demonstrations, plans or rehearsals for projects (Saunders, Perspectives on Accreditation 2008, 307), they can use other institutional data sources to explore possible correlations with other forms of student data such as major, GPA, test scores, or time to graduation. According to Morest (2009, 21), "the student information system is the primary repository of institutional data that institutional researchers can translate into research and analysis. These systems contain the full range of records of student enrollment, course taking, financial aid, and family background.... In order to begin to develop a culture of evidence, it is essential that...data [can be accessed] quickly and reliably." Yet, academic librarians have not collected individual student data or accessed institutional student information systems, despite the fact that these data sources could be used to demonstrate library value. Note: No higher education professionals care more deeply about privacy and confidentiality, are more committed to using data ethically, or are more responsible about stripping personally identifying information from records than librarians. Therefore, once sufficient protections are in place, librarians can use individual student data to not only gain evidence of academic library value, but also find ways to increase that value.

Participating in National Higher Education Assessments

Another way academic librarians can demonstrate value is to participate in national higher education assessments of student learning. These include common reporting forms and initiatives like the AAC&U VALUE project.

For the last decade, higher education institutions have worked to produce common reporting forms to increase transparency, accountability, and improvements throughout higher education and enable state-by-state comparisons of student learning (National Center for Public Policy and Higher Education 2000, iv; Kuh, Risky Business 2007, 32). To this end, the National Forum on College Level Learning collected information from institutions such as licensure and graduate school admission tests (Miller and Ewell 2005, 31). (Initially, they also included student engagement surveys, but dropped them because they are indirect measures of learning and also because they are not revealing for comparisons between institutions (Miller and Ewell 2005, 4). NSSE variations between institutions are less than 10%; 95% of the variance occurs at the student level within institutions (Kuh, Risky Business 2007, 32-33).) Despite these efforts to create common reporting forms, comparisons of student learning are still not possible because there are no real benchmarks for that learning (National Center for Public Policy and Higher Education 2008). There are a few exceptions; South Dakota has a mandatory exam of college juniors, the GRE assesses students pursuing graduate study, nursing students take licensure tests, and WorkKeys evaluates students in some vocational fields (National Center for Public Policy and Higher Education 2008). However, these options are limited and fall short of the goal of state-by-state student learning comparisons.

Now, efforts are focused on campus-level assessments such as the VSA, VFA, and U-CAN. Critics of these systems point out that they oversimplify student learning by comparing schools on limited indicators of learning, such as graduation rate, test scores (e.g., the Measure of Academic Proficiency and Progress (MAPP), the College Assessment of Academic Proficiency (CAAP), and the Collegiate Learning Assessment (CLA) tests), and satisfaction measures (Kuh, Risky Business 2007, 33; Keeling, et al. 2008, 29). Other authors register concern over the focus on tests (Rhodes 2008; Maki, Moving Beyond 2009; Hamilton-Pennell, et al. 2000). Rhodes acknowledges that the tests have worth (Rhodes 2008, 63), but also writes:

> The initial reaction to the national accountability demands for indicators of student learning has resulted in calls to use tests that have some basic characteristics in common: they are in some way standardized, they result in a score or quantitative measurement that summarizes how well a group of students has performed; they test only samples of students at a given institution; they require additional costs for students or institutions to administer; they reflect a snapshot picture at one point in time; they provide an institutional rather than an individual score; and they lack high stakes for students taking the exams. These approaches to accountability have been criticized for their expense, the lack of usefulness of the scores for faculty and others seeking to improve the curriculum and cocurriculum, the lack of useful information for students to refocus their own efforts, the limited number of outcomes addressed by the tests, and the problems of motivating students to perform well on the exams. (Rhodes 2008, 60)

According to Keeling et al. (2008, 29), "while each of these measures has some significance, neither individually nor in the aggregate do they effectively or meaningfully portray the breadth" of student learning. Thus, many believe they are incomplete, don't allow for real institutional comparisons, don't highlight institutional differences (Lederman 2010), and cannot be used to rank institutions or justify funding cuts (Kuh, Risky Business 2007, 33). According to Lederman (2010), "if existing flaws are not resolved, the nation runs the risk of ending up in the worst of all worlds: the appearance of higher education accountability without the reality."

One possible method for augmenting or supplanting test measures of student learning is the AAC&U VALUE project. The VALUE project is based on a set of rubrics that assess essential learning outcomes (Maki, Moving Beyond 2009; E. A. Jones 2009, 4; Association of American Colleges and Universities 2010) using students authentic work, including research projects and papers, lab reports, creative products, internships, service learning activities, capstone projects, and e-portfolios (Maki, Moving Beyond 2009). This approach offers several benefits, including the abilities to capitalize on existing rubric assessments and data sources (Rhodes 2008), to adapt rubrics locally to reflect individual campus cultures, to reinforce the skills institutions want students to learn (Smart, Feldman and Ethington 2006, 37), and to draw internal and external comparisons (Rhodes 2008, 61, 67). For these reasons, IMLS has recently awarded a grant (RAILS) to examine the potential of VALUE rubrics in demonstrating the contributions of academic libraries to student learning.

Assessment Management Systems

Higher education institutions can adopt new or "add-on" assessment methods, but they can save resources if they "generate data on actual student learning directly out of [their] regular program" (Shupe 2007, 48). To do that, institutions require "electronic system[s] or structure[s] that knit these elements together as steps in a single and simple process, with information on all the necessary new elements of information flowing through the process. [Such] structure[s] focus on expected and actual outcomes with the same systematic precision that the enrollment-based systems keep track of student enrollment…and course grades" (Shupe 2007, 51). These structures are called "assessment management systems."

Assessment management systems make assessment "easier, faster, less intrusive, more useful, and cost effective" (Hutchings 2009, 28). Several assessment management systems exist, including WeaveONLINE, TracDat, eLumen, ILAT, Blackboard Learn's assessment module, LiveText, Tk20, Waypoint Outcomes, and others (Oakleaf, Writing Information Literacy Assessment Plans 2010; Oakleaf, Are They Learning? 2011). Each assessment management system has a slightly different set of capabilities. Some guide outcomes creation, some develop rubrics, some score student work, or support student portfolios. All manage, maintain, and report assessment data (Hutchings 2009, 28). However, institutions still need to identify course and program goals, evaluate student learning, and determine how to use assessment data to improve learning (Hutchings 2009, 30).

In addition to decreasing resource expenditures and increasing organizational efficiencies, assessment management systems allow higher education institutions to link outcomes vertically (within units) and horizontally (across divisions, colleges, departments, programs, and libraries) (Keeling, et al. 2008, 8). In this way, assessment management systems recognize the reality that students do not gain knowledge, skills, or abilities from just one course, just in their major, or just in the classroom; rather they enable institutions to capture student learning through all their interactions with institutional units (Keeling, et al. 2008, 8). According to Shupe (2007, 51), "it is [this] element—a learning outcomes information structure—that makes this process feasible. In fact, the academic process is dependent on the structure to work well, delivering everyone web-based access from his or her desktop/laptop and permitting everyone to play his or her authorized role(s). This provides a college or university with a new capacity to distribute information on expected outcomes across the institution and to generate data on actual student learning wherever and whenever it chooses to use this approach—capacities that are still unimagined by most colleges and universities…. the more consistently this process is applied, the more academic benefits begin to accrue." Furthermore, assessment management systems help institutions create and support horizontal structures (e.g., first-year programs, advising, service learning), structures that encourage students to transfer learning out of their general education or major courses into other areas. Supporting these horizontal structures using an assessment management system helps institutions "increase coherence between and among for-credit and not-for-credit learning activities; foster the development of a student body that collectively understands and supports the mission of the institution; generate a synthesis of institutional data sets that provides a more robust and multidimensional understanding of student experience; and produce a complex, yet clear, assessment portfolio" (Keeling, et al. 2008, 58-59).

Faculty Teaching

Academic libraries impact students, but they also provide value for teaching faculty. According to Bundy (2004, 2), instructional content, methods, and assessments "can no longer be the sole province of individual academic teachers"; instead, librarians can become instructional partners and help faculty "improve the quality of their courses…develop innovative curricula, and save time on teaching-related activities" (Simmel 2007, 91). While some in higher education may argue that librarians are not teachers, others would counter that "librarians have always been educators because the most enduring and flexible agency for learning is the library—organized for well over two millennia—predating the first universities by well over one millennium" (Bundy 2004, 2).

Many faculty welcome library instructional support. One study describes the results of course-integrated library instruction from a faculty perspective (Simmel 2007, 90). The study involved interviews of faculty who spent time with librarians to determine how to integrate info lit instruction in their classes; "while estimates ranged from 15 minutes to two hours, depending on project and course, every faculty member interviewed considered the time spent on this activity a negligible price to pay in light of the benefits they realized." In this study, librarians helped improve the quality of courses by providing "a higher caliber of discipline-based research instruction" that allowed faculty to "1) develop and implement new curricula by targeting and customizing access to relevant information resources, 2) improve their own research productivity since they learn new techniques and become familiar with new resources, and 3) save time in preparing research classes, interacting with students about information resources, and grading both individual assignments and group projects" (Simmel 2007, 90). Librarians can also add value to faculty teaching by participating in institutional efforts to increase faculty instructional skills (e.g., grants for faculty projects or teaching workshops and seminars) (Levinson-Rose and Menges 1981, 403).

Assessments of co-created instruction effectiveness should be designed and scored collaboratively (Nimon 2001, 50; Warner 2008, 5), but students are not the only ones who can be assessed when librarians and faculty work together. Faculty can also be queried about the impact of academic library support for faculty teaching. In one study of this kind, three out of five faculty felt that librarians had assisted their students in finding appropriate information for course assignments, and nearly half said that librarians had "supported their teaching objectives" (Dickenson 2006, vi). Similar numbers reported the positive impact of library resources on their instructional goals, including preparation of lectures, student reading assignments, and conceptual frameworks for courses (Dickenson 2006, vi).

Faculty Research

Academic libraries contribute to faculty research productivity in both straightforward and subtle ways (Case 2008). In the past, library contributions to faculty research were primarily collections-based. However, as online collections grow and discovery tools evolve, that role has become less critical (Schonfeld and Housewright 2010; Housewright and Schonfeld, *Ithaka's 2006 Studies of Key Stakeholders* 2008, 256). Now, libraries serve as research consultants, project managers, technical support professionals, purchasers, and archivists (Housewright, Themes of Change 2009, 256; Case 2008). Although librarian roles are changing, research collaborations between faculty and librarians continue to benefit both partners. Faculty benefit from library resources and librarian expertise. The importance of these benefits is underscored by faculty who have been impacted by library resource cuts; these faculty believe that the cuts have negatively impacted their ability to conduct research (Dickenson 2006, v; Pittas 2001). On the other side of the partnership, librarians benefit from the opportunity to "secure the library's future as a significant partner in research and scholarship" (Case 2008).

When academic libraries impact faculty research productivity, they also impact institutional quality. Traditional library measures can be linked to faculty research productivity; for instance, Wolff (1995) linked research activity to reference inquires, and other authors suggested grants and publications as indicators of faculty productivity that could be connected to library factors (Pritchard, Determining Quality in Academic Libraries 1996; Gratch-Lindauer, Defining and Measuring 1998). Another author suggests that number of library books and journal may be correlated to faculty research productivity (Dundar and Lewis 1998, 614). In contrast, Rosenblatt suggested traditional library inputs/outputs were ill suited for documenting library contribution to faculty research (Rosenblatt 1998).

Some traditional input/output measures may indeed be useful for correlating library value to the outcome of faculty research productivity. Researchers might examine how library characteristics can be connected to faculty:

- publication output
- grant proposals

- funded grants
- conference output (Patrick and Stanley 2006, 40)
- textbook (Middaugh 2001)
- national juried show exhibits (R. Kaufman 2001, 5)
- national or international awards (R. Kaufman 2001, 5)
- citation impact (Australian Research Council 2008, 8-9)
- patents (Australian Research Council 2008, 8-9)
- consultancy/advisory work (Cook, et al. 2001, 10)

Much of this data can be obtained from individual institutional research offices or by using software packages such as Academic Analytics (Academic Analytics LLC 2010). Of course, there are many other predictors of faculty productivity not included on this list (R. Kaufman 2001, 5; Dundar and Lewis 1998, 610); many faculty productivity predictors are personal characteristics or related to institutional, not library, characteristics (Dundar and Lewis 1998, 610; Center for Measuring University Performance 2007; Charleston Observatory 2009).

Other traditional approaches to the assessment of library impact on faculty research productivity are also viable. Librarians can count citations of faculty publications (Dominguez 2005). Budd used a citation database to discover connections between the number of publications faculty produce and library volume counts, total expenditures, materials expenditures, and professional staffing (Budd, Faculty Publishing Productivity 1995; Budd, Increases in Faculty 1999). Baughman and Kieltyka also found a positive relationship between faculty publications and library holdings (Baughman and Kieltyka 1999). Librarians can also investigate how many citations faculty use that could have been accessed via the institutional library (Poll and Payne, Impact Measures 2006, 332), a practice that can decrease faculty research cycle time (Webster and Flowers 2009, 306). Ahtola (2002) and Smith (2003) employed this approach to study dissertations. Yet another study showed that a particular library supplied 95% of the journals in which their faculty publish, and 90% of faculty citations were available from campus libraries (Wilson and Tenopir 2008, 1407). In other research, library expenditures (Dundar and Lewis 1998; Franklin 2002) and "perceived adequacy of university library facilities" (Fairweather 1998) were connected to increased research productivity.

In addition to input/output assessments of faculty research productivity, some researchers have investigated the connection between faculty research and reading, a connection that may be explored in future academic library value research. Faculty productivity and award recognition have both been linked to increased reading (Tenopir and King, Perceptions of Value 2007, 203). In one study, researchers questioned faculty about the last scholarly article they read and about how much time they spent identifying, obtaining, and reading the article (Tenopir and King, Perceptions of Value 2007, 201). They found that faculty spend about 8-17 minutes reading to identify and obtain articles and 34 minutes actually reading the articles; this adds up to 143-159 hours of reading annually (Tenopir and King, Perceptions of Value 2007, 202). More than half stated that their reason for reading was research; 20% attributed reading to teaching preparation. Other purposes included grant proposal preparation, current awareness, and consulting (Tenopir and King, Perceptions of Value 2007, 202). They also stated that reading helped them develop new ideas, improve research results, or alter the focus of their research work (Tenopir and King, Perceptions of Value 2007, 203). Studies like this one can be replicated or adapted to further explore the nature of academic library value in the context of faculty research productivity.

Library Valuation

A few academic libraries have attempted to estimate their monetary value. For example, at California State University Northridge, Oviatt Library conducted a valuation study. They showed that, "if our users had to pay for [library] resources and services, in FY 2006/07, they would have paid at least $31,977,586" (Oviatt Library 2008, 1). At Cornell University, librarians estimated library value at $90,648,785 in 2008/2009. However, they did not attempt to value some electronic collections, public computers, library instruction, and some special collections (Cornell University Library 2010).

Such large-scale valuation studies are challenging and may not be feasible for all libraries. According to Poll, assessment "is most difficult when one tries to measure the effect of the library as an entity"; it is more feasible to measure outcomes of individual services (Impact/Outcome Measures for Libraries 2003, 331).

Reference Services

Reference assessments have focused on different aspects of quality reference service provision. One study covered the skills that make librarians "great" (Quinn 1994). Another study researched the amount of time needed for quality reference transactions (Stalker and Murfin 1996). Still another explored how reference librarians conceptualize reference work (Gerlich, Work in Motion 2006). Additional studies focus on how much effort reference transactions require (Gerlich and Berard, Testing the Viability 2010, 118), the friendliness of reference staff, and student confidence after transactions occur (Gerlich and Berard, Testing the Viability 2010, 137).

Several studies have estimated the "functional cost" of reference services, an approach described in detail by Abels, Kantor, and Saracevic (Abels, Kantor and Saracevic 1996) using data from Kantor, Saracevic, and D'Esposito-Wachtmann (Kantor, Saracevic and D'Esposito-Wachtmann, Studying the Cost 1995). Through an interview protocol, researchers identified labor costs associated with staff times, direct costs, and the annual number of reference transactions (Abels, Kantor and Saracevic 1996, 224). In 1995 dollars, Abels, Kantor, and Saracevic found that reference costs range from $1.24 to $38.00 (Abels, Kantor and Saracevic 1996, 225). Previous studies identified different ranges: $9.00 to $28.00 (Kantor, Three Studies 1986), $0.86 to $8.93 (Association of Research Libraries 1980, 1994), and an average of $14.29 (Cable 1980). These studies reveal a wide range of variation, probably attributable to quality of the service, operational policies and procedures, or a mismatch between capacity and demand (Abels, Kantor and Saracevic 1996, 226).

Electronic resources help library users, especially faculty, to be more productive. For example, electronic resources allow faculty to integrate resources into their proposals, articles, and reports regardless of location and to explore interdisciplinary research (Luther 2008, 3). Consequently, a number of studies have investigated the value provided by academic library electronic resources. These studies have explored usage counts, contingent valuation, return-on-investment calculations, and cost/benefit analyses.

Academic librarians often equate use and value; therefore, many seek to capture the usage of electronic resources. Two sources for e-resources usage data are vendor supplied datasets and web log use statistics Usage logs and vendor reports show usage, which could indicate value. However, they "do not show why someone used or requested a source or the outcomes on their work from using that source. Downloads may not equal actual use or satisfaction—someone may download an article and find it worthless for their task or they may be unhappy because they did not find what they needed" (Tenopir, Measuring the Value 2009, 10). Also, "the utility of vendor statistics is hampered by inconsistent measurement frames, differing metrics, and different definitions for the same metrics (Counter 2007). Web logs suffer from a lack of granularity, standardized metrics and reporting protocols that allow comparison among institutions. More importantly, neither method captures the 'why,' or the purpose of the use. Without this information, it is virtually impossible to determine if the resources are being used to advance student learning or any other desirable outcome. One established solution is the ARL MINES for Libraries protocol. It is an online 'transaction-based survey that collects data on the purpose of use of electronic resources and the demographics of users' (Association of Research Libraries 2005)" (Ackermann 2007).

Contingent valuation compares the time or other costs of not having a service with the time or cost of the service. This method has been used to estimate the value of electronic resources, especially journals. One study asked library users to indicate what they would do if the last journal article they read was not available to them from the library and estimate the costs to get it another way. The results showed that the library journal collection saved over 100 FTE faculty, having electronic access saved another 23 FTE faculty—an overall return-on-investment of 2.9:1 (King, Aerni, et al. 2004). Another study "estimated [the value of] the Portuguese electronic scientific information consortium B-on, using the estimated value of time saved to measure the benefits, obtaining a ratio of [5.35:1]" (Melo and Pires 2009, 8). Kantor and Saracevic also developed a model for the evaluation of digital library impact that includes "the assigned dollar value of the service, the length of time spent using the service, and the question 'was the value worth the time?'" (Kantor and Saracevic, Quantitative Study 1999).

Return-on-investment can be defined as "income received as a percent of the amount invested" or "return value for the life of [an] investment, not just a gain or loss, or a year-to-date return" (Luther 2008, 5). The goal of academic library return-on-investment studies is to "establish a relationship between the library and its university that could be expressed in quantifiable terms that could satisfy administrators" (Tenopir, Measuring the Value 2009, 111). Perhaps the best known academic library return-on-investment study took place at the University of Illinois at Urbana-Champaign (UIUC). At that institution, university administrators have numerous strategic goals; one is to attract and retain top faculty (Luther 2008, 4). A key factor in recruiting top faculty is the ability of an institution to obtain grants (Luther 2008, 4) and, indirectly, prestige (Weiner 2009, 4). Therefore, the UIUC study set out to link the library to grant income generation (Luther 2008, 7) by connecting citations to resources in the library collection to successful grant proposals and the income they generate (Luther 2008, 3). Researchers focused on the ways in which electronic resources increase faculty productivity, productivity increases grant applications, and grant funding generates an environment that is attractive to top faculty recruits (P. T. Kaufman, Library as Strategic Investment 2008, 31). The UIUC study demonstrated that the library produced a return-on-investment of 4.38:1 (P. T. Kaufman, Library as Strategic Investment 2008, 433) in 2006.

In a similar international study, Kaufmann, Luther, Mezick, and Tenopir measured the value of electronic journal collections in academic libraries focusing on grant income. ROIs ranged from under 0.27:1 to 15.54:1 (Tenopir, Love, et al. 2009, 3). According to Tenopir, "this variation has much to do with the purpose of the institution, with the high being for a pure research institute and lower for teaching/research universities in countries without a high number of competitive grant funds. [The researchers recommend] caution…when comparing ROI across institutions" (Measuring the Value 2009, 12).

In light of these studies, librarians can examine the degree to which citations impact whether or not faculty are awarded grants. Certainly, many nonlibrary factors impact grant funding (Lehner 2009, 1). Grant literature indicates that "the whole [grant] system rests on the assumption that the best proposals or the best researchers are winning in the competitive grant application game" (Laudel 2006, 376). According to Laudel (2006, 398, "empirical findings demonstrate that a scientist's successful acquisition of competitive grants is influenced by a variety of factors such as a country's general investment in research, a scientist's research field, the availability of enabling funds, and the continuity of the research trail. These factors depend either partly or not at all on a scientist's or a proposal's quality….Rejecting the quality-only assumption casts doubt on external funding per se as a useful performance indicator. It seems especially problematic to use it in a comparative manner or to aggregate it" (Laudel 2006, 400). Neither of these uses are the intention of current library return-on-investment studies; future researchers can investigate the merits of various data uses.

In the future, researchers might expand library contributions to return-on-investment targets, including patents or technology transfer (P. T. Kaufman, Library as Strategic Investment 2008, 32). They might also explore nonincome outcomes (Lehner 2009, 2), like tuition (Luther 2008, 12), learning outcomes, civic engagement, and campus relations with local, state, national, and international communities (P. T. Kaufman, Library as Strategic Investment 2008, 32).

A substantial volume of literature explains why institutional rank is not a valid indicator of quality. Rankings-based cross-institutional comparisons "can drain time and energy from more significant—and more often internally motivated—assessments of learning, effectiveness, and outcomes" (Keeling, et al. 2008, 3). From an institutional perspective (Capaldi, Lombardi and Abbey, et al. 2008, 3). maintains that they trap many institutions in "a self-defeating effort to manipulate data to make us look better than we are. We can find ourselves pursuing the false god of ranking instead of the true goal of institutional improvement." According to Keeling et al. (2008, 3):

> It is unlikely that the annual ranking of colleges and universities by popular magazines have improved student learning or educational outcomes....There is no evidence that institutions with 'higher rankings' have better student outcomes....and there is certainly no evidence that rankings in magazines have any relationship to the ability of institutions of higher education to serve the public good.

Still other authors argue that institutional rankings do not measure the "real value" of a university (Guskin, Reducing Student 1994; Guskin, Restructuring 1994; Guskin, Facing 1996; Pike, Measuring Quality 2004). The real value of an institution of higher education is "the processes and outcomes of what we do...not what is taught, but what is learned" (Levesque 2002, 3). Pike believes that "educational quality seems to have little to do with resources and reputation" (Pike, Measuring Quality 2004) citing the lack of alignment between institutional NSSE benchmark scores and *U.S. News and World Report* rankings.

Even so, many students make application and matriculation decisions based, at least in part, on institutional rank; changes in *U.S. News and World Report* rankings impact admission outcomes. Faculty also are influenced; *U.S. News and World Report* rankings affect faculty recruitment (Lang 2005) and faculty retention (Matier 1989). They can also impact and university pricing policies (Monks and Ehrenberg 1999), especially at public institutions (Meredith 2004, 459), as well as donations to institutions and other economic factors (Brewer, Brewer and Goldman 2002; Griffith and Rask 2004; Machung 1998; Dahlin-Brown 2005; Zhang 2005; Marginson 2006; Smith-Doerr 2006; Lang 2005). Because "most rankings have some value for some observers interested in some characteristics of higher education institutions" (Capaldi, Lombardi and Abbey, et al. 2008, 3), institutional rankings maintain their importance.

According to *U.S. News and World Report*, they assign greatest weight in their ranking formula to academic reputation; however, many authors dispute this claim. For example, one study found that "the most significant ranking criterion is the average SAT scores of enrolled students" (T. J. Webster 2001, 235), and after SAT, the next most important ranking criterion is graduation rate (T. J. Webster 2001, 243). For top national doctoral universities, one more factor is especially significant: endowment funds. Endowment funds are positively associated with almost all the variables used to rank these institutions. Endowment per student provided an even stronger positive association (Michael 2005, 365). This indicates that "money plays a significant role in how an institution is ranked" (Michael 2005, 365).

Not only is institutional rank a controversial topic in higher education, it is problematic from a library perspective. It is difficult to demonstrate the impact of the library on institutional rank because library services and resources are "intertwined" with other institutional activities (see Figure 4) and hard to isolate (Bertot and McClure 2003; Thompson, Cook and Kyrillidou 2005). For example, studies exist that indicate that higher per student expenditures affect student learning (Toutkoushian and Smart 2001), graduation rates (Goener and Snaith 2003/2004; Blose, Porter and Kokkelenberg 2006), prestige (Grunig 1997; Volkwein and Sweitzer 2006; Francis and Hampton 1999), and library resources (Goener and Snaith 2003/2004; Weiner 2009, 8). In fact, Weiner shows that the contribution of the library to institutional reputation is "disproportionately high" relative to its cost (Weiner 2009, 9). However, common sense suggests that institutions that spend more money per student are better in many areas and none of those areas can take "credit" for their value.

In a similar situation in the United Kingdom, a university's academic excellence (based on its Research Assessment Exercise (RAE)) and its library expenditures have been proven to be indirectly linked (Oppenheim and Stuart 2004, 156). However, this correlation could mean at least three different things: the RAE rating is affected by library expenditures, the RAE rating leads to increased library expenditures, or both are caused by a third factor that increases them both (Oppenheim and Stuart 2004, 163). According to Oppenheimer and Stuart (2004, 164), "the most likely reason for the positive correlation…is that the best institutions have both the best RAE ratings and the best libraries" (Oppenheim and Stuart 2004, 163). Oppenheimer and Stuart conclude, "There needs to be a more detailed study as to *how* the money is spent rather than just *how much* money is spent."

Liu demonstrates a connection between university prestige and library collections and library serials collections. The study purports to "reconfirm that indeed library collections contribute significantly to the prestige of universities" (Liu 2003, 277). Liu argues that "academic research libraries seek to maximize their utility by expanding the size of their library collections" and "the results show that there is a fairly strong association between library volume and serial collections and prestige of universities. Library volume and serials collections accounted for a significant amount of the contribution [26-40%] to prestige of universities" (Liu 2003, 290).

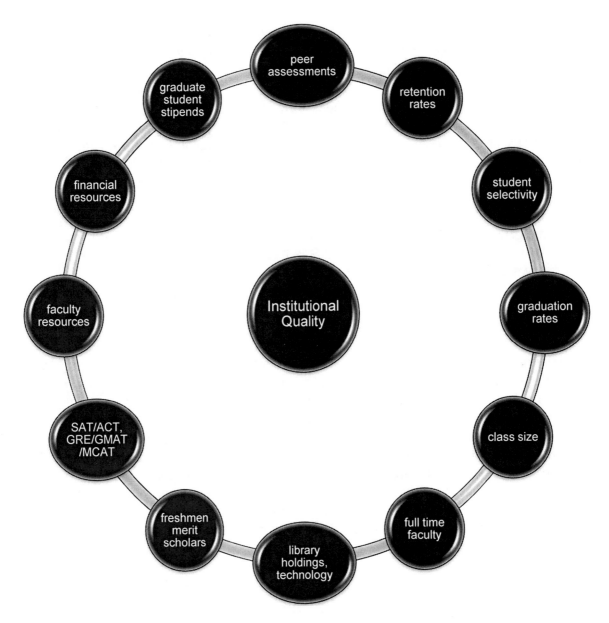

Figure 4. Potential Surrogates of Institutional Quality (Michael 2005, 368)

What About Accreditation?

Although the focus of any assessment effort should be future improvement, there is no denying the persistent emphasis on accreditation as a major driver of assessment in colleges and universities (National Institute for Learning Outcomes Assessment 2009). Regional accrediting agencies motivate institutions to continuously improve. They outline guidelines that serve as a structure for ongoing assessment and improvement; they encourage colleges to articulate goals and demonstrate proof that they are using those goals to seek feedback and improve (Commission on Colleges and Universities 1999). They want educators to respond to broad questions like, "What are students learning? What difference are you making in their lives? What evidence do you have that you're worth our investment?" (Council of Regional Accrediting Commissions 2003).

"All [regional accrediting bodies] seem to place a high value on...information literacy outcomes" (Saunders, Regional Accreditation 2007, 323) rather than traditional library inputs and outputs (Ratteray 2002, 375). According to Saunders, references to information literacy are "scattered" throughout accreditation documents. Librarians can become familiar with their institution's accreditation guidelines in their entirety, and look for terms synonymous with information literacy (Oakleaf, Are They Learning? 2011). Librarians can take the initiative to communicate the presence and importance of information literacy language in accreditation documents and leverage them to integrate information literacy skills into teaching and assessment processes throughout campus (Saunders, Regional Accreditation 2007, 325). They need not act independently. Rather, librarians can ensure that information literacy extends "beyond the walls of the library and into the classroom...[so that] it is the institution as a whole that [provides data to] assure accreditors and other constituents that, upon graduation, students are information literate" (Ratteray 2002, 375). Doing so can improve the library's status on campus and increase its perceived value to the mission of the institution (Saunders, Regional Accreditation 2007, 325).

In fact, Gratch-Lindauer (Comparing the Regional Accreditation Standards 2001) and Rader (2004) suggest that librarians work with regional accreditors to increase the presence of information literacy content in future iterations of accreditation standards. This would not only augment student learning of information literacy content, but promote the role of librarians in the academy (Saunders, Perspectives on Accreditation 2008, 312).

It is important to note that an emphasis on greater articulation of information literacy in accreditation documentation is not a push to artificially standardize the treatment of information literacy on a regional or national basis. Differentiation of outcomes across institution types and cultures is desirable; differences allow individual institutions to tailor content areas to match their students' learning needs. However, explicit language about information literacy in accreditation documents is critical for future assessments as it is difficult to assess a construct that is not clearly understood. Of course, regional accreditation agencies do not determine institutional missions, goals, or outcomes; nor do they require use of specific assessment tools or methods (Baker 2002, 5). Those decisions are left to local stakeholders (Steadman 2001).

Societal Contribution

Libraries of all types value service to society. Academic libraries are underpinned by their value of an "educated populace for a democratic society" (Hisle 2005, 4). Therefore, it is not surprising that some authors suggest "positive societal return" and "social return-on-investment" as frameworks for identifying criteria for examining the value of academic libraries (R. Kaufman 2001, 1). Positive societal return is the return-on-investment to society for what a university spends (R. Kaufman 2001, 1).

Currently, societal contributions are not a part of institutional ranking schemes (R. Kaufman 2001, 8); however, societal outcomes relate to payoffs and consequences of interest to many higher education stakeholders. These outcomes include student survival, quality of life (R. Kaufman 2001, 10), higher pay, and the enjoyment of education itself (Barr 2000, 34). According to Blanchflower and Oswald (2000), "education is associated with greater recorded levels of life satisfaction" and job satisfaction." In addition, community residents who have access to academic library services and resources benefit personally and professionally. This benefit increases when academic libraries partner with school libraries and public libraries to reach more community members (Stoffle, Guskin and Boisse 1984, 12).

Institutions of higher education contribute to societal benefits through the outcomes of funded research. However, it is challenging to isolate the impact of academic libraries on these contributions, in part because the benefits of funded research are diverse (e.g., economic, health, environmental, social, cultural benefits) (Australian Research Council 2008, 2). For example, the National Academies is currently working to define the impact of government funded research in four categories: economic growth (measured by indicators, including patents and business start-ups), workforce outcomes (measured by student mobility into the workforce and employment markers), scientific knowledge (measured by publications and citations), and social outcomes (measured by long-term health and environmental impacts) (Academies 2010). Furthermore, there is extensive lead time between the research itself and its benefits (Australian Research Council 2008, 2). According to the Australian Research Council (2008, 2), there are also many other entities that also impact funded research; "in the process of going from knowledge generation to markets or use, other complementary investments will have been made, which raises issues of attribution of benefits to particular…sources." Still, it is possible that the role libraries play in research contributes to the creation of "thousands of jobs…and help[s]…core industries stay completive in a changing world" (Wisconsin Technology Council 2009, 1).

Academic library contributions to society have not been widely identified or researched. However, once librarians know more about how they contribute to the primary areas of institutional missions—learning, research, and service—they can use the lessons they learn to assess the societal value of those contributions.

A Reminder Regarding Scope

This report is focused on the value of academic libraries and how librarians can demonstrate their impact on learning, research, and service from an institutional perspective. To maintain this focus, some topics had to be omitted, even ones of substantial current interest to librarians, such as library spaces, institutional repositories (Howard 2008), scientific data management (Carlson 2006), embedded librarianship (Dewey 2005), etc. For instance, library spaces are not included in this report, although many library spaces (e.g., learning commons spaces) are designed to support learning and research. Learning commons service models help libraries become campus community centers (Hisle 2005, 13); however, they are a "means to an end."

Developing such useful, even "boutique," services and resources can help libraries "valuably complement [other] services and integrate [themselves] even more deeply into the scholarly life of...campus[es]" (Housewright, Themes of Change 2009, 267). However, this report emphasizes the "ends" or outcomes of academic libraries within an institutional context, not the "means." Consequently, not all topics of interest are included.

Note: Despite efforts to uncover all relevant publications, it is likely that some excellent exemplars of library value research have been missed. The author invites those who have not been included to identify themselves so that their efforts can contribute to the ongoing conversation about academic library value.

What's Next for Academic Library Value Studies?

Recommendations for future academic libraries studies are in the "Next Steps" and "Research Agenda" sections at the end of this report. Many recommendations are based on lessons learned from school, public, and special libraries. Selected library value literature from these environments is included in the sections below.

Academic librarians can learn a great deal about assessing library value from their colleagues in school, public, and special libraries. In particular, school libraries and academic libraries share a mandate to help students learn and teachers teach; they have similar missions and, consequently, similar assessment challenges.

School library literature is dominated by efforts to demonstrate the impact of school libraries and librarians on student learning. According to Harada, "the worth of any school program is based on its contribution to student achievement" (Working Smarter 2005, 8). Schools are in the business of student achievement. When school librarians take part in the assessment of student learning, they align themselves with the goals of their school community (D. K. Logan 2010, 7). Thus librarians can use assessment to address several questions:

- What do school libraries and librarians teach?
- What do students learn from their instruction?
- What record is there of the learning that is produced? (Wiegand 2007)

In answering these questions, librarians shift assessment from their historical focus on inputs and outputs to outcomes, changing "the focus from the medium to the message—from articulating what school librarians do in their day-to-day work to articulating their effect on what students become" (R. J. Todd, A Question of Evidence 2008, 21). This shift has the potential to change the long held view that "school librarians are predominantly library managers and information/resource specialists, rather than instructional partners (R. Todd, School Administrators' Support 2007, 14).

Working with Teachers and Principals

School library literature reveals that school librarians reach and teach students in numerous ways and require both teacher and principal support to be most effective (ASCD 2003). While informal and individualized interactions occur between librarians and students, librarians depend on teachers for instructional access to students. Partnerships between librarians and teachers occur in three forms: cooperation, coordination, and collaboration (Levitov 2006). In some cases, librarians and teachers *cooperate* by communicating informally about student assignments, but work independently to support students. Other librarians and teachers *coordinate* their work by meeting together to discuss student learning, but set goals separately, plan learning experiences separately, teach and assess separately. *Collaboration* occurs when teachers and librarians "jointly set goals, design learning experiences, teach, and evaluate" student studies (R. Todd, Collaboration: From Myth to Reality 2008). According to Immroth and Lukenbill (2007), "collaboration can not only improve student achievement but...it is

Do academic librarians who truly collaborate with faculty impact student learning more significantly than librarians who only coordinate?

essential in improving students' information literacy skills and behaviors." Loertscher and Woolls (2003, 6) outline several benefits to librarian-teacher collaborations: teaching in a technology-rich environment, adding information literacy skills to subject learning standards, increasing the amount students read (Lange, Magee and Montgomery 2003, 5), bringing a systematic approach to research, and producing a positive impact on learning. However, true collaboration can be difficult to achieve. Indeed, "available data show that the concept of collaboration is more espoused than practiced" by school librarians (R. Todd, Collaboration: From Myth to Reality 2008). Librarians who are active in school leadership, attend meetings, communicate with principals, and serve on committees are more likely to collaborate with teachers (D. Achterman 2007, 51). These collaborations in practice can be measured by a "repeat customer" count that tracks the percentage of teachers who collaborate with librarians on a regular basis (Lange, Magee and Montgomery 2003, 5).

School librarians also benefit from the cooperation of school principals. According to McGregor, librarians require visible principal support when attempting to connect with teachers. They need principals to integrate the school library into the whole school plan, support librarian and teacher collaborations, regard librarians as essential to learning, and encourage librarian-led staff development (Henri, Hay and Oberg 2002). When librarians provide professional development in-services for teachers, there is a positive impact on

To what extent does library director or academic dean support impact academic librarians' ability to add value to student learning and faculty research?

teaching strategies (Anderson 2002, 34). In fact, when principals expect and support librarian-teacher collaborations, including librarian-led in-services, higher student achievement is attained (McGregor 2002). Unfortunately, one study found that "only 47% [of principals] saw a direct link between the school library and student achievement, and even fewer, 41%, agreed strongly that the school library had a positive impact on test scores" (R. Todd, School Administrators' Support 2007, 14). Still, school librarians are taking an active approach to securing principal support of school libraries (Institute for Library and Information Literacy Education 2010).

Evidence-Based Practice and Action Research

In order to capture evidence of the impact of school libraries on student achievement, school librarians have embraced evidence-based practice and action research approaches.

Evidence-based practice is the "collection, interpretation, and evaluation of the research on a particular issue and using that evaluation to make a decision concerning the issue" (Reeder, Where's the Evidence? 2008, 30). Broadly defined, evidence-based practice is "fundamentally about professional practice being informed and guided by best available evidence of what works" (Bogel 2008, 15). Evidence-based practice in school libraries is "an approach to professional practice in school libraries that systematically engages research-derived evidence, school librarian-observed evidence, and user reported evidence in iterative processes of decision-making, development, and continuous improvement to achieve the school's mission and goals, which fundamentally center on student achievement, quality learning, and quality teaching" (R. J. Todd, Evidence Based Practice 2007). In a departure from asking stakeholders and the public to "believe" in school libraries, evidence-based practice moves from a "rhetorical warrant to an evidential warrant...from a tell me framework to a show me framework, from a persuasive or advocacy framework to a declarative framework" (R. J. Todd, Hearing the Voices 2007). By using evidence-based practice, librarians can answer questions like:

- What are the learning outcomes of your school library?
- How do the learning outcomes measurably impact student achievement?
- If the principal asks for evidence of your impact on student achievement, how would you produce the data? (Geitgey and Tepe 2007, 10)

Rather than prescribing one approach to answering these questions, evidence-based practice recognizes the value of "multiple sources, types of evidence, and ways of gathering evidence. The use of multiple sources facilitates triangulation—and approach to data analysis that synthesizes data from multiple sources. By using and comparing data from a number of sources, you can develop stronger claims about your...impact and outcomes" (R. Todd, The Evidence-Based Manifesto 2008, 40). In fact, researchers at Syracuse University, Rutgers, and Florida State University plan to create a digital library to collect evidence-based practices and research, such as data collection tools, evaluation tools, best practice tutorials, video testimonials, and research reports (Whelan, Up, Up, and Away 2010, 36).

Evidence-based practice encourages librarians to conduct their own research (Koufogiannakis and Crumley 2006), often according to an action research model. Action research is "used for the analysis and reflection of everyday problems in the practitioner's specific situation...[in action research, a librarian] reflects on an existing practice or problem, collects data, analyzes the data, and subsequently implements a plan of action" (Burger and McFarland 2009, 38). When action research is completed in collaboration with other teachers or schools, it "strengthens the meaning of the data...[and] the results are more easily seen as fact rather than opinion" (Dickinson 2001, 17). Action research and evidence-based practice both help school librarians give "local school context" to large-scale research findings (Dickinson 2001, 19).

Assessment Tools

School librarians have used a variety of assessment tools to demonstrate their impact on local student learning (Lance and Loertscher, Powering Achievement 2001). Although the school library literature describes these tools and their benefits, it includes little specific data on what these assessment tools have revealed about student achievement. Still, the assessment tools are designed in the context of outcomes, goals, guidelines, and standards (Castonguay 2004, 9). Standards-based assessments are particularly important because they "bring credibility...[and] rich teaching partnerships" to the school library program and increase student achievement (Jewett 2003, 4). These assessments demonstrate to stakeholders that school librarians are valuable to students and staff (Marie, From Theory to Practice 2005, 20) and can give a local facet to larger-scale school library studies. Assessment tools found in school library literature are listed below. In most cases, these assessment tools mark a departure from previous evaluation measures. To gather data about student achievement, school librarians have altered what they collected in the past, moving from collection and usage statistics to tools that demonstrate what students have learned (Geitgey and Tepe 2007, 11; Loertscher and Todd 2003; Champlin, Loertscher and Miller 2008). Examples include:

- Mission monitoring (McGriff, Harvey II and Preddy, Collecting the Data 2004)
- Focus groups
- Rubrics identifying criteria and levels of successful learning performance (Harada, Working Smarter 2005, 10)
- Evidence folders (Harada, From Eyeballing to Evidence 2007)
- Tests
- Control group studies
- Surveys
- Observations
- Checklists of desired learning behaviors (Harada, Working Smarter 2005, 10)

Which of these assessment tools can most effectively assess student learning produced by academic libraries?

- Rating sales (Harada, Working Smarter 2005, 10)
- Worksheets (Edwards 2007)
- Examinations of student work (Everhart, Evaluation of School Library 2003)
- Graphic organizers synthesizing student work characteristics (Harada, Working Smarter 2005, 10)
- Plus/Delta charts (Vandeventer 2007)
- Formal and informal conferences
- Reflection journals, logs, letters, and notes (Harada, Working Smarter 2005, 10)
- Process journals, logs, letters, and notes (Harada, Working Smarter 2005, 10)
- Interviews of students
- Usage statistics
- Large-scale test score analysis (Valenza 2004, 8)
- Comment cards (Geitgey and Tepe 2007, 12)
- Minute papers (Geitgey and Tepe 2007, 12)
- Portfolios
- Case studies (Lance and Russell, Scientifically Based 2004, 14)
- Critical incidents (Lance and Russell, Scientifically Based 2004, 14)
- General student data (R. Todd, The Evidence-Based Manifesto 2008, 40; Geitgey and Tepe 2007, 12)
- Lesson plans (Harada, Librarians and Teachers 2005, 53)
- Anecdotal evidence

A number of these assessment tools merit a bit more detail; they follow below:

Mission Monitoring

Mission monitoring uses program data "to affirm that the library...activities and services...are consistent with the library's...stated mission" (McGriff, Harvey II and Preddy, Collecting the Data 2004). To use this tool, school librarians create a grid with three main areas: "what we say," "evidence we have," "evidence we need." This approach ensures that librarians focus on "data that relates to the stated mission of the library media center" (McGriff, Harvey II and Preddy, Collecting the Data 2004). This technique is even more effective when librarians and principal share the responsibility for matching data collection with espoused values (D. Johnson 2001, 14).

> *Are academic libraries efforts consistent with their missions? Their institutions' missions? Do academic librarians' espoused values match their enacted values?*

Evidence Folders

Library evidence folders are compiled by school librarians to document evidence of the value of school libraries. They might include:

- Descriptions of how the library mission connects with the school mission
- Descriptions of major library learning targets
- Descriptions of how library instruction connects with learning targets
- Sample lesson plans
- Samples of student work
- Compiled assessment data
- Comments from teachers and students about future improvements (Harada, Building Evidence 2006).

These folders help librarians collect and reflect on assessment efforts, demonstrate the library's contribution to student achievement, and summarize the learning that results from library instruction. In addition, they are "intended as communication tools with key stakeholder groups in the school community" (Harada, Building Evidence 2006).

A related tool is the "literacy autobiography" described in (Collier 2007, 31-32). Such teaching autobiographies serve as reflective guides to good teaching practice. According to a study by Collier, over 50% of pre-service teacher autobiographies make positive mention of school libraries or librarians.

Focus Groups

Focus groups are helpful tools for assessing school library value; they can be used to "discover the perceptions, feelings, and beliefs of students"; "generate lists of problems, unmet needs, or ideas for new services or programs; [or] test and refine new products, services, and programs (Hughes-Hassell and Bishop 2004, 8). Data that results from focus groups can be used "in planning, making decisions, evaluating programs, products, or services, [and] enriching findings from other research methods" (Hughes-Hassell and Bishop 2004, 8). For example, Bishop used focus groups to "understand what impact projects that were collaboratively developed between…librarians and teachers had on student learning" (Hughes-Hassell and Bishop 2004, 11), and Hughes-Hassell used them to "gather data from teachers about their students, the curriculum, and methods of instruction used in their classrooms" to build a new library collection (Hughes-Hassell and Bishop 2004, 12).

Rubrics

Rubrics are a mainstay of K-12 educational assessment, especially when authentic assessment approaches are used to measure student learning. Many educators feel that, "overreliance on traditional assessments, such as multiple-choice tests, limits the type and quality of information we can gather" (Wiggins 1998). Consequently, teachers and librarians employ other examples of student work for

> *How might academic librarians expand rubric use to better capture the impact of libraries on learning and research?*

assessment, such as: research papers, posters, oral presentations, videos, Web sites (Mueller 2005, 16), worksheets (Edwards 2007), or reflective responses (Todd, Kuhlthau and Heinstrom, School Library Impact Measure 2005). In order to analyze student work samples, librarians can work independently or with teachers (Mueller 2005, 16, 18) to create rubrics. Rubrics help communicate learning expectations to students and parents (Shaw 2004, 16), promote scoring consistency (Shaw 2004, 18), align librarian and teacher instructional agendas, help teachers view librarians as true instructional partners (Loertscher and Woolls 2003, 7), and "satisfy the current public demand for greater transparency in student evaluation" (Shaw 2004, 19). In addition to assessing student skill levels, rubrics can also be designed to evaluate entire school library programs (Sample Evaluation Checklists 2003).

Control Groups

According to the U.S. Department of Education, randomized control trials are the gold standard of research quality (Bogel 2008, 12). They should be "well designed and implemented" (Coalition for Evidence-Based Policy 2003). As early as the 1960s, control

> *What types of randomized control trials are needed to demonstrate the impact of academic libraries?*

group studies demonstrated that student performance and reading habits are improved when students participate in library-centered teaching (Neelameghan 2007). In more recent times, one study found that school libraries have an impact on student reading habits, use of materials for non-school-related activities, and academic performance (Dent 2006). Another revealed decreased plagiarism and increased sophistication of information integration in research papers (Daniels 2007).

Tests

The most well known test in school library literature is TRAILS. The TRAILS test was designed to be "a class assessment tool that was standards-based; provided both class and individual outcomes; assured privacy; and was web-based, easy to use, and available at no cost" (Schloman and Gedeon 2007, 45). There are multiple test forms available, so it can be used as a pre- and post-test (Geitgey and Tepe 2007, 12). In general, TRAILS data shows that high school seniors perform better than ninth graders (Schloman and Gedeon 2007, 46). Students have higher scores on the portions of TRAILS that focus on "identifying potential sources and recognizing how to use information responsibly, ethically, and legally" (Schloman and Gedeon 2007, 46). They tend to struggle with areas that ask them to "develop, use, and revise search strategies," identify or focus a topic, and evaluate information according to criteria (Schloman and Gedeon 2007, 47). One school-specific study reports that most ninth grade students understood the concept of primary resources, 91% know to ask a librarian for help, and 95% correctly identified the public library as the best source for new fiction books (Owen 2010, 37-38).

> *What impact on student learning might be revealed by connecting student academic library interactions to test scores in higher education?*

Another school librarian deployed a locally developed test via a learning management system, Blackboard, to assess ninth grade student skills at the beginning and end of the school year. The test showed improvement over the year, although no specific details are provided. The librarian does detail benefits of using a test embedded in a learning management system, including viewing scores in real time and maintaining records without excessive paperwork (Dando 2005, 24). Clearly, such test scores can aid school librarians seeking to assess student information skills. Even so, Achterman believes that "standards-based test scores alone are an extremely narrow definition of academic achievement" (2007, 52) that must be augmented by other assessment tools both qualitative and quantitative.

Surveys

School library literature is replete with survey-based assessment data; most surveys are large scale in scope and covered in the section below. However, some small scale survey data is also available. For example, Marie and Weston recount a survey taken at one high school. Forty-nine percent of student respondents said they received higher grades due to the library, 69% said they completed assignments more quickly, and 67% said they felt more confident using other libraries (Marie and Weston, Survey Says 2009, 53). In another school, the librarian also has students analyze and report survey results to their peers (D. K. Logan 2006). McGriff, Harvey, and Preddy (2004) suggest numerous ideas for single school surveys.

A variety of large-scale studies of school libraries exist: some conducted by professional associations, some by independent researchers, and many organized according to states. One well-known large scale tool is the American Association of School Libraries (AASL) "School Libraries Count" survey. The "School Libraries Count" survey gathers data on library hours, staff levels, staff activities, collections, technology, usage, expenditures, and digital resources (American Association of School Librarians 2010). However, this survey does not collect data directly related to the impact of school libraries on student achievement. An earlier study of the Library Power Initiative investigated 40 schools nationwide and found that a team-teaching approach to inquiry was a key factor in fostering student learning in school libraries (Kuhlthau 2005, 50).

An independent researcher, Krashen conducted a large-scale study that investigated the relationship between libraries and student reading. Krashen examined school and public libraries and connected the availability of information to test scores (S. D. Krashen 1995). He demonstrated that "students who have access to more reading materials...are more likely to read voluntarily, read more and more often, and score better on achievement tests" (S. Krashen, The Power of Reading 2004). Another researcher, Elley, found a positive association between school libraries and reading achievement in 32 countries (Elley 1992).

Test-Correlated State Studies

Other large-scale school library studies are divided by states. State studies have established the relationship between school libraries and state-wide standardized test scores (Hamilton-Pennell, et al. 2000) (Tepe and Geitgey 2002). State studies have shown that libraries impact student achievement when librarians collaborate with teachers to integrate information skills into the curriculum and are supported fiscally and programmatically by the educational community to achieve the school mission (SLW at scholastic.com, p 6).

State	Selected Results
Alaska	<ul><li>Level of librarian staffing, library hours, library staff activities, library usage, online access, and level of collaboration between school and public libraries all have an effect on academic achievement (Lance, Still Making an Impact 1999).</li><li>Higher CAT5 scores are associated with librarians spending more time with students, delivering information literacy instruction, planning with teachers, providing in-service training to teachers, and having a working relationship with public libraries (Lance, Still Making an Impact 1999).</li><li>First study to identify librarians as teachers of information literacy and show the impact on achievement when librarians provide teacher in-service training (Lance, Impact of School Library Media Programs 2002, 33).</li></ul>

California	• Levels of certified staffing are correlated to the level of library service, and the level of library service is related to increases in STAR test scores. This relationship increases with grade level (D. Achterman 2009, 26).
	• Test scores increase in relation to library hours (D. Achterman 2009, 26).
	• Test scores increase when librarians offer curriculum-integrated information literacy instruction, Internet searching and research instruction, and informal instruction on resource use (D. Achterman 2009, 26).
	• These relationships remain significant when school and community variables are accounted for (average parent education level, poverty level, ethnicity, percentage of English language learners, percentage of highly qualified teachers, and average teacher salary) (D. Achterman 2009, 26).
Colorado (1)	• Students at schools with better funded libraries achieve higher average reading scores, whether their schools and communities are rich or poor, well or poorly educated (Lance, Proof of the Power 2004).
	• The size of a library program, as indicated by staff and collection size, is the best predictor of student achievement (Lance, Proof of the Power 2004).
	• Library expenditures predict the size of the staff and collection and, in turn, student achievement (Lance, Proof of the Power 2004).
	• The librarian's instructional role shapes the collection and, in turn, student achievement (Lance, Proof of the Power 2004).
Colorado (2)	• Reading scores increase as library program development increases (hours, print volumes, periodical subscriptions, electronic reference titles, expenditures); information technology; librarian and teacher collaboration (cooperative planning, identifying materials for teachers, providing in-service training); and individual visits to the library. These relationships are not explained away by school or community conditions, such as expenditures per student, teacher/student ratio, average years experience of teachers, average salaries, adult educational attainment in the community, poverty levels, and racial/ethnic demographics (Lance, Rodney and Hamilton-Pennell, How School Librarians Help 2000).
	• When library predictors are maximized, reading scores are 10-18 percent higher (Lance, Rodney and Hamilton-Pennell, How School Librarians Help 2000).
Connecticut	• Required collaborations between librarians and science teachers increase student achievement on the Connecticut Academic Performance Test (Snyder and Roche 2008, 23). Student scores

	increased from 75% to 80.7% in one year (Snyder and Roche 2008, 24).
Florida	• High school FCAT scores are higher when library hours are greater, there are more certified librarians, more interlibrary loans, and more library visits (Baumbach 2003, 5). • FCAT and ACT scores are higher when there are more visits by individual students to the library. Individual visits are increased with library hours, books, subscriptions, and expenditures (Baumbach 2003, 5).
Illinois	• Test scores are higher at schools with more library staffing, librarian and teacher collaboration, current collections, library spending, and circulation (Lance and Loertscher, Powering Achievement 2005).
Indiana	• Higher test scores are connected to full-time school librarians employed in the same school for at least three years (Scholastic 2008). • Higher test scores are related to principal support of school librarian and teacher collaboration (Scholastic 2008).
Iowa	• Higher reading test scores are connected to development of school library programs (Scholastic 2008).
Kentucky	• Study is based on standards-related questionnaire rather than a standardized survey instrument (Houston 2008, 2). • Commonwealth Accountability Testing System scores are connected to data from the state's Library Media Report (Allard and White 2001, 8). • Formal collaboration and promotion of information literacy have a greater impact on test scores than socio-economic status (Houston 2008, 2).
Massachusetts	• High-quality school libraries are linked to high scores on the Massachusetts Comprehensive Assessment System (Glick, Smart State Shortchanges School Libraries 2000, 26). • Students from low-income families who attend schools with good libraries score higher on tests than students from low-income families that do not (Kertesz 2000).
Michigan	• Higher reading test scores are linked to the presence of certified school librarians (Scholastic 2008).
Minnesota	• High test scores are related to increased library spending (Scholastic 2008).
Missouri	• School library services have a 10.6% impact on student achievement (Scholastic 2008).
New Mexico	• Test scores rise with the development of school library programs (Scholastic 2008).
New York	• Study examined student achievement, motivation for learning, and technology use (Small and Snyder 2010, 61-62). • Language test scores in schools with certified librarians are up to

	10% higher than those in schools without librarians (New Study Reaffirms School Library, Academic Link 2008).
North Carolina	• School library programs impact reading and English tests (Scholastic 2008).
Ontario	• Student achievement is linked to well-stocked and professionally staffed libraries. • Students in schools with trained librarians are more likely to enjoy reading and perform better on standardized reading tests (Weiss 2006, 19).
Oregon	• Academic achievement can be predicated by library hours, print volumes, periodical subscriptions, and expenditures (Lance, Impact of School Library Media Programs 2002, 32). • Group and individual library visits can predict test performance (Lance, Impact of School Library Media Programs 2002, 33).
Pennsylvania	• Higher reading scores are associated with school librarian presence, library hours, expenditures, collections, computers, and staff time spent integrating information literacy into school curriculum and determining linkages to academic standards (Lance and Rodney, Impact of School Libraries 2010, 31).
Texas	• Library predictors may account for up to 8% of variance in reading-related test scores (E. G. Smith 2001).
Wisconsin	• Library predictors account for higher test scores at high school level (7.9% reading, 19% language arts) (Lance, The Future of School Librarianship n.d.). • Library predictors of academic achievement include: professional staff, planning with classroom teachers, team teaching with classroom teachers, teaching without classroom teachers, providing in-service training for teachers, developing collections, identifying resources for classroom teachers, meeting regularly with principals, attending faculty meetings, serving on key communities, meeting with other librarians, library hours, library usage, and number of computers (Lance and Loertscher, Powering Achievement 2005).

The Ohio, Delaware, Idaho, and New Jersey studies took different approaches to establishing library value, as described below.

Ohio and Delaware Studies

The Ohio and Delaware studies asked students to describe how school libraries help them in their academic work (R. J. Todd, Hearing the Voices 2007). In these studies, help was "conceptual defined as institutional involvement through advice and assistance in the information seeking and use experiences of people, and the effect of the institution's activities and services on the people it serves" (R. J. Todd, Hearing the Voices 2007). In addition to close-ended questions, these studies included an open-ended question: "Now, remember one time when the school library really helped you. Write about the help that you got, and what you were able to do because of it" (R. J. Todd, Hearing the Voices 2007). Students discussed help from library-based instruction, and student descriptions of "help" fell into seven categories:

- getting information students need;
- getting help using information to complete student school work;
- getting help with their school work in general;
- getting help using computers in the library, at school, and at home;
- getting help with their general reading interests;
- getting help when students are not at school; and
- getting encouragement to work better and get better grades (Lance, How School Library Leave No Child Behind 2002, 4).

In addition, 99.4 percent of students in grades 3 to 12 believe school libraries and their services help them become better learners...88.5 percent...say the school library helps them get better grades on projects and assignments, 74.7 percent say it helps with homework" (Whelan, 13,000 Kids Can't Be Wrong 2004). After the Ohio study was completed, Ohio librarians organized ongoing evidence-based practice professional development sessions to encourage librarians to extend and expand upon the results (Geitgey and Tepe 2007, 10). The survey can be used by individual school librarians, in whole or in part, to get feedback from students in their local institution (Geitgey and Tepe 2007, 12).

Idaho Study

The Idaho study surveyed principals and other administrators. Results indicate that "where administrators value strong library programs and can see them doing their part for student success, students are more likely to thrive academically" (Lance, Impact of School Library Media Programs on Academic Achievement 2002, 14). Researchers recommend that principals should "make it known" that they expect librarian and teacher collaborations to be the norm, not the exception; meet with the librarian regularly; and educate prospective hires on the librarian's role in the school (Lance and Rodney, Impact of School Libraries 2010, 16).

New Jersey Study

While not strictly considered a "state study," a sample of New Jersey librarians participated in a small investigation to determine what learning "looks like" when students use information to complete school assignments. This study revealed two main student behaviors: 1) an "additive approach to knowledge construction, where knowledge development seemed to be characterized by the progressive addition of facts, and it remained on a descriptive level throughout" and 2) an "integrative approach...[where students] manipulated...facts in a number of ways: building explanations, synthesizing facts into more abstract groupings,...organizing facts in more coherent ways, reflecting on facts to build positional, predictive conclusion statements"

(R. J. Todd, Hearing the Voices 2007). This study may be reflective of a coming trend in studies: the development of models describing in detail what students look like when they're learning and when they're not.

Assessment Management Systems

Like academic librarians, school librarians often struggle to document and analyze assessment results. School library literature reveals three different solutions to the problem of managing assessment results. Smith recounts how one school librarian uses logs to track usage data in her library and helped her respond to a Title I audit. Tracking assessment data helped her make the "intangible" value of her library visible, marked a "turning point" in her assessment efforts, and provided information to develop conversations and collaborations previously considered impossible (S. S. Smith 2007, 22).

Groups of school librarians also seek to manage their assessment data. One school library system developed a wiki to track their assessment of the impact of subscription databases on student achievement. Their wiki included research questions, literature reviews, calendars, meeting agendas, notes, reflections, and documented research progress. They used the wiki to share information and findings, comment on work, provide suggestions, brainstorm, collaborate efficiently, compare and contrast results, and, perhaps most importantly, share results with teachers and administrators (Burger and McFarland 2009, 38).

Multiple school districts can also collaborate to manage their assessment information, including the degree of library integration into school curriculum, staffing levels, size/currency of collections, and collaborations between librarians and teachers. Houston-area school librarians developed an online instrument, available to all Texas school librarians, to collect and compare library data related to state-wide standards, identify strengths and weaknesses, and format that data into graphs and goal sheets for presentation to principals and teachers (Dubbin, Beyer and Prueit 2002). Systems like these, allow school librarians to produce information about the impact of school libraries that can be reported widely.

Reporting Results

According to Ballard (2008, 22), school librarians often fail to report assessment data until budget cuts or other problems are imminent. Rather, there are three proactive strategies to employ before an issue arises: creating visibility, engaging in honest assessment, and using evidentiary data. Once librarians produce assessment data that shows the value of their libraries and ability to contribute to student learning, they need to share that data with stakeholders (Hamilton-Pennell, et al. 2000, 47). Geitney and Tepe state, "It is truly important not to keep the data to yourself, and remember never to just drop the data in front of your staff or principal. Early in the data-sharing process, begin by telling your colleagues about the nature of your…project, and then continue to supply them with the data from the students" (Geitgey and Tepe 2007, 12). It also helps to include details about how teacher collaboration was employed, because "if you make your teachers and administrators look good, they'll think you're valuable" (York 2004, 39). Indeed one librarian creates positive feedback forms for collaborative teachers which are shared with the principal and included in yearly appraisals (York 2004, 39).

One reporting challenge is to move data beyond library walls. According to Lance and Russell, "one of the frequent laments of school library advocates is that we spend too much time preaching to the choir. In the end, research on school library impact will have its greatest effect when it reaches the ears of school administrators (school boards, superintendents, principals), other educators (classroom teachers, technology specialists), parents, and students" (Lance and Russell, Scientifically Based 2004, 16). Venues for communicating school library assessment results include staff and parent meetings, school administrator meetings, school library Web sites, school newsletters, community newspapers, association meetings (Todd, Kuhlthau and Heinstrom, School Library Impact Measure 2005, 14), and librarian journals (Dickinson 2001, 16).

What's Next for School Library Value Studies?

Lance summarizes new directions for school librarians seeking to extend research in the area of school library impact on student learning (Enough Already! n.d.). School library research needs to:

- drill down into state achievement tests and complete item-by-item analysis (Geitgey and Tepe 2007, 11);
- establish stronger causal evidence;
- increase randomized control trials;
- determine impact of specific library programs, practices, or policies on student learning;
- track student cohorts over longer periods of time;
- document negative impacts on student achievement linked to reductions in library staffing, services, or sources;
- include an evidence and research track at library conferences (R. Todd, The Evidence-Based Manifesto 2008, 42);
- develop a clearinghouse of assessment exemplars (R. Todd, The Evidence-Based Manifesto 2008, 42);
- influence teachers, principals, administrators, and public officials through their literature, press, and conferences; and
- impact the curriculum of colleges of education and library/information science.

Traditionally, public library value research has been categorized into two broad areas: studies that focus on the economic value, benefits, and impact of public libraries and studies that emphasize their social impact. Academic library value research can be divided in similar ways: financial value and impact value. Consequently, academic librarians can benefit from knowledge of public library value research.

Economic Value

Most public library value literature focuses on the **economic value** of libraries. The goal of this literature is to determine "a financial amount expressing the importance of library services to individuals within the community" (Library Council of New South Wales 2009). Because libraries do not exist primarily to generate economic activity, their economic value can be expressed as an imputed amount involving no exchange of goods and services (Library Council of New South Wales 2009). Thus, when estimating public library economic value, researchers attempt to determine the value that people derive from the library, whether or not they use it (Aabo and Audunson, Rational Choice and Valuation of Public Libraries, 2002, 12), and include the value that nonusers of public libraries assign to their sense of contentment that libraries exist and that they have the option to use them in the future (Jura Consultants 2008). There are two major categories for measuring the economic value of public libraries: consumer surplus and contingent valuation.

Consumer Surplus

Consumer surplus, one measure of public library economic value, emphasizes the "value a consumer (or public library user) places on a good or service in excess of what they must pay to get it….[and] the willingness of a library user to purchase this substitute good when the library service is not available is measured (through the use of survey instruments) and summed, and repeated for other services" (Barron, et al. 2005). For example, library users might be asked, "if you did not have this library available to provide investment information, how much money would you likely spend each year to obtain this information?" In South Carolina's public library survey, 20% of respondents said $500 or more, and 6% said over $1,000 (Barron, et al. 2005, 13). The consumer surplus is equal to "the difference between what consumers would have been willing to pay and the market price…because most consumers are able to enjoy a relative bargain at the market price. In other words, they would have been willing to pay more than the market price. If a good or service is free, then the bargain (the consumer surplus) is even greater. The goal of the approach for valuing free library services is to ascertain the additional consumer surplus that results from providing priced goods for free" (Barron, et al. 2005, 13-14).

One popular type of consumer surplus assessment is known as **contingent valuation** (see Figure 5). Contingent valuation encourages users to "give an opinion or assessment of [a] good directly" (Aabo and Audunson, Rational Choice and Valuation of Public Libraries, 2002, 6) by asking them for "a totally subjective valuation of how much they would pay for library

> *How much would academic library users be willing to pay for library services and resources?*

services, or alternatively how much they would accept in the form of tax savings if library services were eliminated" (Duncan 2008) There are two main forms of questioning: willingness to pay (WTP) and willingness to accept (WTA). WTP elicits how much an individual would be willing to pay for a library service were they required to pay for it; WTA focuses on how much money they would accept in order to forgo the good or service. In general, WTP valuations tend to be lower than WTA valuations, since 'willingness to pay' tends to be influenced by people's budget constraints (Pung, Clarke and Patten 2004, 88). Conversely, WTA is usually higher and sometimes considered inflated (Jura Consultants 2008, 20). The difference may be attributable to "loss aversion"; people value losses higher than they do gains (Jura Consultants 2008, 21). Different valuation approaches produce a range of value estimates, so some studies tend to use both approaches and hope for an estimated, defensible final result (Pung, Clarke and Patten 2004, 88).

Public Library Study	Results
New South Wales Public Libraries	Users WTP $58.20 per year Per capita expenditure was $42.73 Users WTP 36.2% over expenditures
UK Public Libraries	Book loans valued at 30-50 pence, approximately 7-8% of purchase price
British Library	4.4:1
St. Louis Public Library	4:1
Wagga Wagga City Library	1.33:1 overall 2.4:1 technical services (Hider, How Much 2008, 254)
Norwegian Public Libraries	4:1
Bolton Museum, Library And Archive Services	1.60:1 (Bolton Metropolitan Borough Council 2005)
United States	average tax increase Americans are willing to pay to support public libraries: $49 (New York Library Association 2004)
Korea Public Library	0.84:1-2.95:1 depending on method employed (Chung, Contingent Valuation 2008, 76)
New Zealand Public Libraries	Average value of book loans is 25.3% of purchase price

Figure 5. Contingent Valuation Studies Using WTP and/or WTA

The contingent valuation approach to public library value offers several benefits. For instance, it focuses on users (Jura Consultants 2008; Morris, Hawkins and Sumsion, Value of Book 2001; Morris, Sumsion and Hawkins 2002), but offers the potential to have both users and nonusers attribute a value to library services. Because it conveys user perceptions of public library value, it can be used to present a value for money argument (Jura Consultants 2008). However, like other library value assessment approaches, it also presents some challenges. For example, some economists argue that contingent valuation techniques have yet to be proven as valid (Hider, Using the Contingent Valuation 2008, 439). Contingent valuations are also susceptible to potential biases, including yea-saying (the tendency to answer "yes" or overestimate), protest answers (the tendency to refuse to answer at all since respondents oppose the payment vehicle), and information bias (the likelihood of not providing valid answers due to lack of familiarity with library services) (Chung, Contingent Valuation 2008, 72). In addition, WTP is often overstated, especially in response to hypothetical scenarios (Hider, Using the Contingent Valuation 2008, 439); Loomis, et al. 1996). WTA is often even more inflated (Jura Consultants 2008, 20). For example, in one study the WTP estimate was close to the average annual library costs per household in Norway, while the WTA estimate was five times higher (Aabo, Libraries and Return on Investment 2009). Furthermore, contingent valuation requires detailed surveys of library patrons that are expensive in terms of both time and money. Thus, critics see contingent valuation as costly surveys that yield only speculative information (Indiana Business Research Center 2007, 13; Levin, Driscoll, and Fleeter 2006). Fortunately, there are techniques for correcting some of these difficulties (Jura Consultants 22-23; (Chung, Contingent Valuation 2008, 73). According to Hider (2008, 437), if contingent valuation "surveys are carefully designed and administered, they can produce estimates that are as convincing as those produced by other valuation methods."

It is worth noting that not all contingent valuation studies use WTP and WTA strategies. Some surveys ask questions to elicit information on consumer surplus without utilizing the specific CV approach of WTP and WTA (see Figure 6).

Study	Results
St. Louis	Surveyed users to identify consumer surplus using phone surveys. Interviewers asked patrons about the number of books they borrow from the library, the books they purchased, and additional books that they would buy if they could not borrow. By comparing the number of books a patron borrows with the number of books he/she would buy at market price, it is possible to calculate the value that library patrons place on borrowing materials above and beyond any cost of traveling to and the time involved in using the library. This value is a dollar measure of the net benefits provided by the library's borrowing privileges (Holt and Elliott 2003).
South Carolina	Survey questions included: "What dollar value would you assign to this library's investment information resources?" 32% said between $10,000 and $1 million; 2% said over $1 million (Barron, et al. 2005).

Florida	Respondents indicated in dollar terms the value to them of individual library programs and services. The total of these calculations was taken to equal the total benefits received by library users (Chung, Contingent Valuation 2008, 72).

Figure 6. Contingent Valuation Studies Using Techniques Other Than WTP/WTA

Economic Benefit

Public library value strategy literature also focuses on **economic benefit** or "the financial amount saved relative to the cost of obtaining services from alternate sources. It is an imputed amount and involves no exchange of goods and services, thus no economic activity is generated" (Library Council of New South Wales 2009). This strategy is also a consumer surplus approach, but "instead of using stated preference techniques or techniques where users simply state a value estimate," assessing economic benefit means identifying the tangible advantage "that occurs when users utilize library services at a cost lower than the cost of equivalent commercially available services" (Library Council of New South Wales 2009).

Library Valuation

There are two ways to measure value using the economic benefit strategy. The first is **library valuation** or **costs of alternatives**. This method involves measuring the actual costs of alternatives to library services in a local economy. From the actual costs of similar services, researchers can calculate a total value of the library service (see Figure 7). Services typically valued include books, magazines, newspapers, movies, audio books, interlibrary loans, meeting room use, programs attended, computer use, and reference questions. To facilitate this approach of valuing public library services, helpful "value calculators" have been produced. Two examples are the Massachusetts Library Association (http://69.36.174.204/value-new/how.html) and Maine State Library (http://www.maine.gov/msl/services/calculator.htm) value calculators.

Study	Results
New South Wales	4.24: 1
UK	values a "read" of a book rather than a lending transaction (Sumsion, Hawkins and Morris 2002) book purchase estimated at 20 percent (Morris, Hawkins and Sumsion, Value of Book 2001; Morris, Sumsion and Hawkins, Economic Value 2002)
Ohio	2.56:1
New Brunswick and Ontario	user Internet access = $2.53 per capita
Indiana	items checked out = $547.3 million reference questions = $10/question
Florida	reference questions = $2/question
Massachusetts	reference questions = $7/question

Maine	reference questions = $15/question
St. Louis	reference questions = $50/hour

Figure 7. Examples of Public Library Valuation

The library valuation approach to establishing public library value has a major benefit; it demonstrates "the large amount of income that the library is saving and providing for users" to stakeholders (Pasamba 2009). Still, there are challenges associated with public library valuation. First, not all stakeholders equate concepts of value and worth (Debono 2002, 82). Second, the values used in this approach are estimated and sometimes not rooted in economic reality. Thus the values are open to questioning, especially for services (e.g., reference, special events, and programming). Third, library valuation does not account for "non-use" (Indiana Business Research Center 2007, 14-15). Fourth, the results of valuation tend to be very conservative (Levin, Driscoll, and Fleeter 2006, 10).

Investment in Access

Another way to assess economic benefit is by measuring **user investment** or **Investment in access**. This method is based on the idea that libraries "save users millions of dollars each year in time not wasted attempting to recreate data already available, time saved in not duplicating work already done, and time not wasted on erroneous work" (Kraushaar and Beverley 1990, 167). To capture time data, researchers ask users questions that measure the cost of time and travel they invest to use a service (Pung, Clarke and Patten 2004, 86). Some library studies have attempted to estimate library value by assigning a value to the time library patrons spend in the library, utilizing library resources and services (see Figure 8). These cost of time valuations posit that patrons would not spend an hour of time in the library if they did not get at least as much "out of it" as they could get out of an hour of work.

Study	Results
St. Louis	5.50:1
Florida	Users indicated timed saved totaling of 57.6 million hours = $1.3 billion… time savings accrued
British Libraries	Annual average public library valuation of £263 per user

Figure 8. Investment in Access Studies

Not surprisingly, researchers can encounter difficulties measuring the cost of time. For example, this approach "assume[s] implicitly that each hour spent in the library substitutes for an hour spent earning income. This assumption fails to account for the likelihood that library time may substitute for other kinds of recreational time to which no dollar value can easily be assigned" (Levin, Driscoll, and Fleeter 2006, 24). In addition, cost of time and cost of travel research methods are expensive because they require extensive surveys (Indiana Business Research Center 2007, 13).

Public library value can also be measured in terms of **economic activity.** Economic activity can be defined as the "real financial activity in the form of the various exchanges of goods and services and associated **multiplier effects** necessary to provide public library services" (Library Council of New South Wales 2009).

Multiplier Effects

Multiplier effects result from trickle-down effect of spending in an economy. Multiplier effects demonstrate public library impact on employment and the local, regional, and national economy. These effects can include library employee salaries, library purchases of materials which benefit vendors, and the salaries of vendor employees, all of which grow economies (Griffiths, King and Tomer, et al. 2004, ii; Aabo, Libraries and Return on Investment 2009, 313; Americans for the Arts 2010, 5; Imholz and Arns 2007, 15). Other elements of multiplier effects include visitors (Griffiths, King and Tomer, et al. 2004, 17) and relocations. For example, people and businesses may be more willing to visit or move to an area in part because of public libraries (Ontario Libraries and Community Information Branch 1995, 8; Cooper and Crouch 1994, 233). Public library users also tend to combine trips to the library with other activities and these activities often involve spending money at area businesses, a phenomenon known as "halo effect" (Nova Scotia Regional Libraries Funding Formula Review Committee 1993, 36). For example, one study shows that 75% of library users combined library visits and the purchase of goods and services ($500-$600 annually) from retail stores in the library vicinity (Surrey Public Library Administration 1994). According to Griffiths, "the results of multiplier analysis are expressed as full time equivalent (FTE) jobs created/safeguarded or as expenditure generated in the economy" (Griffiths, King and Tomer, et al. 2004, 16; Indiana Business Research Center 2007, 21). They can also be expressed as resident household income and local and state government revenues" (Americans for the Arts 2010) or GDP/GRP: GDP (Griffiths, King and Tomer, et al. 2004, 2).

The multiplier effects approach to public library value allows librarians to assess previously unmeasured benefits and can be used to help determine the economic benefits received from library programs and services (McClure, et al. 2000, 7). However, used alone, the approach is somewhat narrow (Jura Consultants 2008, 3).

Economic Impact

Because individual approaches to assessing public library value have weaknesses, some studies mitigate study design flaws though the use of multiple measures (Pung, Clarke and Patten 2004, 87). The goal of these studies is to develop an overall **economic impact** picture of public libraries.

Two methodologies associated with this approach are return-on-investment and cost/benefit analysis. Return-on-investment is "calculation of the most tangible financial gains or benefits that can be expected from a project versus the costs for implementing the suggested program or solution" (National States Geographic Information Council 2006). The results of return-on-investment studies are usually figures that represent how high the return is on each dollar invested (Matthews, What's the Return; Aabo, Libraries and Return on Investment 2009, 312). National return-on-investment studies have the lowest mean (3.0:1) and median (3.5:1); in contrast, state public library return-on-investment studies have the highest median and return as much as five times per dollar invested. Studies at the individual library and county level fall between these two ends of the spectrum (Aabo, Libraries and Return on Investment 2009, 319).

Cost/benefit analyses are more comprehensive than many return-on-investment studies and they focus on both tangible and intangible costs and benefits (National States Geographic Information Council 2006). The goal is to define the relationship between public library benefits and taxpayer costs (Griffiths, King and Tomer, et al. 2004). Most of the time, cost/benefit analyses focus on areas that can be represented in monetary terms and "seek to establish whether the benefits of an investment outweigh the costs" (Jura Consultants 2008, 16).

Although distinctions can be made between these approaches, in reality, the same tools and methodologies are often used to calculate return-on-investment and cost/benefit analyses; consequently, it can be challenging to distinguish between the two approaches. For example, Aabo reports that over the past decade, 32 public library return-on-investment studies have been performed. These studies incorporated cost/benefit analysis, contingent valuation, consumer surplus methodology and/or multiplier analysis, as well as other methods. Twenty used a combination of cost/benefit analysis and contingent valuation (Aabo, Libraries and Return on Investment 2009, 317-318). According to Aabo, "for each dollar of taxpayers' money invested in public libraries, the libraries—on average—return a value to the citizens of four to five times more" (Libraries and Return on Investment 2009, 322).

In addition to the aforementioned approaches to establishing library value, public library economic impact studies employ a number of methods for data collection, including:

- Staff deployment studies designed to provide information on the amount and cost of staff time for various library services (Kostiak 2002).
- Integrated library system data about specific collections and their use (Kostiak 2002).
- Case files and individual assessments (Ellis 2008, 52).
- Surveys of users/nonusers of public libraries and analysis of library use statistics (Barron, et al. 2005; Holt and Elliott 2003, 100).
- Focus groups of targeted populations, users and nonusers (Kostiak 2002).
- Key informant interviews, which provide detailed information on the value of the library to representatives from the targeted groups (Library Council of New South Wales 2009).

Regardless of approach, public library economic impact studies should have three main characteristics: simplicity, credibility, and detail. Simplicity can be achieved by "developing a methodology that allows value to be expressed in a brief sound byte that expresses rate of return" (Holt and Elliott 2003). According to Holt and Elliott, "A measurement of direct benefits to users provides a solid, simple statement about direct returns flowing from public library tax revenues." Credibility is also key. Reliable cost-benefit studies often do not include indirect benefits because they would force a large amount of estimation and would make all of their claims dubious. According to Holt and Elliott (2003, 99), "credible public communication occurs when a public official does not overstate the case for the institution." Finally, economic impact studies should be detailed. The St. Louis study shows how detailed, narrowly focused methodology can be used to determine the benefits of particular categories of services for different categories of users. This allows spokespersons to define the meaning of the benefits in human terms, market particular services to particular audiences, and assists administrators with strategic planning (Holt and Elliott 2003).

Some indirect economic impacts are perceived as difficult to quantify despite their importance. For example, librarians struggle to articulate the economic impacts of career support, community development, and small business support (Imholz and Arns 2007). In fact, some researchers fear that the inclusion of financial equivalents for any indirect economic impact has the potential to damage the institution's credibility (Holt and Elliott 2003, 99) because they're difficult to quantify with exact dollar amounts (Levin, Driscoll, and Fleeter 2006, 33). Because the goal of many economic impact studies is to develop a cost/benefit ratio, researchers tend to lean towards conservativism to avoid stakeholder skepticism (Indiana Business Research Center 2007, 13).

Social Impact

In addition to economic impact, public libraries can demonstrate their **social impact** as well. According to Jesse Shera, "the objectives of the public library are directly dependent upon the objectives of society itself" (Hillenbrand, Public Libraries as Developers of Social Capital 2005, 5). In one public library study, respondents stated that the following were the *most important* reasons for using limited public funds on libraries:

- Libraries help individuals and companies solve problems.
- Libraries offer individuals enjoyment via leisure time reading.
- Libraries proliferate knowledge which everyone should know.
- Libraries promote democracy (Aabo and Audunson, Rational Choice and Valuation of Public Libraries 2002, 7).

Definitions of social impact vary. According to Brophy, "impact can be defined in different ways, but in the context of library services it may be thought of as any effect of a service (or other 'event') on an individual or group" (Evaluation of Public Library 2002). Debono (2002, 80) reveals two basic approaches to defining public library social impact. The first investigates any effects, experiences, or differences attributable to public library use or interaction; the other looks for positive impacts only. The latter approach tends to focus on "social benefits" or "social value" rather than objectively measuring "social impacts." However, there are other motives for performing social impact studies, which require the objective examination of both positive and negative impacts, such improving library services (Debono 2002) .

Public library social impact studies employ two general strategies: reporting of noteworthy outputs and measuring outcomes (Durrance and Fisher, How Libraries and Librarians Help 2005; Durrance and Fisher-Pettigrew, Toward Developing Measures 2002). Although outputs numbers (e.g., circulation counts, reference transactions, library program attendance) do not actually convey evidence of social impact, some public library stakeholders find them compelling. For example *How Libraries Stack Up 2010* reports:

How do academic libraries facilitate social outcomes, including community building?

- 2.8 million times every month, business owners, and employees use resources at public libraries to support their small businesses;
- more public libraries offer free public wi-fi than Starbucks, Barnes & Noble or Borders; more public libraries offer career assistance than U.S. Department of Labor One-stop Career Centers (13,000 vs. 3,000);
- more public libraries offer free meeting rooms than there are conference centers, convention facilities, and auditoriums combined; and
- public libraries have a daily circulation of 7.9 million. (OCLC 2010)

Although none of these statistics demonstrate social impact, they may impress stakeholders.

Like other types of libraries, public libraries are also adopting an outcomes-focused perspective on demonstrating social impact. Debono (2002), among others, suggests that public libraries need to "demonstrate rather than assume" that they are culturally significant using "more effective and meaningful methods of monitoring, assessing and reporting on their wider social value to society." This call for demonstration of "wider social value" can be answered through outcomes assessment. Currently, research in area of social value tends to mix outcomes and outputs. For example, Rodger states that libraries should be able to report "how many people use the newly created job center [output], how many actually have found jobs [outcome #1], what percentage of the city's unemployed this represents [outcome #1], and how the resources are used and valued by job seekers and employers [outcome #2]" (Public Libraries: Necessities or Amenities? 2009).

Such outcomes can be more challenging to assess than calculating data on economic impacts for two major reasons: the complexity of social impacts and the difficulty demonstrating that libraries, and not some other entity, caused the impact to occur. However, this effort may be spurred by recent developments in the United Kingdom. There, the Museums, Libraries, and Archives Council (2008) has developed "Generic

Social Outcomes" and "Generic Learning Outcomes" that apply to libraries. These outcomes can easily be applied to U.S. public libraries and serve as a basis for future assessments of public library impact.

Thus far, existing public library outcome studies focus on social inclusion, social capital, community building, and community capacity building. The first public library outcome, social inclusion, can be defined as mutual respect and communication between groups and individuals where everyone has equal access to opportunities. Libraries that strive towards social inclusion strive to "create an environment and services which cater for people who normally do not use the library, particularly those who are marginalized and socially excluded, such as youth, the homeless and the unemployed" (Hillenbrand, A Place for All 2005, 50). Several social impact studies have attempted to assess the library's social inclusiveness (Picco 2008; Leckie and Hopkins 2002; Muddiman, et al. 2000; Audunson 2005).

Other areas of public library social impact are social capital and community building. Research in this area seeks to explore the question: "Does the library contribute to community social capital? In other words, is the use of public libraries associated with greater levels of trust in neighbors and neighborhood institutions, greater community involvement and increased civic engagement?" (C. A. Johnson 2010, 148). What is the "contribution to and impact of [public libraries] on local communities?" (Rosenfeldt 2004). In this research area, multiple studies reveal that the community-building potential of libraries stems from "their provision of an open learning environment and a safe, nondiscriminatory, free and accessible place, their partnerships with other community organizations, and their encouragement of self reliance or helping people to do things for themselves" (Rosenfeldt 2004, 6).

Finally, public libraries can be linked to community capacity building or "the developing or acquiring of skills, competencies, tools, processes and resources that are needed to strengthen a neighborhood or community's processes and systems so that individuals, families, and local groups may take control of their own lives" (Rosenfeldt 2004, 7). Public libraries' impact on skills is demonstrated by their work to support literacy and information competence, lifelong learning, and a reading culture for long-term benefits. The immediate effects of these activities benefit the individuals concerned by increased employment opportunities and improved quality of life. The wider effects include benefits to the society's economic, political, and social well-being attributable to greater employment levels (and resulting taxes available to communities); increased participation in democratic activities; and growing capacity for community members to share resources and develop as sense of belonging (Kerslake and Kinnell 1998).

What's Next for Public Library Value Studies?

The next phase of public library value studies may focus on social return-on-investment (SROI) as a common ground between stakeholders interested in economic value and social impact. Social return-on-investment measures capture the social impact of libraries by "measuring social, environmental and economic outcomes and us[ing] monetary values to represent them" (Nef Consulting 2009, 7). Thus social impacts can be documented in financial terms. According to Jura Consultants, just like any return-on-investment, "SROI gives us a ratio between benefits and costs. The social value created by the programme is assessed against the programme's investment, or the amount it costs to run the programme. The higher the ratio, the higher the social and economic return of the programme" (Jura Consultants 2008, 5).

Social return-on-investment studies follow a five-stage process. First, researchers establish the scope of the study and identify key stakeholders. Second, researchers determine the social outcomes that may be expected to occur. Third, they locate data related to the outcomes and assign them monetary values. Fourth, researchers attempt to isolate the outcomes that are not attributable to other causes. Fifth, they sum all current and future monetary values, subtract negative values, and compare the result to the original investment (Nef Consulting 2009, 7-8).

The challenge of using social return-on-investment is determining monetary values for some social outcomes. According to Jura Consultants, "there will be some benefits that are important to the programme's participants but that cannot be easily monetised (e.g., increased self-esteem, improved family relationships). This value can still be monitored and tracked using qualitative research methods and approaches (e.g., interviews, case studies, etc.)" (Jura Consultants 2008, 4-5). Like other approaches to public library value assessment, social return-on-investment is not a panacea, but it does have promise.

Special libraries have been called the "bellwethers of change" for the library world (Renaud 1997). As the development and proliferation of online resources has enabled users to locate information without librarian assistance, the value proposition of special libraries has changed considerably (Housewright, Themes of Change 2009, 255). Consequently, special librarians moved first from input measures to output measures of library quality. Output measures were, for a time, considered indicators of library "goodness" (Matthews, Determining and Communicating 2003). However, according to (Botha, Erasmus and Van Deventer 2009, 108), "the mere fact that a library service is being used does not mean that the service makes a difference or has a positive impact on the users." In addition, input counts, output measures, and satisfaction feedback are not clearly correlated with the success of special libraries' overarching organizations (Housewright, Themes of Change 2009, 256). Rather, special libraries have found that they must demonstrate their value in terms meaningful to organizational management (Housewright, Themes of Change 2009, 258). Now, academic librarians find themselves with a similar challenge: how to demonstrate their impact on their overarching institutions. Thus, academic librarians can monitor and learn from the efforts of special librarians to demonstrate the library value.

As special libraries have struggled to convey their value to organizational managers, two research strands have emerged (J. G. Marshall 2007, 9). The first strand relies on economic studies and includes return-on-investment and cost/benefit analysis. The second strand focuses on the impact of information employed by user groups. Both strands have advantages and limitations. According to Housewright, "although the efficacy or accuracy of different measurements may be debated, in general, simply choosing to measure value and to adopt a value-oriented mindset lays the ground work for [special] library success" (Housewright, Themes of Change 2009, 257).

Working with Managers

Managerial perceptions are a major challenge for special librarians who seek to demonstrate library value, regardless of their approach. While librarians tend to evaluate their performance based on standard library measures, managers use "far different, often subjective, evaluation criteria" (Matarazzo and Prusak 1995). Matarazzo and Prusak believe that managers maintain a "strong reservoir of good will and affection for the library and librarians—often based on an intuitive 'feel' that the service is valuable." However, Keyes states, "no business will be run on a 'feeling' and that sooner or later, clear evidence, in business terms and with monetary values, will be required…to justify the budget portion taken by the special library" (Keyes 1995, 173).

According to Strand (2004, 13), "management doesn't truly care about [librarians'] work ethic, content resources, and usage statistics," but there is little consensus about how managers should measure library value (Matarazzo and Prusak 1995). Libraries run the risk of appearing to be "black holes" of funding (Housewright, Themes of Change 2009, 261). When managers try to determine the return on their investment, they do not ask

"How good is the library?" Rather they ask, "How much good does the library do?" (Matarazzo and Prusak, Valuing Corporate Libraries 1990).

Unfortunately, managers do not appear to know the answer to the latter question. While managers state that they would like libraries to provide quality information (Matarazzo and Prusak, Valuing Corporate Libraries 1990), save time, and lower corporate costs (Matarazzo and Prusak, Valuing Corporate Libraries 1990, 106), few managers can state the function of the special library within their organization (Matarazzo and Prusak 1995), and most have no procedure for measuring library value (Matarazzo and Prusak, Valuing Corporate Libraries 1990). More than 60% of managers responsible for evaluating library staff and justifying library budgets (Matarazzo and Prusak, Valuing Corporate Libraries 1990) did not know the value of their library (Matarazzo and Prusak, Valuing Corporate Libraries 1990). A more recent study of executives showed they could not easily identify performance measures that demonstrate library value; 82% did not know their organizations had libraries at all (Lustig 2008), findings which confirm Matarazzo's earlier findings (Closing the Corporate Library 1981, 132-135).

Economic Studies

A large portion of special library value research moves beyond input, outputs, and anecdotes to document impact (Aaron 2009, 45) using cost/benefit analysis and return-on-investment. These studies seek to answer questions such as:

- What is the return on the money spent by the library? (Strouse, Demonstrating Value 2003)
- How much does the library save its overarching organization? (Strouse, Corporate Information Centers 2001)
- Why is an in-house library the best option? (Strouse, Corporate Information Centers 2001)

Much of the economic study of special libraries is focused on cost/benefit analysis. There are three major ways of calculating cost/benefit ratios. The first is the most basic; the last is the most conservative.

$$library\ value = \frac{gross\ estimated\ benefits}{library\ production\ costs}$$

$$library\ value = \frac{(gross\ estimated\ benefits)-(gross\ user\ costs)}{library\ production\ costs}$$

$$library\ value = \frac{gross\ estimated\ benefits}{(library\ production\ costs)+(gross\ user\ costs)}$$

In each formula, the costs can be easily identified using library budget figures; in contrast, the benefits must be elicited from library users. These formulas can be used to demonstrate the positive benefits of special libraries in general or specific resources and services (Keyes 1995, 177-178). However, according to Koenig (1992, 203), "the calculations of cost/benefit figures is a complex and disputatious exercise, of rather more subtlety than is often realized…the calculation of cost/benefit figures where a principal commodity is information, a commodity particularly ill addressed by conventional economies, is even more fraught with peril." While some researchers believe that a true cost/benefit analysis is not "practical or even possible" (White 1979, 164), others believe it can be used to "strengthen the position of the special library and should be actively sought out as important evidence promoting the special library and justifying its existence within the [organizational] framework" (Keyes 1995, 180).

Special libraries must define their value in terms that resonate with library users. According to Kantor, Saracevic, and D'Esposito, user value is obtained in three areas: acquisition (getting materials), cognition (intellectual value), and application (value-in-use) (Kantor, Saracevic and D'Esposito-Wachtmann, Studying the Cost 1995, 11). While the process of getting materials easily, learning from them, and applying learned information is valuable to library users, special library value is articulated differently from an organizational perspective. According to Sykes (2001, 15), the "contributions of information professionals may not be perceived to be of high value if results are not measured and presented in terms that resonate within the organization." Return-on-investment metrics that are significant to organizations include:

- Time saved (multiplied by salary rate) (Mason and Sassone 1978)
- Industrial productivity (Hayes and Erickson 1982; Braunstein 1985)
- Shortened product cycle (Kassel 2002)
- Reduced parts costs (Strouse, Demonstrating Value 2003)
- Labor savings (Strouse, Demonstrating Value 2003)
- Improved quality (Strouse, Demonstrating Value 2003)
- Increased sales (Kassel 2002)
- Quicker response to threats (Kassel 2002)
- Return on shareholder value (Kassel 2002)
- Willingness to pay (Griffiths and King, Manual on the Evaluation 1990)
- Value of reading (Griffiths and King, Information Audit 1988)
- Readings forgone by requirement to spend more time seeking information (Griffiths and King, Manual on the Evaluation 1990)
- Money saved over alternative information sources (Griffiths and King, Manual on the Evaluation 1990; Griffiths and King, Information Audit 1988)
- Risk of irrelevant or inappropriate information decreased (Henczel 2006, 9)

Of all return-on-investment metrics, time savings is the "most easily and credibly quantified benefit measure" (Aaron 2009, 41), although different studies vary in their details. First, any work completed by a librarian leads in cost reductions because the cost of librarian time is less than other professionals' time (Keyes 1995, 174). Second, librarians save other professionals many hours of information-seeking time. For example, one Outsell publication states that special library users save an average of nine hours and $2,218 per library interaction (Information Management Under Fire 2007). Outsell also suggests that the average amount of time spent seeking information is at least 12 hours per week (Outsell's Neighborhoods of the Information Industry: A Reference Guide 2004). Environmental Protection Agency librarians save their users as much as 16 hours per question answered and $600-$777 per reading (Stratus Consulting 2004, 4-5). Other sources suggest that corporate library users save more than $35 in time, $777 in revenue generated, and $42 in other monies per library use (Strouse, Demonstrating Value 2003).

> *How much faculty or student time do academic libraries save? How can that be conceptualized monetarily?*
>
> *What would it cost (time and money) for faculty or students to use alternative sources?*

Many other return-on-investment metrics attempt to capture the concept of productivity. According to Koenig (1992, 199), "the reason organizations build and maintain information services is to enhance the effectiveness and

> *Do academic librarians reduce costs when they complete work otherwise done by faculty? If so, by how much?*

productivity of people and units supported by those services." The difficulty is accurately assessing the productivity of those people and units and the relationship between their productivity and information supplied by the special library (Koenig 1992; Keyes 1995, 177). However, special library literature demonstrates that "more productive individuals make greater access to and greater use of information services" (Koenig 1992, 206). For example, King Research documented a significant and positive relationship between professional productivity and time spent reading at Oak Ridge National Laboratories. Indicators of productivity in this study included: number of formal records, publications, proposals, research plans, oral presentations, and consultations (Koenig 1992, 205). In a separate study, Mondschein revealed scientists who use current awareness services and alerts appear to be more productive than their colleagues who don't use these services or use them infrequently (Mondschein 1990). After completing a review of the literature, Koenig also states that "access to information is a very critical component in the productivity of information workers and consequently the productivity of the information dependent organization employing [them]" (Koenig 1992, 206). He concludes that, to maximize productivity, organizations should increase their investments in libraries (Koenig 1992, 206).

> *Do library alert services make faculty and students more productive?*

Because organizations do not increase their investments in libraries without solid evidence of increased productivity, additional research in this area is needed (Keyes 1995, 179).

Griffiths and King have conducted the major research in the area of cost/benefit analysis and return-on-investment to date. They have emphasized savings in time and costs using three approaches:

- willingness of users to pay (as shown by what they pay in terms of time spent seeking information and reading) (Griffiths and King, The Value of Information Centers 1996),
- general time and cost savings, and
- costs to the user of alternative sources (including extra money spent due to loss of organizational purchasing power and additional information seeking costs).

Griffiths and King have shown the rate of return to be 4:1 using the first approach, 15:1 using the second approach, and 2.5:1 using the third (Griffiths and King, Manual on the Evaluation 1990). In other work, Griffiths and King show rate of returns on "savings achieved from reading" ranging from 7.8:1-14.2:1 and returns for "what professionals are willing to pay for library services" of about 8.5:1 (Griffiths and King, Special Libraries 1993, 25, 78-79). In general, Griffiths and King's findings reveal "an average overall figure 2.3 times more expensive to provide information from other sources than...[a] special library" (Keyes 1995, 179). Additional return-on-investment ratios are included in Figure 9. Of course, their research assumes that users will seek out other sources, but users' level of persistence was not investigated (Keyes 1995, 176). Even so, Griffiths and King conclude that it is "abundantly clear that library services pay for themselves by orders of magnitude" (Special Libraries 1993, 190). According to Koenig (1992, 206), such findings demonstrate that organizations should "substantially increase their investment in special libraries."

One variant on Griffiths and King's work is also worth noting. Edgar proposes a model of special library value that conceptualizes library impact as taking place in the lives of the organization's customers, not the organization itself. Thus library value is manifested as a "change in the customers' life for the better" (Edgar 2004, 124-125). Edgar writes, "The...intellectual problem often not addressed in the research done so far on the value and influence created by the [special] library is that the ultimate value provided by the...library has not been conceptualized holistically as customer value...rather than being something provided to individual...library users or some profit earned by the [organization], this customer value occurs outside of the [organization] within the lives of the [organization's] individual customers" (2004, 136). This reconceptualization of library value merits further investigation.

Subject of Study	Return-on-investment
Exxon Research Center **(Weil 1980)**	11:1
NASA **(Mogavero 1979)**	1.98:1
Private Corporations and Government Agencies (Griffiths and King, A Manual on the Evaluation of Information Centers and Services 1990; Griffiths and King, An Information Audit of Public Service Electric and Gas Company Libraries and Information Resources 1988; Griffiths and King, The Contribution Libraries Make to Organizational Productivity 1985; Roderer, King and Brouard 1983; Koenig 1992)	2.5:1-26:1

Manufacturing (**Hayes and Erickson 1982**)	**2.54:1**
Manufacturing (**Braunstein 1985**)	**2.50:1**
Energy Data Base (**King, Griffiths, et al. 1982**)	**2.2:1**
Accenture Knowledge Management (**Aaron 2009, 43**)	**18.6:1**
Environmental Protection Agency (**Stratus Consulting 2004**)	(Library services in general) **2:1-5.7:1** (Reference service) **4.4:1** (Public access) **6:1** (Readings delivered) **2.3:1-5.7:1**
Korea Development Institute (**Chung, Measuring the Economic Value of Special Libraries 2007, 38**)	(Physical resources) **2.44: 1** (Facility use) **5.71:1** (Loan and in-library use) **2.97:1**
Pharmaceuticals (**Portugal 2000**)	**54:1**
Texas Instruments (**Manning 1987**)	**5.15:1**

Figure 9. Special Library Return-on-Investment Examples

While return-on-investment studies have effectively demonstrated the value of special libraries, they are not without challenges. One of the limitations of this approach is that it can appear abstract and "distant form the actual services provided to users in particular libraries" (J. G. Marshall 2007, 9). Calculating time savings is difficult because the time periods for incurring costs differ greatly from those for gaining benefits (Keyes 1995, 174); the latter is usually spread over long periods of time (Matthews, Bottom Line 2002, 78). Indeed, Cohen (2006) suggests that calculations based on time savings are "flawed" without evidence of how the saved time was spent. Another challenge is that costs are usually measured in dollar amounts, but not all benefits can be calculated in dollars (Keyes 1995, 174). According to Keyes (1995), "there are several other barriers to the development of valuation data, such as the cost in terms of additional time required by the librarian to gather and analyze...data; lack of confidence in the data gathered; or, a lack of belief in the impact that any such data will have on day-to-day operations." Perhaps that is why so few special libraries gather return-on-investment data (Strouse, Demonstrating Value 2003); it can be time consuming, require external consultants, and—in special libraries—the results would be protected as proprietary and privileged information (Keyes 1995, 173).

Impact Studies

Most of the impact studies in special libraries use a survey-based critical incident technique, where survey respondents are asked to request information on a topic of current interest from a special library and then talk about the impact that information had on their practice. One of the first of these studies focused on physicians in the Chicago area (D. N. King 1987). In this study, almost 2/3 of the physicians responded that they would definitely or probably handle their cases differently based on information provided by the library (D. N. King 1987, 291). This first study served as the basis for Marshall's impact studies. Marshall studied a number of populations beginning with Rochester physicians (J. G. Marshall, Impact of the Hospital Library 1992, 169). In this study, 80% of physicians said they probably or definitely handled patient care differently. Areas of difference included diagnosis, choice of tests, choice of drugs, length of hospital stay, and advice given to patients. They were able to avoid hospital admissions, patient mortality, hospital-acquired infections, surgeries, as well as additional tests and procedures. In addition, physicians rated the library information higher than any other information source (J. G. Marshall, Impact of the Hospital Library 1992, 169). Marshall found two challenges with this study: 1) getting adequate response rates (J. G. Marshall, Impact of the Hospital Library 1992, 171) and 2) lacking information about nonclinical information with longer term impacts (J. G. Marshall, Impact of the Hospital Library 1992, 176).

Numerous follow-ups to the Marshall Rochester study exist in the health care field (Weightman and Williamson 2005). In one similar study of hospital clinicians in the United Kingdom, 89% said the information "did or would in the future assist in clinical decision making" (Urquhart and Hepworth 1995, 14). Another found that, in addition to patient-care outcomes, special libraries lead to time savings for health care professionals and to general health care savings (Urquhart 2004; Winning and Beverley 2003; Wagner and Byrd 2004). A third found that the cost for a library to answer a health care question is roughly equivalent to a chest x-ray (Veenstra and Gluck 1992). Researchers noted that these studies could benefit from an established, core set of questions validated at the national or international level to facilitate comparisons and benchmarking (Weightman and Williamson 2005, 22).

Marshall conducted a similar study of Canadian financial institutions using the same critical incident technique. Eighty-four percent of respondents reported better informed decision making as a consequence of receiving library information (J. G. Marshall, The Impact of the Special Library on Corporate Decision-Making 1993, v). Respondents stated that the information helped them proceed to the next step in a project or task, decide upon a course of action, improve the image of the organization, improve relations with clients, and exploit new business opportunities. It also helped them avoid time lost, poor business decisions, loss of funds, or other resource wastes (J. G. Marshall, The Impact of the Special Library on Corporate Decision-Making 1993, vi). Fifty-four percent reported that they probably or definitely handled decision making differently. In cases where there was a financial transaction involved, 74% estimated that the value of the transaction was over $1 million.

In the United Kingdom, five additional critical incident studies analyzed the role of information provision in other sectors, although not all respondents had in-house special libraries. The sectors included physiotherapy (Ashcroft 1998), banking (Reid, Thomson and Wallace-Smith 1998), insurance (Smith, Winterman and Abell 1998), pharmaceuticals (Bouchet, et al. 1998), and government (Winterman, Smith and Abell 1998). The results are summarized below:

> In all cases a very high value was placed on the information sought and provided with 96% of the respondents in the pharmaceuticals and government department

studies saying that it was of value and the lowest figure of 81% being physiotherapists. That the information led to better informed decision making was confirmed by 97% of respondents in government departments, 96% in pharmaceuticals and 94% in banking, but only 74% in physiotherapy.... On the question of whether the decision making process had been handled differently...banking was highest with 78% of respondents confirming this statement, followed by physiotherapists (74%), government departments (61%), pharmaceuticals (58%), and insurance (46%).... Ninety-eight percent of those in pharmaceuticals and 96% in government departments thought that it provided new knowledge.... Where respondents were asked if the information had added a new dimension this was supported by 69.8% of those in banking and 56% in government departments.... Respondents in all the sectors felt that the information had saved them time, and this was as high as around 80% in banking and pharmaceuticals. (Grieves 1998, 79-81)

An impact study following a different protocol investigated the impact of library service on natural science researchers. This study employed focus group, survey, and interview methods (Botha, Erasmus and Van Deventer 2009, 108). The results showed that 80% of the researchers believed the most important indicators of impact are 1) time saved in information retrieval and delivery and 2) higher success rate in research.

While impact studies reveal a great deal about the impact of special libraries, they also face challenges (Keyes 1995, 179). For example, value and impact are "soft" terms (Markless and Streatfield 2006) that are difficult to define precisely (J. G. Marshall 2007, 7) and cannot easily be translated into dollar amounts (Keyes 1995, 174). Some value and impact measures occur only at the individual level and must be summed up to produce a cumulative effect on the overarching organization (Matthews, Determining and Communicating 2003). Furthermore, there can be multiple influences on individual or organizational impact and it can be difficult to track value back to the library (Poll, Quality Measures for Special Libraries 2007). Despite these challenges, frameworks for measuring library value is essential for good decision making and rationales for continuing and investing in special libraries (Housewright, Themes of Change 2009, 258). According to Henczel (2006, 9), where there is confusion about their value, special libraries have an uncertain future. Consequently, impact studies are necessary to show how special libraries contribute to their organizations' "bottom line, however the bottom line is measured" (Matthews, Determining and Communicating 2003).

Reporting Results

According to Housewright, one characteristic of successful special libraries is that they are able to communicate their value to their overarching organizations (Housewright, Themes of Change 2009, 256). The special library literature is replete with ideas for communicating value, and a few are listed below:

- Identify, know, and communicate with organizational "winners," influencers, decision makers, strategic planners, and administrative assistants.

- Monitor current areas of research need by contacting library users regularly. Anticipate and proactively fulfill these users' needs. Visit with them in offices, at sites, and at functions.
- Develop reports and evaluation data based on organizational priorities (Strand 2004).

As one example, one organization represents and reports the value of its information services to stakeholders using a "V measurement" structure with six levels (Aaron 2009, 37):

1. System status—reports the operational status of resources and services
2. Access systems—describes level user access to information
3. Locate information—identifies the extent to which the right information gets to the right people at the right time
4. Apply knowledge—articulates the work done to create value for users
5. Business results—explains the outcomes of applying created knowledge
6. Return-on-investment—presents a ration of results to costs

Strouse provides examples of traditional and value-based report summaries to educate special librarians about how to report library information to organizational managers:

Library A: The Library's budget for last year was $5 million. We have ten employees who are very busy, and we'd like to add three more to help with workload and turnaround times, so we need more money for added headcount. During last year, the Library performed 500 research projects. We updated intranet content 50 times each on four portal sites. The Library managed a collection of 230 periodicals, and 225 new books were bought and processed. Seven hundred items were circulated from the Library's collection. All this work is very time-consuming, but the Library staff works very hard and at 100% capacity, so we're happy to say we managed all this last year with only 10 on staff.

Library B: The Library budget for last year was $5 million, an investment for which the Company received a $7.5 million return. Ten Library employees generated this $2.5 million profit, and we believe adding three more employees will increase that margin. Last year, the Library performed 500 research projects. Library users tell us that the Library's participation on those projects saved them an average of 14 hours per project, which translates to $168,000; that we saved them on average $2,500 in direct costs per project ($1,250,000); and that, on 50 of the projects, we found information that led to an average sale or increased sale of $85,000 ($4,250,000). Intranet site content, which the Library pays for and posts, resulted in 14 known new sales, each valued on average at $131,000 ($1,834,000). (Strouse, Corporate Information Centers 2001)

Finally, Matthews suggests using a balanced scorecard approach for tracking and reporting value information. According to Matthews, "the value of the library balanced scorecard approach is that it assists librarians in identifying what measures are important and supports the presentation of these measures in a cogent and understandable form for the management team of a larger organization" (Matthews, Bottom Line 2002, 115).

What's Next for Special Library Value Studies?

According to Marshall, librarians at every level need to commit to ongoing value research. Practitioners need to actively engage in demonstrating the impact of their work in terms their overarching organizations will value. Library directors should support these efforts by providing their professional staff with the necessary time and resources. Library and information science faculty should partner with practitioners in the effort to demonstrate library impact as well as teach pre-service librarians the skills they need to engage in value research. Finally, "research funding agencies, government bodies that support libraries, library advocacy organizations, and professional associations should prioritize value and impact research and its related areas of evidence-based practice, performance measurement, and valuation research in the future" (J. G. Marshall 2007, 10-11).

The sections below outline the "Next Steps" in articulating academic library value to institutional stakeholders. Noticeably absent from this list are traditional library measures. Despite their value in internally managing services and resources, inputs, outputs, process measures, satisfaction measures, and service quality measures are not designed to demonstrate achievement of outcomes; therefore, they may be less effective in demonstrating the institutional value of academic libraries. Consequently, the steps below focus on how librarians can accelerate their efforts to demonstrate academic library value by embracing an outcomes approach that reveals the impact of libraries on users.

Get Started

The most important step is to start. Librarians who seek to create perfect value studies may be stymied, and likely let great be the enemy of good. Librarians who are feeling ambitious can partner with research experts and conduct large-scale studies on a national or international scale. But most librarians do not need large-scale studies; in fact, small-scale local studies are often more powerful within individual institutions. The latter group can start by identifying one area of impact, collecting data, analyzing the data, and reporting results, even if the results are not ideal, keeping in mind that, "assessment is an ongoing process. One need not wait for the perfect opportunity, the perfect instrument, or the perfect time" (Carter 2002, 41).

For example, a small library that wants to know whether they help their institution recruit the best possible students might seek to add questions to an admissions survey about the role of the library in prospective students' decision to submit an admissions application. Even if the library turns out not to have a significant role in students' decision making, the library can use those results to spur innovation. What might the library do to increase its contribution to the institutional goal of recruiting students? Should library tours be made a mandatory part of prospective student events? Would library user testimonials help as part of a prospective student event? Should the library consider contacting students and parents of prospective students and identify how the library can help them be successful at the institution? Once changes are attempted, future assessments may reveal a greater library impact on this institutional goal. Then, the library has demonstrated its value.

Not only can librarians get started demonstrating their value in institutional terms, they can communicate their experiences, whether they are effective or ineffective, to their colleagues. If each library identifies some part of the Research Agenda in this document, collects data, and communicates it through publication or presentation, the profession will develop a body of evidence that demonstrates library impact in convincing ways.

Once librarians commit to getting started, they can define the outcomes they wish to explore. Libraries cannot demonstrate their institutional value to maximum effect until they define outcomes of institutional relevance and then work to measure the degree to which they attain them (Kaufman and Watstein 2008, 227). Librarians throughout higher education can establish, assess, and link academic library outcomes to institutional outcomes related to the following areas: student enrollment, student retention and graduation rates, student success, student achievement, student learning, student engagement, faculty research productivity, faculty teaching, service, and overarching institutional quality. The final outcome list should be long enough to represent the ways in which the library enables institutional goals, but short enough to be clearly communicated to stakeholders. The final outcomes should also be mapped to institution, department, and accreditation outcomes (Oakleaf, Writing Information Literacy Assessment Plans 2010). (This process may be complicated because these organizations are likely not to use the term "information literacy"; instead they may use synonyms for the concept (Oakleaf, Are They Learning? 2011).) Outcome maps reveal shared foci across and among institutions. Outcome map creation is facilitated by the development or purchase of an assessment management system.

Use Assessment Management Systems

Assessment management systems have been developed over the last several years to support higher education assessment; currently there are several commercial products available for purchase (Oakleaf, Writing Information Literacy Assessment Plans 2010; Oakleaf, Are They Learning? 2011). Assessment management systems help educators manage their outcomes (learning outcomes as well as strategic/organizational outcomes), record and maintain data on each outcome, facilitate connections to similar outcomes throughout an institution, and generate reports. Assessment management systems are helpful for documenting progress toward strategic/organizational goals, but their real strength lies in managing learning outcomes assessments. Individual librarians have assessed student learning for decades. Because assessment efforts are typically "one-shot," they tend to capture limited amounts of information, e.g., only one librarian's class, one group of students, or one assessment method. Such assessments are so limited that they are very difficult to use to demonstrate the impact of the library on student learning in a broad sense. In contrast, assessment management systems allow multiple librarians to enter assessment data, focus on different student groups (or the same groups over time), and use different assessment methods. Because they aggregate data by outcomes, they generate reports that demonstrate how well the library is achieving its outcomes as well as contributing to the mission of its overarching institution (Oakleaf, Are They Learning? 2011).

Gather New Data

Academic libraries can learn from their school, public, and special library colleagues and adapt the best of their approaches to demonstrating value. For example, school librarians have conducted test audits to identify individual test items that measure student information skills; they have also conducted "help" studies to collect, in student voices, qualitative data about the impact of libraries on student learning. Academic librarians can pursue both of these approaches.

Public and special librarians have conducted groundbreaking studies on library return-on-investment. Special librarians in particular have explored the dichotomy of a "business" perspective and an "impact" perspective; both perspectives offer great potential to demonstrate library value. Academic librarians should also pursue two paths to library value, as their stakeholders have two different perceptions of that value.

For some academic library stakeholders, higher education is in many ways a business, and money is the bottom line. For them, library value can be calculated using cost/benefit analysis, like the one represented in the formula below. According to this

$$library\ value = \frac{benefits}{costs}$$

formula, libraries can increase their value in one of two ways. First, they can decrease costs by managing their finances well. Second, they can increase their benefits. Increasing benefits may mean bringing more money into the institutions. It could also mean offering beneficial services and resources—ideally ones that offer value that can be represented in financial terms. Of course, it is challenging to simultaneously increase benefits and decrease costs. Therefore, to reach financially minded stakeholders, librarians must demonstrate that they keep costs down, bring money into the institution, or offer benefits that have financial value. The charts included in the Research Agenda section of this report can be used to create cost/benefit analyses and calculate return-on-investment information to provide evidence of library value according to this perspective.

Other academic library stakeholders focus on the contribution higher education makes through producing learning, research, and service, rather than as a money-making enterprise. For these stakeholders, an impact-focused, evidence-gathering process is more meaningful. There are numerous methods for gathering evidence of library impact. Regardless of specific research methodology, this process involves eliciting information from users about what the services and resources librarians provide enable them to do. This second approach also may be more meaningful to librarians who are focused on what library users actually accomplish following their academic library interactions and how they might be changed for the better.

Both paths to articulating library value have potential; however, to achieve that potential, librarians need to collect new and different data. Some data is easy to capture. In other cases, data not currently collected, could be.

- Librarians can undertake systematic reviews of course content, readings, reserves, and assignments. Using this data, librarians can identify students who have had substantial library exposure and compare them to those who have not. Simultaneously, librarians should use this process to track the integration of library resources into the teaching and learning processes of their institution. Not only should this information be used in collections decisions, it can also be used to answer additional questions, such as: What percent of readings used in courses are available and accessed through the library? How much do these materials save students? What contributions do they make to student learning? How many assignments do students complete that require use of information skills? What do library services and resources enable students to do or do better? Are faculty assessing these skills in their own ways, and if so what have they learned about student skill levels? Of course, this type of information is also useful for designing proactive, rather than passive, library services designed to provide "just-in-time" and "just-for-me" assistance to users.

- Librarians can explore the range of products like MINES for Libraries with the potential to ask library users about how they will use the resources they find though the library. This kind of contextual information allows librarians to report, "Ten percent of the student access to business resources is attributable to company researching for interview preparation" rather than saying, "Library users downloaded 5,000 articles today." The former sentence demonstrates library impact on student job placement, an institutional goal. The latter does not provide the context necessary to show library value to the institution.

- Librarians can develop systems that will allow data collection on individual user library behavior. A number of potential correlations included in the Research Agenda section below are not possible unless librarians can identify and compare user groups with different types or levels of library interactions. For instance, until libraries know that student #5 with major A has downloaded B number of articles from database C, checked out D number of books, participated in E workshops and online tutorials, and completed courses F, G, and H, libraries cannot correlate any of those student information behaviors with attainment of other outcomes. Until librarians do that, they will be blocked in many of their efforts to demonstrate value.

Clearly, data systems need to protect the privacy of individuals by stripping individual information from records, information that is not necessary to demonstrate library value. For example, because libraries do not assign students grades, there is no need to know about information behavior of individual, named students. However, it would be helpful to know that students who have participated in three or more library instructional episodes over the course of their college career have a significantly higher GPA. Or it would be helpful to know that faculty who work with a librarian to prepare their tenure or promotion package have a 25% higher pass rate, but it may not be necessary to know what departments these faculty are in. However, cleaned data is crucial; demonstrating the full value of academic libraries is only possible when libraries possess evidence that allows them to examine the impact of library user interactions.

In some cases, potentially useful library impact data exists and is collected by nonlibrary entities, but requires effort to access and analyze. A few examples are:

- NCES institutional data and academic library data are currently maintained in different databases with separate searching capabilities. NCES could combine the Academic Libraries Survey with IPEDS data. Doing so would facilitate meaningful exploration of connections between academic libraries and institutional outcomes. When examining IPEDS data for this category, librarians can begin by investigating retention, graduation, completion, and transfer rate categories. Librarians can also investigate the utility of similar NSC data. Integrating library data with institutional data is critical; without joined data, joint analysis is not possible. Without joint analysis, libraries will find it more difficult to demonstrate their value.
- Librarians can monitor K-12 assessment efforts, including the assessment of the Common Core College and Career-Readiness Standards (Achieve 2008), as it is a "well-known phenomenon for a state legislature or governor's office to initially base any…reporting proposal for colleges and universities on what the state is already doing in K-12 education" (P. T. Ewell, "Shovel-Ready" Data 2009, 11).
- Librarians can seek to impact current efforts to track longitudinal data across K-12, postsecondary, and workforce systems, as such databases increase stakeholder ability to ask more specific questions about student development (P. T. Ewell, "Shovel-Ready" Data 2009, 11-12).
- Efforts to augment national surveys (e.g., NSSE, CCSSE) with information and library questions can be continued and expanded. The same is true for local surveys, especially senior and alumni surveys.

Engage in Higher Education Assessment External to Libraries

Academic librarians, in general, do not participate on a broad scale in higher education assessment activities. There are exceptions, to be sure, but academic librarians need to use their skills to remain aware of current philosophies and movements in higher education assessment, as well as to ensure that higher education is aware of library assessment. In general, higher education literature "consistently portrays librarians as ancillary to the academic enterprise" (Gratch-Lindauer, Defining and Measuring 1998), rendering the library "largely invisible" when it comes to accomplishing institutional missions (Boyer 1987; Hardesty 2000).

One way for librarians to engage rigorously in higher education assessment is to become involved in program review (Schwartz 2007) and accreditation processes, especially by influencing accreditation guidelines (Gratch-Lindauer, Comparing the Regional Accreditation Standards 2001; Rader 2004). Accreditation guidelines motivate institutions; increasing integration of information literacy into the guidelines may result in increased integration of information literacy into institutional curricula (Saunders, Perspectives on Accreditation 2008, 310). It is important to keep in mind that infusing information literacy content into accreditation guidelines is not an effort to homogenize learning. Accreditation processes seek to encourage institutions to meet their own missions and goals, to "ensur[e]...the distinctive mission of the institution" (Bogue 1998).

In some situations, librarians may be able to influence higher education assessment initiatives (e.g., adding information skill-centric questions to national surveys and tests). For example, librarians can become involved in Tuning USA's effort to develop common postsecondary learning standards in disciplinary areas; they can also be aware of the new national "College and Career Readiness" standards that describe the learning outcomes that incoming college students should master. Librarians can also familiarize themselves with national movements, such as the VSA, VFA, U-CAN, and NILOA initiatives, as well as international efforts, such as AHELO. They can participate in these activities whenever possible; for example, several institutions are at work integrating the new VALUE information literacy rubric into their institutional assessment processes and IMLS has funded the RAILS project to address the same goal.

Furthermore, librarians can publish and present in higher education venues rather than limiting themselves to library-centric conferences and journals. In addition, select academic library journals may pursue indexing in databases that include higher education literature.

Finally, academic libraries can appoint a liaison librarian to the senior leadership of their institutions and/or their offices of assessment or institutional research. Providing top-notch liaison services to key decision makers within an institution will help contribute to efficient administrators (Neal 2009) and may make library value less abstract and, over time, indispensible.

Create Library Assessment Plans

Librarians can develop assessment plans that organize assessment efforts, keep them on track, and record assessment results and lessons learned. Excellent resources for creating assessment plans, a topic outside the scope of this report, are available to aid librarians in their planning efforts (Kerby and Weber 2000; Maki, Developing an Assessment Plan 2002; Oakleaf, Writing Information Literacy Assessment Plans 2010; Rubin 2006; Matthews, Library Assessment in Higher Education 2007, 119).

Mobilize Library Administrators

Library administrators can move assessment forward by taking the following actions: tying library value to institutional missions (Lynch, et al. 2007, 226-227); communicating assessment needs and results to library stakeholders (Fister 2010); using evidence-based decision making; creating confidence in library assessment efforts; dedicating assessment personnel and training (Durrance and Fisher, How Libraries and Librarians Help 2005, 321-322); and fostering environments that encourage creativity and risk taking (Stoffle, Guskin and Boisse 1984, 9). Library administrators can integrate library assessment within library planning, budget (Hoyt 2009, 10), and reward structures (Dow 1998, 279). They also can ensure that assessment efforts have requisite resources. Assessment processes that have insufficient resources risk being "incomplete, wasteful, frustrating, not illuminative, or perceived as invalid" (Keeling, et al. 2008, 75). According to Keeling et al., "A process that has limited resources in money, time, and organizational commitment is likely to yield results that are narrow, and the report of that work will likely sit on a shelf or never escape the confines of somebody's hard drive" (Keeling, et al. 2008, 76). A key resource is access to professional development opportunities. Furthermore, administrators can mitigate employee anxiety by creating "psychological safety or emotional security by providing direction, encouragement, and coaching, as well as fostering norms that reward innovative thinking and encourage acceptance of mistakes" (Worrell 1995, 355). Thus, by supporting their employees in numerous ways, library administrators avoid the major pitfalls of higher education assessment: trivializing the effort, underestimating the necessary change of perspective, adding assessment duties without reassigning other work tasks (Keeling, et al. 2008, 61); under-resourcing assessment efforts, and failing to ensure that employees feel comfortable with uncertainty and complexity (Barnett, University Knowledge 2000, 420).

Engage in Professional Development

Librarians learning to demonstrate their value to their overarching institutions will require training and support to acquire new assessment skills (Oakleaf, Are They Learning? 2011). Their attendance at existing assessment professional development opportunities, such as the ARL Library Assessment Conference and the ACRL Assessment Immersion program, can be encouraged and supported. In some cases, inviting consultants, participating in webinars, and establishing assessment resource collections will be required to update librarian skills. Example assessment resource collections include: *Measuring Quality in Higher Education* (Association for Institutional Research 2010) and the American Library Association and Illinois Library Association value Web sites (American Library Association 2010; Illinois Library Association 2010).

Furthermore, librarians can participate in professional development opportunities outside the academic library sphere. For example, librarians can attend conferences that focus on higher education assessment like the IUPUI Assessment Institute. They can also benefit from general higher education assessment literature; faculty and student affairs professionals face similar assessment challenges and librarians can learn from their experiences. For instance, one student affairs resource lists the following questions as a starting point for contributing to institutional missions:

- How do I contribute to student learning [or another institutional outcome] at my institution?
- Is student learning one of my daily top priorities?
- What are the programs that I am responsible for that have been shown to have a tenuous impact on student learning?

- Have I taken the initiative to create opportunities to establish and maintain professional relationships with faculty and academic administrators on my campus?
- Have I exploited opportunities to demonstrate my interest in and support for faculty work?
- Have I thought about what I can offer faculty members to assist them in fulfilling their instructional goals?
- Do I regularly analyze institutional data on the student learning that occurs through the program and activities sponsored by my department or area?
- In what specific way can I work this year to remove a barrier that has prevented me from fostering…learning? (R. P. Keeling 2006, 50-51)

These questions, while intended to spur student affairs professionals to engage in reflective practice, can also help librarians examine how their work contributes to institutional missions.

According to Durrance and Fisher (How Libraries and Librarians Help: A Guide to Identifying User-Centered Outcomes 2005, 324), libraries should use professional development to conduct assessment skill inventories, capture librarian assessment skill gaps, continuously update librarians' assessment skills, and allocate assessment resources. Additional lists of necessary skills are also available (Keeling, et al. 2008; Oakleaf, Are They Learning? 2011). Library administrators who support this type of professional development will find themselves armed with better evidence to guide decision making and influence institutional administrators.

Leverage Professional Library Associations

Major professional associations can play a crucial organizing role in the effort to demonstrate library value. First, they can create online support resources and communities to serve as a nexus of value demonstration activities. Second, they can serve a "pulse taking" role, learning how member libraries are showing value and communicating this information to the membership. One example of this approach might be a one-question survey in C&RL News akin to the one-question surveys published in Library Media Connection, a school library publication. Third, they can orchestrate an "all hands on deck" approach to assessment, helping librarians determine which part of the Research Agenda might be best suited to their institutions and ensuring that the agenda is covered. Fourth, they can encourage library-centric publications and conferences to index their work in library and education literature databases. Finally, they can identify expert researchers and grant-funding opportunities that can partner with librarians to take on the most challenging aspects of the Research Agenda.

Note: The research agenda below focuses on areas of academic library impact on institutional missions (see Figure 10). Each section lists an essential question, surrogates (also known as hallmarks or indicators) for library impact (Markless and Streatfield 2006, 65), data sources, and potential correlations. As the research agenda is explored, librarians may find that some surrogates are stronger than others (Botha, Erasmus and Van Deventer 2009, 110); that some correlations exist or do not; that some causative relationships emerge.

A Bit About Methods

As librarians investigate elements of the research agenda, they may find that some approaches are more or less useful in the effort to articulate and establish library value. Certainly, the true utility of a particular assessment method is based less on the attributes of the method and more on the fit between a method and the research question under investigation. For example, librarians may find that satisfaction surveys are not as useful in the library value arena as outcomes-based surveys; but the actual method—a survey—is not inherently useless or useful. Indeed, a survey can be used to elicit user satisfaction levels (less useful) or self-reported outcomes data (more useful).

When it comes to selecting assessment methods and approaches, academic librarians can learn from their school, public, and special library counterparts. School librarians have established the effectiveness of critical incident surveys that elicit what libraries enable users to do and test audits that identify the impact of libraries on popular measures of student learning. Public librarians have demonstrated the political power of economic value estimations. Special librarians lead the way in showing the value of a library within a larger organization; they pair economic value calculations with critical incident surveys that capture what librarians enable users to do. Taken together, these examples suggest that academic librarians should investigate methods that allow them to capture what academic libraries enable users to do (using surveys or similar methods such as focus groups or interviews); show evidence of student learning (auditing tests and authentic assessments of student learning); and calculate the economic value of libraries (employing established financial value formulas). Academic librarians should also explore promising new approaches to assessment, including balanced scorecards (Brophy 2006, 160; Bielavitz 2010; Wilson, Del Tufo and Norman 2008) and rubrics.

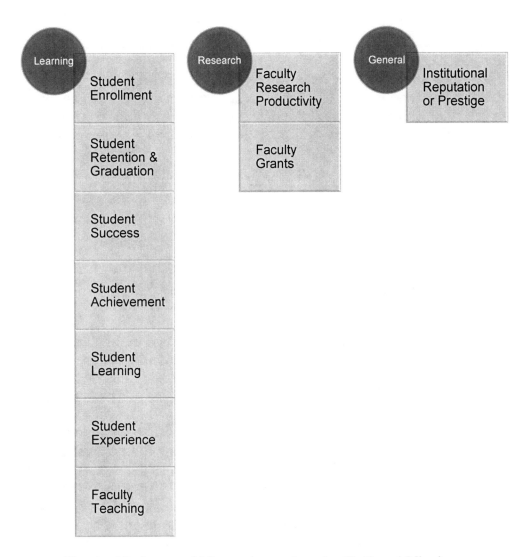

Figure 10. Areas of Library Impact on Institutional Missions

Student Enrollment

Essential Question—How does the library contribute to student enrollment?

Institutions of higher education want to admit the strongest possible students at both the undergraduate and graduate levels. Entering student class characteristics are major predictors of institutional rank, prestige, graduation, alumni donations, and other positive markers. According to the Association of Higher Education Facilities Officers, libraries are an important consideration when students select a university or college (Association of Higher Education Facilities Officers 2006), and, as a result, academic libraries can help institutional admissions boost enrollment (Simmel 2007, 88).The library ranked second in terms of facilities important in the selection decision process; only facilities for students' majors ranked higher. Libraries were ranked ahead of technology facilities, the student union center, and even recreational facilities (Michigan Academic Library Council 2007). Even *U.S. News and World Report* suggests libraries should impact college selection (Greer 2010).

Libraries can help their institutions attract the best possible prospective students as well as matriculate the best possible admitted students in a variety of ways depending on the institution type, size, profile, etc. Libraries are often housed in attractive facilities and librarians typically take part in campus-wide recruiting and orientation efforts. In addition, some libraries are taking even more direct steps to help their institutions attract and matriculate the best students. At the University of Washington, librarians act as advisors to entering honors students—a service that likely captures the attention of top-notch students and their parents alike. In the future, libraries can take a prominent campus role in reaching key prospective student groups and communicating the ways in which librarians can help students attain academic success. One can imagine assigning incoming students to librarians as "research advisors" and envision librarians innovating ways to provide just-in-time and just-for-you assistance based on students' enrollment records or individual characteristics. Academics conceive of a time when librarians send students instructional content relevant to their newly assigned projects proactively, rather than waiting passively to be asked to help (Eisenberg 2010; Shupe 2007, 53). Such service can target both students of great need and of great potential and possibly increase the strength of enrolling students (institutional outcome), while at the same time delivering excellent information literacy instruction (library outcome).

Surrogates for Library Impact

Surrogates for library impact on student enrollment include **recruitment of prospective students**, **matriculation of admitted students**, and **recommendations of current students**.

Data Sources

To investigate the ways in which libraries currently (or in the future) contribute to student enrollment, librarians can partner with campus colleagues in order to leverage existing data sources unique to the issue of enrollment, including **admissions data**, **admissions student and parent surveys** ("What were the most exciting, inspiring aspects of our campus?"), and student self-reported information on **student engagement surveys** ("Would you attend this institution again? Would you recommend it to a friend?").

Potential Correlations

Librarians need to determine areas for potential connections between surrogates for library impact on institutional mission or outcomes and descriptive library data elements. Are any of the surrogates of library impact on institutional mission or outcomes (listed in the first column) correlated, related, or linked to any descriptive library data elements (in the second column)? Libraries that do not collect data on these surrogates or areas for potential correlations may wish to expand their data collection practices.

Surrogates of library impact on institutional mission/outcomes(s)	Possible Areas of Correlation
Recruitment of prospective students	Are there correlations, relationships, or linkages to these macro-level areas? Note: Macro-level areas are fertile territory for ROI calculations. ✓ Library expenditures ✓ Collection value ✓ Collection use, physical and online, may divide by subject area or other criteria ✓ Space use ✓ Service use, including reference, ILL, reserves, etc. ✓ Service use, including instruction, integration of library resources and services into course syllabi, course Web sites, lectures, labs, reserve readings, etc. ✓ Library ranking ✓ Library awards ✓ Librarian staffing levels or ratio of user group to librarian ✓ Librarian skills or participation in professional development
Matriculation of admitted students	Are there correlations, relationships, or linkages to these macro-level areas? Note: Macro-level areas are fertile territory for ROI calculations. ✓ Library expenditures ✓ Collection value ✓ Collection use, physical and online, may divide by subject

	area or other criteria ✓ Space use ✓ Service use, including reference, ILL, reserves, etc. ✓ Service use, including instruction, integration of library resources and services into course syllabi, course Web sites, lectures, labs, reserve readings, etc. ✓ Library ranking ✓ Library awards ✓ Librarian staffing levels or ratio of user group to librarian ✓ Librarian skills or participation in professional development
Recommendations of current students	Are there correlations, relationships or linkages to individual student behavior in these areas? Note: These library user interactions must be captured in order to be correlated, related, or linked to surrogates of library value. ✓ Circulation counts ✓ Tutorial logins ✓ Resources logins, including MyLibrary, MINES data, e-resources, etc. ✓ Resource login/logout surveys ✓ Self-reported usage ✓ Self-reported time saved ✓ Swipe cards on building, library instruction classrooms ✓ Enrollment in courses identified as having high library collections and services usage ✓ Enrollment in for-credit library instruction course ✓ Cohort studies Are there correlations, relationships, or linkages to these macro-level areas? Note: Macro-level areas are fertile territory for ROI calculations. ✓ Library expenditures ✓ Collection value ✓ Collection use, physical and online, may divide by subject area or other criteria ✓ Space use ✓ Service use, including reference, ILL, reserves, etc. ✓ Service use, including instruction, integration of library resources and services into course syllabi, course Web sites, lectures, labs, reserve readings, etc. ✓ Library ranking ✓ Library awards ✓ Librarian staffing levels or ratio of user group to librarian ✓ Librarian skills or participation in professional development

Student Retention

Essential Question—How does the library contribute to student retention and graduation rates?

Most retention and graduate rate studies have focused on explanations for student persistence or departure, either due to personal characteristics or institutional practices (Bailey 2006, 10). Because most librarians are not in positions that enable them to influence students' personal traits, they can focus on creating institutional environments that foster retention and eventual graduation. To this end, librarians can integrate library services and resources into high-impact educational practices (Kuh, High-Impact Educational Practices 2008) and embrace "proactive early warning and intervention strategies for students with academic deficiencies. There is a substantial difference between providing academic support as a service for students to elect to participate in voluntarily and [an] approach in which student progress is monitored actively in detail, with mandatory intervention if difficulties are encountered" (Ewell and Wellman 2007, 9).

Currently, retention and graduation rates are attracting attention at all levels. Consequently, librarians can investigate the major predictors of persistence and departure, which are largely outside the scope of this report. Librarians can also be well versed in the difficulties of obtaining accurate graduation data.

Surrogates for Library Impact

Surrogates for library impact on student retention and graduation include student **fall-to-fall retention, graduation rates (four-year, six-year, at institution of origin, at another institution)**, transfer rates, certificate completion.

Data Sources

To investigate the ways in which libraries currently (or in future) contribute to student retention and graduation rates, librarians can partner with campus colleagues in order to leverage existing data sources, including **registrar records, records of individual students' library behaviors, IPEDS/NSC data**, and the **Academic Libraries Survey**.

Potential Correlations

Librarians can determine areas for potential connections between surrogates for library impact on institutional mission or outcomes and descriptive library data elements. Are any of the surrogates of library impact on institutional mission or outcomes (listed in the first column) correlated, related, or linked to any descriptive library data elements (in the second column)? Libraries that do not collect data on these surrogates or areas for potential correlations may wish to expand their data collection practices.

Surrogates of library impact on institutional mission/outcomes(s)	Possible Areas of Correlation
Fall-to-fall retention	Are there correlations, relationships or linkages to individual student behavior in these areas? Note: These library user interactions must be captured in order to be correlated, related, or linked to surrogates of library value. ✓ Circulation counts ✓ Tutorial logins ✓ Resources logins, including MyLibrary, MINES data, e-resources, etc. ✓ Resource login/logout surveys ✓ Self-reported usage ✓ Self-reported time saved ✓ Self-reported course material costs saved ✓ Swipe cards on building, library instruction classrooms ✓ Enrollment in courses identified as having high library collections and services usage ✓ Enrollment in for-credit library instruction course ✓ Cohort studies Are there correlations, relationships, or linkages to these macro-level areas? Note: Macro-level areas are fertile territory for ROI calculations. ✓ Library expenditures ✓ Collection value ✓ Collection use, physical and online, may divide by subject area or other criteria ✓ Space use ✓ Service use, including reference, ILL, reserves, etc. ✓ Service use, including instruction, integration of library resources and services into course syllabi, course Web sites, lectures, labs, reserve readings, etc. ✓ Library ranking ✓ Library awards ✓ Librarian staffing levels or ratio of user group to librarian ✓ Librarian skills or participation in professional development
Graduation rates (four-year, six-year, at institution of origin, at another institution)	Are there correlations, relationships or linkages to individual student behavior in these areas? Note: These library user interactions must be captured in order to be correlated, related, or linked to surrogates of library value. ✓ Circulation counts ✓ Tutorial logins ✓ Resources logins, including MyLibrary, MINES data, e-

	resources, etc. ✓ Resource login/logout surveys ✓ Self-reported usage ✓ Self-reported time saved ✓ Self-reported course material costs saved ✓ Swipe cards on building, library instruction classrooms ✓ Enrollment in courses identified as having high library collections and services usage ✓ Enrollment in for-credit library instruction course ✓ Cohort studies Are there correlations, relationships, or linkages to these macro-level areas? Note: Macro-level areas are fertile territory for ROI calculations. ✓ Library expenditures ✓ Collection value ✓ Collection use, physical and online, may divide by subject area or other criteria ✓ Space use ✓ Service use, including reference, ILL, reserves, etc. ✓ Service use, including instruction, integration of library resources and services into course syllabi, course Web sites, lectures, labs, reserve readings, etc. ✓ Library ranking ✓ Library awards ✓ Librarian staffing levels or ratio of user group to librarian ✓ Librarian skills or participation in professional development

Student Success

Essential Question—How does the library contribute to student success?

The term "student success" is often used very generally and broadly. Here, the term is used to denote student ability to do well in internships, secure job placements, earn salaries, gain acceptance to graduate/professional schools, or obtain marketable skills. Although it may be challenging to make direct and clear connections between academic libraries and students' educational and professional futures, librarians can acknowledge that these outcomes are of critical importance to institutions and their stakeholders. Consequently, librarians can investigate the linkages between academic libraries and student success, and—if no linkages currently exist—librarians should form them. For example, institutions place emphasis on students' job placements immediately after college and most invite employers to campus to interview students. Librarians can help students prepare for these interviews by sharing resources, such as company profiles, market analyses, etc., with career resources units on campus and with students directly. When librarians help students secure jobs, their value to their overarching institutions is clear. This principle translates to other student success issues—academic librarians can focus their services on directly and actively supporting institutional outcomes.

Surrogates for Library Impact

Surrogates for library impact on student success include **internship success, job placement, job salaries, professional/graduate school acceptance**, and **marketable skills**.

Data Sources

To investigate the ways in which libraries currently (or in the future) contribute to student success, librarians can partner with campus colleagues in order to leverage existing data sources, including **internship evaluation reports, career services records, alumni surveys, and records of individual students' library behaviors**.

Potential Correlations

Librarians can determine areas for potential connections between surrogates for library impact on institutional mission or outcomes and descriptive library data elements. Are any of the surrogates of library impact on institutional mission or outcomes (listed in the first column) correlated, related, or linked to any descriptive library data elements (in the second column)? Libraries that do not collect data on these surrogates or areas for potential correlations may wish to expand their data collection practices.

Surrogates of library impact on institutional mission/outcomes(s)	Possible Areas of Correlation
Internship success	Are there correlations, relationships, or linkages to individual student behavior in these areas? Note: These library user interactions must be captured in order to be correlated, related, or linked to surrogates of library value. ✓ Circulation counts ✓ Tutorial logins ✓ Resources logins, including MyLibrary, MINES data, e-resources, etc. ✓ Resource login/logout surveys ✓ Self-reported usage ✓ Self-reported time saved ✓ Swipe cards on building, library instruction classrooms ✓ Enrollment in courses identified as having high library collections and services usage ✓ Enrollment in for-credit library instruction course ✓ Cohort studies Are there correlations, relationships, or linkages to these macro-level areas? Note: Macro-level areas are fertile territory for ROI calculations. ✓ Library expenditures ✓ Collection value ✓ Collection use, physical and online, may divide by subject area or other criteria ✓ Space use ✓ Service use, including reference, ILL, reserves, etc. ✓ Service use, including instruction, integration of library resources and services into course syllabi, course Web sites, lectures, labs, reserve readings, etc. ✓ Library ranking ✓ Library awards ✓ Librarian staffing levels or ratio of user group to librarian ✓ Librarian skills or participation in professional development
Job placement	Are there correlations, relationships or linkages to individual student behavior in these areas? Note: These library user interactions must be captured in order to be correlated, related, or linked to surrogates of library value. ✓ Circulation counts ✓ Tutorial logins ✓ Resources logins, including MyLibrary, MINES data, e-resources, etc. ✓ Resource login/logout surveys ✓ Self-reported usage ✓ Self-reported time saved

	✓ Swipe cards on building, library instruction classrooms ✓ Enrollment in courses identified as having high library collections and services usage ✓ Enrollment in for-credit library instruction course ✓ Cohort studies Are there correlations, relationships, or linkages to these macro-level areas? Note: Macro-level areas are fertile territory for ROI calculations. ✓ Library expenditures ✓ Collection value ✓ Collection use, physical and online, may divide by subject area or other criteria ✓ Space use ✓ Service use, including reference, ILL, reserves, etc. ✓ Service use, including instruction, integration of library resources and services into course syllabi, course Web sites, lectures, labs, reserve readings, etc. ✓ Library ranking ✓ Library awards ✓ Librarian staffing levels or ratio of user group to librarian ✓ Librarian skills or participation in professional development
Job salaries	Are there correlations, relationships or linkages to individual student behavior in these areas? Note: these library user interactions must be captured in order to be correlated, related, or linked to surrogates of library value. ✓ Circulation counts ✓ Tutorial logins ✓ Resources logins including MyLibrary, MINES data, e-resources, etc. ✓ Resource login/logout surveys ✓ Self-reported usage ✓ Self-reported time saved ✓ Swipe cards on building, library instruction classrooms ✓ Enrollment in courses identified as having high library collections and services usage ✓ Enrollment in for-credit library instruction course ✓ Cohort studies Are there correlations, relationships, or linkages to these macro-level areas? Note: Macro-level areas are fertile territory for ROI calculations. ✓ Library expenditures ✓ Collection value ✓ Collection use, physical and online, may divide by subject area or other criteria ✓ Space use

	✓ Service use, including reference, ILL, reserves, etc.
	✓ Service use, including instruction, integration of library resources and services into course syllabi, course Web sites, lectures, labs, reserve readings, etc.
	✓ Library ranking
	✓ Library awards
	✓ Librarian staffing levels or ratio of user group to librarian
	✓ Librarian skills or participation in professional development
Professional/graduate school acceptance	Are there correlations, relationships, or linkages to individual student behavior in these areas? Note: These library user interactions must be captured in order to be correlated, related, or linked to surrogates of library value.
	✓ Circulation counts
	✓ Tutorial logins
	✓ Resources logins, including MyLibrary, MINES data, e-resources, etc.
	✓ Resource login/logout surveys
	✓ Self-reported usage
	✓ Self-reported time saved
	✓ Swipe cards on building, library instruction classrooms
	✓ Enrollment in courses identified as having high library collections and services usage
	✓ Enrollment in for-credit library instruction course
	✓ Cohort studies
	Are there correlations, relationships, or linkages to these macro-level areas? Note: Macro-level areas are fertile territory for ROI calculations.
	✓ Library expenditures
	✓ Collection value
	✓ Collection use, physical and online, may divide by subject area or other criteria
	✓ Space use
	✓ Service use, including reference, ILL, reserves, etc.
	✓ Service use, including instruction, integration of library resources and services into course syllabi, course Web sites, lectures, labs, reserve readings, etc.
	✓ Library ranking
	✓ Library awards
	✓ Librarian staffing levels or ratio of user group to librarian
	✓ Librarian skills or participation in professional development
Marketable skills	Are there correlations, relationships, or linkages to individual student behavior in these areas? Note: These library user interactions must be captured in order to be correlated, related, or linked to surrogates of library value.
	✓ Circulation counts
	✓ Tutorial logins

	✓ Resources logins, including MyLibrary, MINES data, e-resources, etc. ✓ Resource login/logout surveys ✓ Self-reported usage ✓ Self-reported time saved ✓ Swipe cards on building, library instruction classrooms ✓ Enrollment in courses identified as having high library collections and services usage ✓ Enrollment in for-credit library instruction course ✓ Cohort studies Are there correlations, relationships, or linkages to these macro-level areas? Note: Macro-level areas are fertile territory for ROI calculations. ✓ Library expenditures ✓ Collection value ✓ Collection use, physical and online, may divide by subject area or other criteria ✓ Space use ✓ Service use, including reference, ILL, reserves, etc. ✓ Service use, including instruction, integration of library resources and services into course syllabi, course Web sites, lectures, labs, reserve readings, etc. ✓ Library ranking ✓ Library awards ✓ Librarian staffing levels or ratio of user group to librarian ✓ Librarian skills or participation in professional development

Essential Question—How does the library contribute to student achievement?

Like the term "student success," "student achievement" is often used very generally and broadly. In this context, student achievement refers to GPA and professional/educational test scores. Librarians can conduct test item audits of major professional/educational tests to determine correlations between information skills and specific test items. As an example, the box below reveals possible connections between the CAAP test and the Information Literacy Competency Standards for Higher Education. These connections are based on an analysis of CAAP practice exams.

CAAP Reading	ACRL Standard 3, Performance Indicator 1: The information literate student summarizes the main ideas to be extracted from the information gathered.
CAAP Critical Thinking	ACRL Standard 3, Performance Indicator 2: The information literate student articulates and applies initial criteria for evaluating both the information and its sources; ACRL Standard 3, Performance Indicator 3: The information literate student synthesizes main ideas to construct new concepts; ACRL Standard 3, Performance Indicator 4: The information literate student compares new knowledge with prior knowledge to determine the value added, contradictions, or other unique characteristics of the information.
CAAP Science Reasoning	ACRL Standard 3, Performance Indicator 1: The information literate student summarizes the main ideas to be extracted from the information gathered; ACRL Standard 3, Performance Indicator 3: The information literate student synthesizes main ideas to construct new concepts.

Surrogates for Library Impact

Surrogates for library impact on student enrollment include course completions, **GPA** and **professional/educational test scores** such as the GRE, MCAT, LSAT, CAAP, CLA, MAPP, and other licensure tests.

Data Sources

To investigate the ways in which libraries currently (or in the future) contribute to student achievement, librarians can partner with campus colleagues in order to leverage existing data sources, including **registrar records, institutional test score reports, test item audits, and records of individual students' library behaviors**.

Potential Correlations

Librarians can determine areas for potential connections between surrogates for library impact on institutional mission or outcomes and descriptive library data elements. Are any of the surrogates of library impact on institutional mission or outcomes (listed in the first column) correlated, related, or linked to any descriptive library data elements (in the second column)? Libraries that do not collect data on these surrogates or areas for potential correlations may wish to expand their data collection practices.

Surrogates of library impact on institutional mission/outcomes(s)	Possible Areas of Correlation
GPA	Are there correlations, relationships, or linkages to individual student behavior in these areas? Note: These library user interactions must be captured in order to be correlated, related, or linked to surrogates of library value. ✓ Circulation counts ✓ Tutorial logins ✓ Resources logins, including MyLibrary, MINES data, e-resources, etc. ✓ Resource login/logout surveys ✓ Self-reported usage ✓ Self-reported time saved ✓ Swipe cards on building, library instruction classrooms ✓ Enrollment in courses identified as having high library collections and services usage ✓ Enrollment in for-credit library instruction course ✓ Cohort studies Are there correlations, relationships, or linkages to these macro-level areas? Note: Macro-level areas are fertile territory for ROI calculations. ✓ Library expenditures ✓ Collection value ✓ Collection use, physical and online, may divide by subject area or other criteria ✓ Space use ✓ Service use, including reference, ILL, reserves, etc. ✓ Service use, including instruction, integration of library resources and services into course syllabi, course Web sites, lectures, labs, reserve readings, etc. ✓ Library ranking ✓ Library awards ✓ Librarian staffing levels or ratio of user group to librarian ✓ Librarian skills or participation in professional development
Professional/educational test	Are there correlations, relationships, or linkages to individual

scores	student behavior in these areas? Note: These library user interactions must be captured in order to be correlated, related, or linked to surrogates of library value.
	✓ Circulation counts
	✓ Tutorial logins
	✓ Resources logins, including MyLibrary, MINES data, e-resources, etc.
	✓ Resource login/logout surveys
	✓ Self-reported usage
	✓ Self-reported time saved
	✓ Swipe cards on building, library instruction classrooms
	✓ Enrollment in courses identified as having high library collections and services usage
	✓ Enrollment in for-credit library instruction course
	✓ Cohort studies
	Are there correlations, relationships, or linkages to these macro-level areas? Note: Macro-level areas are fertile territory for ROI calculations.
	✓ Library expenditures
	✓ Collection value
	✓ Collection use, physical and online, may divide by subject area or other criteria
	✓ Space use
	✓ Service use, including reference, ILL, reserves, etc.
	✓ Service use, including instruction, integration of library resources and services into course syllabi, course Web sites, lectures, labs, reserve readings, etc.
	✓ Library ranking
	✓ Library awards
	✓ Librarian staffing levels or ratio of user group to librarian
	✓ Librarian skills or participation in professional development

Essential Question—How does the library contribute to student learning?

Although the literature of information literacy instruction and assessment is voluminous, most of the literature is sporadic, disconnected, and reveals limited snapshots of the impact of academic libraries on learning. Academic librarians require systematic, coherent, and connected evidence to establish the role of libraries in student learning. Assessment management systems provide the structure that is absolutely critical to establishing a clear picture of how academic libraries contribute to student learning.

In addition to direct measures of student learning (made coherent through use of an assessment management system), it is often helpful to gather faculty judgments of student work and any changes in quality that result from library instruction and interaction.

Surrogates for Library Impact

Surrogates for library impact on student learning include **learning assessments**, and **faculty judgments** of student learning gains. Learning assessments should be authentic, integrated performance assessments focused on campus learning outcomes including information literacy. However, their formats are flexible and may include research journals reflective writing, "think alouds," self or peer evaluations, research drafts or papers, open-ended question responses, works cited pages, annotated bibliographies, speeches, multimedia presentations, and other formats (Oakleaf, Writing Information Literacy Assessment Plans 2010). In order to give order and structure to a variety of learning assessments enacted by different librarians and completed by different students, librarians can develop or purchase **assessment management systems**. Without assessment management systems, student learning assessments tend to be disorganized and defy attempts to massage them into meaningful reports that can be shared campuswide. With them, evidence of the student learning impact of libraries can be managed, documented, shared, and used to make future instructional improvements.

Data Sources

To investigate the ways in which libraries currently (or in future) contribute to student learning, librarians can partner with campus colleagues in order to leverage existing data sources, including **assessment management systems, faculty surveys, and records of individual students' library behaviors**.

Potential Correlations

Librarians can determine areas for potential connections between surrogates for library impact on institutional mission or outcomes and descriptive library data elements. Are any of the surrogates of library impact on institutional mission or outcomes (listed in the first column) correlated, related, or linked to any descriptive library data elements (in the second column)? Libraries that do not collect data on these surrogates or areas for potential correlations may wish to expand their data collection practices.

Surrogates of library impact on institutional mission/outcomes(s)	Possible Areas of Correlation
Learning assessments	Are there correlations, relationships, or linkages to individual student behavior in these areas? Note: These library user interactions must be captured in order to be correlated, related, or linked to surrogates of library value. ✓ Circulation counts ✓ Tutorial logins ✓ Resources logins, including MyLibrary, MINES data, e-resources, etc. ✓ Resource login/logout surveys ✓ Self-reported usage ✓ Self-reported time saved ✓ Swipe cards on building, library instruction classrooms ✓ Enrollment in courses identified as having high library collections and services usage ✓ Enrollment in for-credit library instruction course ✓ Cohort studies Are there correlations, relationships, or linkages to these macro-level areas? Note: Macro-level areas are fertile territory for ROI calculations. ✓ Library expenditures ✓ Collection value ✓ Collection use, physical and online, may divide by subject area or other criteria ✓ Space use ✓ Service use, including reference, ILL, reserves, etc. ✓ Service use, including instruction, integration of library resources and services into course syllabi, course Web sites, lectures, labs, reserve readings, etc. ✓ Library ranking ✓ Library awards ✓ Librarian staffing levels or ratio of user group to librarian ✓ Librarian skills or participation in professional development
Faculty judgments	Are there correlations, relationships, or linkages to individual student behavior in these areas? Note: These library user

	interactions must be captured in order to be correlated, related, or linked to surrogates of library value.
	✓ Circulation counts
	✓ Tutorial logins
	✓ Resources logins, including MyLibrary, MINES data, e-resources, etc.
	✓ Resource login/logout surveys
	✓ Self-reported usage
	✓ Self-reported time saved
	✓ Swipe cards on building, library instruction classrooms
	✓ Enrollment in courses identified as having high library collections and services usage
	✓ Enrollment in for-credit library instruction course
	✓ Cohort studies
	Are there correlations, relationships, or linkages to these macro-level areas? Note: Macro-level areas are fertile territory for ROI calculations.
	✓ Library expenditures
	✓ Collection value
	✓ Collection use, physical and online, may divide by subject area or other criteria
	✓ Space use
	✓ Service use, including reference, ILL, reserves, etc.
	✓ Service use, including instruction, integration of library resources and services into course syllabi, course Web sites, lectures, labs, reserve readings, etc.
	✓ Library ranking
	✓ Library awards
	✓ Librarian staffing levels or ratio of user group to librarian
	✓ Librarian skills or participation in professional development

Student Experience, Attitude, and Perception of Quality

Essential Question—How does the library contribute to the student experience?

What can libraries do to enhance student engagement? Libraries can integrate their resources and services into any high-impact activities their institutions offer (Kuh, High-Impact Educational Practices 2008, 19). High-impact practices include: first-year seminars and experiences, common intellectual experiences, learning communities, writing-intensive courses, collaborative assignments and projects, undergraduate research, diversity/global learning, service learning/community-based learning, internships, capstone courses and projects (Kuh, High-Impact Educational Practices 2008, 9-11).

Student experience studies tend to focus on the entire student experience and often do not include questions directly related to libraries. However, there are questions that are at least tangentially related to information behaviors, and these questions may reveal information about the impact of the academic library on student impact. Librarians can continue to work to develop library-related questions to augment these national surveys as well as local institutional surveys, especially aimed at seniors and alumni. Finally, librarians can deploy "help" studies to explore how academic libraries contribute to student experiences.

Surrogates for Library Impact

Surrogates for library impact on student engagement include **self-report engagement studies**, **senior/alumni surveys**, **help surveys** and **alumni membership, donations, or endowments**.

Data Sources

To investigate the ways in which libraries currently (or in future) contribute to student learning, librarians can partner with campus colleagues in order to leverage existing data sources, including **self-report engagement surveys, senior/alumni surveys, help surveys, alumni donations, and records of individual students' library behaviors**.

Examples of national engagement survey questions that can serve as data sources are included below.

National Survey of Student Engagement
NSSE 1. *In your experience at your institution during the current school year, about how often have you done each of the following?*

NSSE 1d. Worked on a paper or project that required integrating ideas or information from various sources.

NSSE 2. *During the current school year, how much has your coursework emphasized the following mental activities?*

NSSE 2b. Analyzing the basic elements of an idea, experience, or theory, such as examining a particular case or situation in depth and considering its components.

NSSE 2c. Synthesizing and organizing ideas, information, or experiences into new, more complex interpretations and relationships.

NSSE 2d. Making judgments about the value of information, arguments, or methods, such as examining how others gathered and interpreted data and assessing the soundness of their conclusions.

NSSE 3. *During the current school year, about how much reading and writing have you done?*

NSSE 3b. Number of books read on your own (nonassigned) for personal enjoyment or academic enrichment.

NSSE 3c. Number of written papers or reports of 20 pages or more.

NSSE 3d. Number of written papers or reports between 5 and 19 pages.

NSSE 3e. Number of written papers or reports of fewer than 5 pages.

NSSE 7. *Which of the following have you done or do you plan to do before you graduate from your institution?*

NSSE 7d. Work on a research project with a faculty member.

NSSE 7h. Culminating senior experience (capstone course, senior project or thesis, comprehensive exam, etc.)

NSSE 10. *To what extent does your institution emphasize each of the following?*

NSSE 10b. Providing the support you need to help you succeed academically.

NSSE 11. *To what extent has your experience at this institution contributed to your knowledge, skills, and personal development in the following areas?*

NSSE 11b. Acquiring job or work-related knowledge and skills.

NSSE 11e. Thinking critically and analytically.

NSSE 11g. Using computing and information technology.

NSSE 13. *How would you evaluate your entire educational experience at this institution?*

NSSE 14. *If you could start over again, would you go to the same institution you are now attending?*

NSSE 25. *What have most of your grades been up to now at this institution?*

Faculty Survey of Student Engagement

FSSE *To what extent does your institution emphasize each of the following?*

Providing students the support they need to help them succeed academically.

FSSE *About how many hours do you spend in a typical 7-day week doing each of the following?*

Research and scholarly activities.

Working with undergraduates on research.

Reflecting on ways to improve my teaching.

FSSE *In your selected course section, about how much reading and writing do you assign students? Or do you estimate the typical student has done?*

Number of books read on his or her own (not assigned) for personal enjoyment or academic enrichment

Number of written papers or reports of 20 pages or more.

Number of written papers or reports between 5 and 19 pages.

Number of written papers or reports of fewer than 5 pages.

FSSE *In your selected course section, how important to you is it that your students do the following?*

Work on a paper or project that requires integrating ideas or information from various sources.

FSSE *In your selected course section, how much emphasis do you place on engaging students in each of these mental activities?*

Analyzing the basic elements of an idea, experience, or theory, such as examining a particular case or situation in depth and considering its components.

Synthesizing and organizing ideas, information, or experiences into new, more complex interpretations and relationships.

Making judgments about the value of information, arguments, or methods, such as examining how others gathered and interpreted data and assessing the soundness of their conclusions.

FSSE *To what extent do you structure your selected course section so that students learn and develop in the following areas? To what extent has the typical student's experience at this institution contributed to his or her knowledge, skills, and personal development in the following areas?*

Learning effectively on his or her own.

Thinking critically and analytically.

Using computing and information technology.

Developing a personal code of values and ethics.

Acquiring a broad general education.

Acquiring job or work-related knowledge and skills.

FSSE *How important is it to you that undergraduates at your institution do the following?*

Work on a research project with a faculty member outside of course or program requirements.

Independent study or self-designed major.

Culminating senior experience (capstone course, senior project or thesis, comprehensive exam, etc.).

Beginning College Survey of Student Engagement

BCSSE 7. *During your last year of high school, about how much reading and writing did you do?*

BCSSE 7b. Books read on your own (not assigned) for personal enjoyment or academic enrichment.

BCSSE 7c. Writing short papers or reports (5 or fewer pages).

BCSSE 7d. Writing longer papers or reports (more than 5 pages).

BCSSE 13. *During the coming school year, about how many hours do you think you will spend in a typical 7-day week doing each of the following?*

BCSSE 13a. Preparing for class (studying, reading, writing, doing homework or lab work, analyzing data, rehearsing, and other academic activities).

BCSSE 14. *During the coming school year, about how often do you expect to do each of the following?*

BCSSE 14c. Work on a paper or project that requires integrating ideas or information from various sources.

BCSSE 15. *During the coming school year, how certain are you that you will do the following?*

BCSSE 15b. Find additional information for course assignments when you don't understand the material.

BCSSE 17. *How prepared are you to do the following in your academic work at this college?*

BCSSE 17c. Think critically and analytically.

BCSSE 17e. Use computing and information technology.

BCSSE 17g. Learn effectively on your own.

BCSSE 18. *How important is it to you that your college or university provides each of the following?*

BCSSE 18a. A challenging academic experience.

BCSSE 18b. Support to help you succeed academically.

BCSSE 21. *What do you expect most of your grades will be at this college during the coming year?*

BCSSE 23. *What is the highest academic degree that you intend to obtain at this or any college?*

Community College Survey of Student Engagement
CCSSE 4. *In your experience at this college during the current school year, about how often have you done each of the following?*
CCSSE 4d. Worked on a paper or project that required integrating ideas or information from various sources.
CCSSE 4j. Used the Internet or instant messaging to work on an assignment.
CCSSE 5. *During the current student year, how much has your coursework at this college emphasized the following mental activities?*
CCSSE 5b. Analyzing the basic elements of an idea, experience, or theory.
CCSSE 5c. Synthesizing and organizing ideas, information, or experiences in new ways.
CCSSE 5d. Making judgments about the value or soundness of information, arguments, or methods.
CCSSE 5f. Using information you have read or heard to perform a new skill.

Academic librarians might also explore an approach school librarians pioneered: surveys that ask library users to describe what the academic library has enabled them to accomplish. Special library impact studies are also good models for this approach. A pilot study of this type was conducted in spring 2010 at Trinity University, and the text is included below.

1. Think about a time when the university library helped you. What help did you receive? What did the help enable you to do? [text box, 1,000 characters]
2. Think about a time when the university library didn't help you. What help would you have liked to receive? What would that help have enabled you to do? [text box, 1,000 characters]
3. What is your year in school?
    a. First-Year
    b. Sophomore
    c. Junior
    d. Senior
    e. Other: [text box, 50 characters]
4. What is your major? [Drop down]
5. What is your GPA on 4.0 scale? [Drop down]

6. Do you expect to graduate on time? [Y/N]
7. If you could start over again, would you go to the institution you're attending now? [Y/N]
8. Would you recommend attending your institution to a friend? [Y/N]

Thank you for your participation in this survey. Your responses will help the university library be more helpful in the future!

Potential Correlations

Librarians can determine areas for potential connections between surrogates for library impact on institutional mission or outcomes and descriptive library data elements. Are any of the surrogates of library impact on institutional mission or outcomes (listed in the first column) correlated, related, or linked to any descriptive library data elements (in the second column)? Libraries that do not collect data on these surrogates or areas for potential correlations may wish to expand their data collection practices.

Surrogates of library impact on institutional mission/outcomes(s)	Possible Areas of Correlation
Self-report engagement surveys	Are there correlations, relationships or linkages to individual student behavior in these areas? Note: These library user interactions must be captured in order to be correlated, related, or linked to surrogates of library value. ✓ Circulation counts ✓ Tutorial logins ✓ Resources logins, including MyLibrary, MINES data, e-resources, etc. ✓ Resource login/logout surveys ✓ Self-reported usage ✓ Self-reported time saved ✓ Swipe cards on building, library instruction classrooms ✓ Enrollment in courses identified as having high library collections and services usage ✓ Enrollment in for-credit library instruction course ✓ Cohort studies Are there correlations, relationships, or linkages to these macro-level areas? Note: Macro-level areas are fertile territory for ROI calculations. ✓ Library expenditures ✓ Collection value ✓ Collection use, physical and online, may divide by subject area or other criteria ✓ Space use ✓ Service use, including reference, ILL, reserves, etc. ✓ Service use, including instruction, integration of library resources and services into course syllabi, course Web

	sites, lectures, labs, reserve readings, etc. ✓ Library ranking ✓ Library awards ✓ Librarian staffing levels or ratio of user group to librarian ✓ Librarian skills or participation in professional development
Senior/alumni surveys	Are there correlations, relationships, or linkages to individual student behavior in these areas? Note: These library user interactions must be captured in order to be correlated, related, or linked to surrogates of library value. ✓ Circulation counts ✓ Tutorial logins ✓ Resources logins, including MyLibrary, MINES data, e-resources, etc. ✓ Resource login/logout surveys ✓ Self-reported usage ✓ Self-reported time saved ✓ Swipe cards on building, library instruction classrooms ✓ Enrollment in courses identified as having high library collections and services usage ✓ Enrollment in for-credit library instruction course ✓ Cohort studies Are there correlations, relationships, or linkages to these macro-level areas? Note: Macro-level areas are fertile territory for ROI calculations. ✓ Library expenditures ✓ Collection value ✓ Collection use, physical and online, may divide by subject area or other criteria ✓ Space use ✓ Service use, including reference, ILL, reserves, etc. ✓ Service use, including instruction, integration of library resources and services into course syllabi, course Web sites, lectures, labs, reserve readings, etc. ✓ Library ranking ✓ Library awards ✓ Librarian staffing levels or ratio of user group to librarian ✓ Librarian skills or participation in professional development
Help surveys	Are there correlations, relationships, or linkages to individual student behavior in these areas? Note: These library user interactions must be captured in order to be correlated, related, or linked to surrogates of library value. ✓ Circulation counts ✓ Tutorial logins ✓ Resources logins, including MyLibrary, MINES data, e-resources, etc. ✓ Resource login/logout surveys

	✓ Self-reported usage ✓ Self-reported time saved ✓ Swipe cards on building, library instruction classrooms ✓ Enrollment in courses identified as having high library collections and services usage ✓ Enrollment in for-credit library instruction course ✓ Cohort studies Are there correlations, relationships, or linkages to these macro-level areas? Note: Macro-level areas are fertile territory for ROI calculations. ✓ Library expenditures ✓ Collection value ✓ Collection use, physical and online, may divide by subject area or other criteria ✓ Space use ✓ Service use, including reference, ILL, reserves, etc. ✓ Service use, including instruction, integration of library resources and services into course syllabi, course Web sites, lectures, labs, reserve readings, etc. ✓ Library ranking ✓ Library awards ✓ Librarian staffing levels or ratio of user group to librarian ✓ Librarian skills or participation in professional development
Alumni memberships, donations, or endowments	Are there correlations, relationships, or linkages to individual student behavior in these areas? Note: These library user interactions must be captured in order to be correlated, related, or linked to surrogates of library value. ✓ Circulation counts ✓ Tutorial logins ✓ Resources logins, including MyLibrary, MINES data, e-resources, etc. ✓ Resource login/logout surveys ✓ Self-reported usage ✓ Self-reported time saved ✓ Swipe cards on building, library instruction classrooms ✓ Enrollment in courses identified as having high library collections and services usage ✓ Enrollment in for-credit library instruction course ✓ Cohort studies Are there correlations, relationships, or linkages to these macro-level areas? Note: Macro-level areas are fertile territory for ROI calculations. ✓ Library expenditures ✓ Collection value ✓ Collection use, physical and online, may divide by subject

	area or other criteria ✓ Space use ✓ Service use, including reference, ILL, reserves, etc. ✓ Service use, including instruction, integration of library resources and services into course syllabi, course Web sites, lectures, labs, reserve readings, etc. ✓ Library ranking ✓ Library awards ✓ Librarian staffing levels or ratio of user group to librarian ✓ Librarian skills or participation in professional development

Faculty Research Productivity

Essential Question—How does the library contribute to faculty research productivity (or tenure and promotion decisions)?

Librarians contribute to faculty research productivity in a number of ways. Some of these ways are collection-focused; others are service-focused. To some degree, librarians have investigated the impact of collections on faculty productivity, but much work is left to be done in the service sector. How do librarians serve faculty who are preparing publications, presentations, or patent applications? How do librarians help faculty prepare their tenure and promotion packages? Happily, surrogates for faculty research productivity are well established (see Faculty Productivity section in Review and Analysis of the Research section earlier in this report); the challenge for librarians is to collect data on those surrogates for individual faculty and correlate them to individual faculty behavior and library characteristics.

Surrogates for Library Impact

Surrogates for library impact on faculty productivity include **numbers of publications, numbers of patents, number of research-generated products, value of technology transfer**, and **tenure/promotion judgments**.

Data Sources

To investigate the ways in which libraries currently (or in future) contribute to faculty research productivity, librarians can partner with campus colleagues in order to leverage existing data sources, including **curriculum vitae analysis, publication citation analysis, institutional faculty records, tenure/promotion records**, and **records of individual faculty members' library behaviors, including records of faculty/librarian research collaborations**.

Potential Correlations

Librarians can determine areas for potential connections between surrogates for library impact on institutional mission or outcomes and descriptive library data elements. Are any of the surrogates of library impact on institutional mission or outcomes (listed in the first column) correlated, related, or linked to any descriptive library data elements (in the second column)? Libraries that do not collect data on these surrogates or areas for potential correlations may wish to expand their data collection practices.

Surrogates of library impact on institutional mission/outcomes(s)	Possible Areas of Correlation
Numbers of publications, numbers of patents, number of research-generated products, or value of technology transfer	Are there correlations, relationships, or linkages to individual faculty behavior in these areas? Note: these library user interactions must be captured in order to be correlated, related, or linked to surrogates of library value. ✓ Circulation counts ✓ Resources logins, including MyLibrary, MINES data, e-resources, etc. ✓ Resource login/logout surveys ✓ Self-reported usage ✓ Self-reported time saved Are there correlations, relationships, or linkages to these macro-level areas? Note: Macro-level areas are fertile territory for ROI calculations. ✓ Library expenditures ✓ Collection value ✓ Collection use, physical and online, may divide by subject area or other criteria ✓ Space use ✓ Service use, including reference, ILL, reserves, etc. ✓ Service use, including instruction, integration of library resources and services into course syllabi, course Web sites, lectures, labs, reserve readings, etc. ✓ Library ranking ✓ Library awards ✓ Librarian staffing levels or ratio of user group to librarian ✓ Librarian skills or participation in professional development
Tenure/promotion judgments	Are there correlations, relationships or linkages to individual faculty behavior in these areas? Note: These library user interactions must be captured in order to be correlated, related, or linked to surrogates of library value. ✓ Circulation counts ✓ Resources logins, including MyLibrary, MINES data, e-resources, etc. ✓ Resource login/logout surveys ✓ Self-reported usage ✓ Self-reported time saved Are there correlations, relationships, or linkages to these macro-level areas? Note: Macro-level areas are fertile territory for ROI calculations. ✓ Library expenditures ✓ Collection value ✓ Collection use, physical and online, may divide by subject

	area or other criteria ✓ Space use ✓ Service use, including reference, ILL, reserves, etc. ✓ Service use, including instruction, integration of library resources and services into course syllabi, course Web sites, lectures, labs, reserve readings, etc. ✓ Library ranking ✓ Library awards ✓ Librarian staffing levels or ratio of user group to librarian ✓ Librarian skills or participation in professional development

Faculty Grants

Essential Question—How does the library contribute to faculty grant proposals and funding?

Librarians contribute to faculty grant proposals in a number of ways. Recent studies have documented the contribution of library resources to citations in grant applications (P. T. Kaufman, Library as Strategic Investment 2008). In addition, academic librarians can investigate other ways in which libraries contribute to the preparation of grant proposals, funded and unfunded.

Surrogates for Library Impact

Surrogates for library impact on faculty grants include **numbers of grant proposals** and **numbers of grants funded**.

Data Sources

To investigate the ways in which libraries currently (or in future) contribute to faculty grant proposals and funding, librarians can partner with campus colleagues in order to leverage existing data sources, including **office of sponsored programs records**, and **records of individual faculty members' library behaviors, including records of faculty/librarian grant collaborations**.

Potential Correlations

Librarians can determine areas for potential connections between surrogates for library impact on institutional mission or outcomes and descriptive library data elements. Are any of the surrogates of library impact on institutional mission or outcomes (listed in the first column) correlated, related, or linked to any descriptive library data elements (in the second column)? Libraries that do not collect data on these surrogates or areas for potential correlations may wish to expand their data collection practices.

Surrogates of library impact on institutional mission/outcomes(s)	Possible Areas of Correlation
Numbers of grant proposals (funded or unfunded), value of grants funded	Are there correlations, relationships or linkages to individual faculty behavior in these areas? Note: These library user interactions must be captured in order to be correlated, related, or linked to surrogates of library value.

	✓ Circulation counts ✓ Resources logins, including MyLibrary, MINES data, e-resources, etc. ✓ Resource login/logout surveys ✓ Self-reported usage ✓ Self-reported time saved Are there correlations, relationships, or linkages to these macro-level areas? Note: Macro-level areas are fertile territory for ROI calculations. ✓ Library expenditures ✓ Collection value ✓ Collection use, physical and online, may divide by subject area or other criteria ✓ Space use ✓ Service use, including reference, ILL, reserves, etc. ✓ Service use, including instruction, integration of library resources and services into course syllabi, course Web sites, lectures, labs, reserve readings, etc. ✓ Library ranking ✓ Library awards ✓ Librarian staffing levels or ratio of user group to librarian ✓ Librarian skills or participation in professional development

Essential Question—How does the library contribute to faculty teaching?

Librarians contribute to faculty teaching in a variety of ways. Most librarians think only of their contributions to library instruction, such as guest lectures, online tutorials, and LibGuides. However, libraries contribute to faculty teaching in a variety of ways. They provide resources that are integrated into course materials on a massive scale (a value that is long overdue to be adequately captured and communicated). They collaborate with faculty on curriculum, assignment, and assessment design. They also provide resources that cover the scholarship of teaching and learning; some libraries also partner in campus-wide teaching and learning support centers. Finally, librarians often contribute to teaching and learning outside the traditional classroom by partnering with student affairs professionals on campus.

Surrogates for Library Impact

Surrogates for library impact on faculty teaching include **integration of library resources and services into course syllabi, course Web sites, lectures, labs, texts, reserve readings, co-curricular activities, etc.**; **faculty/librarian or student affairs professional/librarian instructional collaborations**; **cooperative curriculum, assignment, project, or assessment design**; and **resources on the scholarship of teaching and learning**.

Data Sources

To investigate the ways in which libraries currently (or in future) contribute to faculty teaching, librarians can partner with campus colleagues in order to leverage existing data sources, including **course syllabi, Web sites, reserves etc.**, and **records of individual faculty members' library behaviors, including records of faculty/librarian or student affairs professional/librarian instructional collaborations**, and **records of cooperative curriculum, assignment, project, or assessment design**.

Potential Correlations

Librarians can determine areas for potential connections between surrogates for library impact on institutional mission or outcomes and descriptive library data elements. Are any of the surrogates of library impact on institutional mission or outcomes (listed in the first column) correlated, related, or linked to any descriptive library data elements (in the second column)? Libraries that do not collect data on these surrogates or areas for potential correlations may wish to expand their data collection practices.

Surrogates of library impact on institutional mission/outcomes(s)	Possible Areas of Correlation
Integration of library resources and services into course syllabi, Web sites, lectures, labs, texts, reserve readings, co-curricular activities, etc.	Are there correlations, relationships or linkages to individual faculty behavior in these areas? Note: These library user interactions must be captured in order to be correlated, related, or linked to surrogates of library value. ✓ Circulation counts ✓ Resources logins, including MyLibrary, MINES data, e-resources, etc. ✓ Resource login/logout surveys ✓ Self-reported usage ✓ Self-reported time saved Are there correlations, relationships, or linkages to these macro-level areas? Note: Macro-level areas are fertile territory for ROI calculations. ✓ Library expenditures ✓ Collection value ✓ Collection use, physical and online, may divide by subject area or other criteria ✓ Space use ✓ Service use, including reference, ILL, reserves, etc. ✓ Service use, including instruction, integration of library resources and services into course syllabi, course Web sites, lectures, labs, reserve readings, etc. ✓ Library ranking ✓ Library awards ✓ Librarian staffing levels or ratio of user group to librarian ✓ Librarian skills or participation in professional development
Faculty/librarian instructional collaborations; student affairs professional/librarian collaborations; cooperative curriculum, assignment, project, or assessment design	Are there correlations, relationships, or linkages to individual faculty behavior in these areas? Note: These library user interactions must be captured in order to be correlated, related, or linked to surrogates of library value. ✓ Circulation counts ✓ Resources logins, including MyLibrary, MINES data, e-resources, etc. ✓ Resource login/logout surveys ✓ Self-reported usage ✓ Self-reported time saved Are there correlations, relationships, or linkages to these macro-level areas? Note: Macro-level areas are fertile territory for ROI calculations. ✓ Library expenditures ✓ Collection value ✓ Collection use, physical and online, may divide by subject

	area or other criteria ✓ Space use ✓ Service use, including reference, ILL, reserves, etc. ✓ Service use, including instruction, integration of library resources and services into course syllabi, course Web sites, lectures, labs, reserve readings, etc. ✓ Library ranking ✓ Library awards ✓ Librarian staffing levels or ratio of user group to librarian ✓ Librarian skills or participation in professional development

Institutional Reputation or Prestige

Essential Question—How does the library contribute to overall institutional reputation or prestige?

Academic libraries can augment their institution's reputation and prestige in four main ways not mentioned elsewhere in this Research Agenda. First, they can help department chairs to recruit instructors (Simmel 2007, 88). Traditionally, libraries contributed to faculty recruitment (Cluff and Murrah 1987) by building collections that support faculty activities. In the future, librarians have opportunities to be more proactive in this area by actively engaging in dialogue with "star" faculty recruits prior to their hiring. Second, strong libraries, especially those that win awards or other distinctions, may also impact institutional rank by bringing attention to the institution and therefore potentially influencing the peer assessments that make up a large portion of well-known ranking entities. (Note: Libraries also have the potential to contribute substantially to other portions of institutional ranking formulae.) Third, libraries that include renowned special collections may bring significant prestige to their institutions (Fister 2010). Special collections can be the "differentiating characteristic of research universities, the equivalent of unique laboratory facilities that attract faculty and research projects" (Pritchard, Special Collections Surge to the Fore 2009). Finally, library services and resources support institutional engagement in service to their communities by providing community members with "helpful, valuable, valid, and reliable information" (R. Kaufman 2001, 13) locally, nationally, and globally.

Surrogates for Library Impact

Surrogates for library impact on institutional reputation or prestige include **faculty recruitment**, **institutional ranking**, attention-getting **special collections**, and **institutional community engagement**.

Data Sources

To investigate the ways in which libraries currently (or in future) contribute to institutional reputation or prestige, librarians can partner with campus colleagues in order to leverage existing data sources, including **human resources records**, *U.S. News and World Report* **or other institutional rankings, special collections value estimates**, and **records that document institutional community engagement**.

Potential Correlations

Librarians can determine areas for potential connections between surrogates for library impact on institutional mission or outcomes and descriptive library data elements. Are any of the surrogates of library impact on institutional mission or outcomes (listed in the first column) correlated, related, or linked to any descriptive library data elements (in the second column)? Libraries that do not collect data on these surrogates or areas for potential correlations may wish to expand their data collection practices.

Surrogates of library impact on institutional mission/outcomes(s)	Possible Areas of Correlation
Faculty recruitment	Are there correlations, relationships, or linkages to these macro-level areas? Note: Macro-level areas are fertile territory for ROI calculations. ✓ Library expenditures ✓ Collection value ✓ Collection use, physical and online, may divide by subject area or other criteria ✓ Space use ✓ Service use, including reference, ILL, reserves, etc. ✓ Service use, including instruction, integration of library resources and services into course syllabi, course Web sites, lectures, labs, reserve readings, etc. ✓ Library ranking ✓ Library awards ✓ Librarian staffing levels or ratio of user group to librarian ✓ Librarian skills or participation in professional development
Institutional rankings	Are there correlations, relationships, or linkages to these macro-level areas? Note: Macro-level areas are fertile territory for ROI calculations. ✓ Library expenditures ✓ Special collections expenditures ✓ Collection value ✓ Special collections value ✓ Collection use, physical and online, may divide by subject area or other criteria ✓ Special collections use, physical and online, may divide by subject area or other criteria ✓ Space use ✓ Special collections space use ✓ Service use, including reference, ILL, reserves, etc. ✓ Service use, including special collections reference, ILL, reserves, etc. ✓ Service use, including instruction, integration of library resources and services into course syllabi, course Web sites, lectures, labs, reserve readings, etc.

	✓ Service use, including special collections instruction, integration of library resources and services into course syllabi, course Web sites, lectures, labs, reserve readings, etc. ✓ Library ranking ✓ Library awards ✓ Special collections awards ✓ Librarian staffing levels or ratio of user group to librarian ✓ Special collections librarian staffing levels or ratio of user group to special collections librarian ✓ Librarian skills or participation in professional development ✓ Special collections librarian skills or participation in professional development
Community engagement	Are there correlations, relationships, or linkages to these macro-level areas? Note: Macro-level areas are fertile territory for ROI calculations. ✓ Library expenditures ✓ Collection value ✓ Collection use, physical and online, may divide by subject area or other criteria ✓ Space use ✓ Service use, including reference, ILL, reserves, etc. ✓ Service use, including instruction, integration of library resources and services into course syllabi, course Web sites, lectures, labs, reserve readings, etc. ✓ Library ranking ✓ Library awards ✓ Librarian staffing levels or ratio of user group to librarian ✓ Librarian skills or participation in professional development

CONCLUSION

According to Hisle, academic librarians need to "spend as much time thinking about our future as we spend remembering our past...and... work toward our vision of the future...knowing our results will be rooted in the values of our profession" (2005, 14). One way to work toward a positive vision of the future is to engage in the demonstration of library value, recognizing that the process is not one of *proving* value, but rather continuously *increasing* value. The Council on Library and Information Resources asks, "Can we move from the need to survive to something better? Can we change how we go about our work, rather than just continue to seek more money?" (2008, 4). Indeed, librarians can shift from asking "Are libraries valuable?" to "*How* valuable are libraries?" or "How could libraries be *even more valuable*?" Making this shift is **the right thing to do**, for both users and librarians. Why? Because as librarians learn about library value—that is, what library services and resources enable users to do, what outcomes libraries enable users to achieve—they improve. When academic librarians learn about their impact on users, they increase their value by proactively delivering improved services and resources—to students completing their academic work; to faculty preparing publications and proposals; to administrators needing evidence to make decisions. Indeed, **the demonstration of value is not about *looking* valuable; it's about *being* valuable**. By seeking their best value, librarians do their jobs even better, and that's a goal worth pursuing all the time. By learning from higher education colleagues and expanding their efforts to not only *show* value but *be* valuable, librarians can do just that—move from a future of a surviving academic library, to a thriving one.

BIBLIOGRAPHY

Aabo, Svanhild. "Libraries and Return on Investment (ROI): A Meta-Analysis." *New Library World* 110, no. 7/8 (2009): 311-324.

Aabo, Svanhild, and Ragnar Audunson. "Rational Choice and Valuation of Public Libraries: Can Economic Models for Evaluating Non-Market Goods be Applied to Public Libraries?" *Journal of Librarianship and Information Science* 34, no. 5 (2002): 5-15.

Aaron, Bruce C. "Determining the Business Impact of Knowledge Management." *Performance Improvement* 48, no. 4 (2009): 35-45.

Abels, Eileen G., Paul B Kantor, and Tefko Saracevic. "Studying the Cost and Value of Library and Information Services: Applying Functional Cost Analysis to the Library in Transition." *Journal of the American Society for Information Science* 47, no. 3 (1996): 217-227.

"Ab's Blog." *Liveblogging Carol Tenopir's Keynote 'Measuring the Value of the Academic Library: Return on Investment on Other Value Measures'.* June 6, 2009. http://abigailbordeaux.net/abs/2009/06/06/carol-tenopir-nasig/ (accessed May 10, 2010).

Academic Analytics LLC. *Academic Analytics.* 2010. http://www.academicanalytics.com/ (accessed May 10, 2010).

Achieve. "Cross Disciplinary Proficiencies in the American Diploma Project Benchmarks." 2008. http://www.adlit.org/article/32492 (accessed May 10, 2010).

Achterman, Doug. "The Sower." *School Library Journal* 53, no. 10 (2007): 50-53.

———. "A New California Study: School Libraries Give Students a Better Chance at Success." *CSLA Journal* 33, no. 1 (2009): 26-27.

Ackermann, Eric. "Program Assessment in Academic Libraries." *Research & Practice in Assessment* 1, no. 2 (2007): 1-9.

ACT. "National Curriculum Survey." 2009. http://www.act.org/research/policymakers/pdf/NationalCurriculumSurvey2009.pdf (accessed May 10, 2010).

Ahtola, A. Anneli. "How to Evaluate and Measure the Impact of the Library's Collection on the Learning Outcome?" *68th IFLA Council and General Conference.* 2002.

Alexander, F. King. "The Changing Face of Accountability: Monitoring and Assessing Institutional Performance in Higher Education." *Journal of Higher Education* 71, no. 4 (2000): 411-431.

Allard, Suzie, and Jackie White. "Summary: Comparison of CATS Scores and Library Media Report." *Kentucky Libraries* 65, no. 2 (2001): 8-9.

Allen Consulting Group, The. "A Wealth of Knowledge: The Return on Investment form ARC-Funded Research." 2003. http://www.arc.gov.au/pdf/ARC_wealth_of_knowledge.pdf (accessed May 10, 2010).

Allen, Nancy. "Assessment in Higher Education." *The Reference Librarian* 17, no. 38 (1992): 57-68.

American Association of Community Colleges. *Voluntary Framework of Accountability.* 2010. http://www.aacc.nche.edu/Resources/aaccprograms/vfa/Pages/default.aspx (accessed May 10, 2010).

American Association of School Librarians. *School Libraries Count Survey.* 2010. http://www.aaslsurvey.org/ (accessed May 10, 2010).

American Association of State Colleges and Universities. *Value-Added Assessment: Accountability's New Frontier.* Washington, D.C.: American Association of State Colleges and Universities, 2006.

American Library Association. *ALA's Core Competencies of Librarianship.* 2009. http://www.ala.org/ala/educationcareers/careers/corecomp/corecompetences/finalco recompstat09.pdf (accessed May 10, 2010).

———. *Articles and Studies Related to Library Value.* 2010. http://www.ala.org/ala/research/librarystats/roi/ (accessed May 10, 2010).

———. *Presidential Committee on Information Literacy: Final Report.* 1989. http://www.ala.org/ala/mgrps/divs/acrl/publications/whitepapers/presidential.cfm (accessed May 10, 2010).

Americans for the Arts. *Arts and Economic Prosperity III: The Economic Impact of Nonprofit Arts and Culture Organizations and Their Audiences.* 2010. http://www.artsusa.org/pdf/information_services/ research/ services/economic_impact/aepiii/national_report.pdf (accessed May 10, 2010).

Anderson, Mary Alice. "The Value of Staff Development." *School Library Journal* 48, no. 11 (2002): 34-35.

ASCD. "School Libraries and their Impact on Student Performance." *ASCD ResearchBrief* 1, no. 18 (2003).

Ashcroft, Maggie. "The Impact of Information Use on Decision Making by Physiotherapists." *Library Management* 19, no. 3 (1998): 174-195.

Association for Institutional Research. *Measuring Quality Inventory.* 2010. http://applications.airweb.org/surveys/ (accessed May 10, 2010).

Association of American Colleges and Universities. *Liberal Education and America's Promise (LEAP).* 2010. http://www.aacu.org/leap/ (accessed May 10, 2010).

———. "New Survey Finds Colleges Moving Away from Pure 'Cafeteria-Style' General Education Requirements." May 15, 2009.

———. *Our Students' Best Work: A Framework for Accountability Worthy of Our Mission.* Washington, D.C.: Association of American Colleges and Universities, 2008.

———. *Rising to the Challenge: Meaningful Assessment of Student Learning.* 2010.

Association of College and Research Libraries. *Charting Our Future: ACRL Strategic Plan 2020.* May 13, 2009. http://www.ala.org/ala/mgrps/divs/acrl/about/whatisacrl/strategicplan/index.cfm (accessed May 10, 2010).

———. *Research Agenda for Library Instruction and Information Literacy.* 2000. http://www.ala.org/ala/mgrps/divs/acrl/about/sections/is/projpubs/researchagendalibrary.cfm (accessed May 10, 2010).

———. *Standards for Libraries in Higher Education.* 2004. http://www.ala.org/ala/mgrps/divs/acrl/standards/standardslibraries.cfm (accessed May 10, 2010).

———. *Task Force on Academic Library Outcomes Assessment Report.* 1998. http://www.ala.org/ala/mgrps/divs/acrl/publications/whitepapers/taskforceacademic.cfm (accessed May 10, 2010).

Association of Higher Education Facilities Officers. "The Impact of Facilities on Recruitment and Retention of Students." 2006.

Association of Research Libraries. *ARL Annual Salary Survey.* Washington, D.C.: Association of Research Libraries, 1980, 1994.

———. *MINES for Libraries, Measuring the Impact of Networked Electronic Services.* 2005. http://www.minesforlibraries.org/ (accessed May 10, 2010).

Astin, Alexander W. "Assessment, Value-Added, and Educational Excellence." In *Student Outcomes Assessment: What Institutions Stand to Gain*, edited by D.F. Halpern. San Francisco: Jossey-Bass, 1987.

Audunson, Ragnar. "The Public Library as a Meeting-Place in a Multicultural and Digital Context." *Journal of Documentation* 61, no. 3 (2005): 429-441.

Australian Research Council. "ERA Indicator Principles." 2008.

Bailey, Thomas R. *Research on Institution Level Practice for Postsecondary Student Success.* National Postsecondary Education Cooperative, 2006.

Baker, Ronald L. "Evaluating Quality and Effectiveness: Regional Accreditation Principles and Practices." *Journal of Academic Librarianship* 28, no. 1 (2002): 3-7.

Ballard, Susan. "What can Teacher-Librarians do to Promote Their Work and the School Library Media Program? Be Visible, Assess, and Provide Evidence." *Teacher Librarian* 36, no. 2 (2008): 22-23.

Banta, Trudy W. "New Opportunities for Pushing the Wheel Forward." *Assessment Update* 21, no. 5 (2009): 3-4, 16.

Barnett, Ronald. *Improving Higher Education: Total Quality Care.* London: Society for Research into Higher Education and the Open University, 1992.

———. "University Knowledge in an Age of Supercomplexity." *Higher Education* 40, no. 4 (2000): 409-422.

Barr, Nicholas. "The Benefits of Education: What We Know and What We Don't." 2000.

Barron, Daniel D., Robert V. Williams, Stephen Bajjaly, Jennifer Arns, and Steven Wilson. *The Economic Impact of Public Libraries on South Carolina.* University of South Carolina, 2005.

Basken, Paul. "Education Department Develops Strategy for Student-Record Databases." *The Chronicle of Higher Education*, February 11, 2010.

Baughman, James C., and Marcus E. Kieltyka. "Farewell to Alexandria: Not Yet!" *Library Journal* 124, no. 5 (1999): 48-49.

Baumbach, Donna. *Making the Grade: The Status of School Library Media Centers in the Sunshine State and How They Contribute to Student Achievement.* Florida Association for Media in Education, 2003.

Bean, John P. "College Student Retention." In *Encyclopedia of Education*, edited by James W. Guthrie, 401-407. New York: Macmillan Reference USA, 2003.

Bell, Steven. "Keeping Them Enrolled: How Academic Libraries Contribute to Student Retention." *Library Issues* 29, no. 1 (2008).

———. "What Academic Libraries Contribute to Productivity." *Library Journal from the Bell Tower,* blog, 2009. http://www.libraryjournal.com/article/CA6676486.html (accessed 10/18/2010).

Bennett, Scott. "Libraries and Learning: A History of Paradigm Change." *portal: Libraries and the Academy* 9, no. 2 (2009): 181-197.

Berg, Susan. "Living the Solution: Using Research Findings for Continual Improvement." *Ohio Media Spectrum* 60, no. 1 (2008): 19-24.

Bertot, John Carlo, and Charles R. McClure. "Outcomes Assessment in the Networked Environment: Research Questions, Issues, Considerations, and Moving Forward." *Library Trends* 51, no. 4 (2003): 590-689.

Bielavitz, Tom. "The Balanced Scorecard: A Systematic Model for Evaluation and Assessment of Learning Outcomes?" *Evidence Based Library and Information Practice* 5, no. 2 (2010).

Biggs, John. "The Reflective Institution: Assuring and Enhancing the Quality of Teaching and Learning." *Higher Education* 41, no. 3 (2001): 221-238.

Blanchflower, David, and Andrew Oswald. "Wellbeing Over Time in Britain and the USA." *National Bureau of Economic Research Summer Workshop.* Cambridge, Massachusetts, 2000.

Blankenship, Emily F. "Aligning the Assessment Process in Academic Library Distance Education Services Using the Nash Model for Improved Demonstration and Reporting of Organizational Performance." *Journal of Library Administration* 48, no. 3 (2008): 317-328.

Blose, Gary L., John D. Porter, and Edward C. Kokkelenberg. "The Effect of Institutional Funding Cuts on Baccalaureate Graduation Rates in Public Higher Education." In *What's Happening to Public Higher Education?*, edited by Ronald G. Ehrenberg, 71-82. Westport, Connecticut: Praeger, 2006.

Bogel, Gayle. "Facets of Practice." *Knowledge Quest* 37, no. 2 (2008): 10-15.

Bogue, E. Grady. "Quality Assurance in Higher Education: The Evolution of Systems and Design Ideals." *New Directions for Institutional Research* 25, no. 3 (1998): 7-18.

Bolton Metropolitan Borough Council. "Bolton's Museum, Library and Archive Services: An Economic Valuation." Bolton, UK, 2005.

Borden, Victor M.H. "Accommodating Student Swirl: When Traditional Students Are No Longer the Tradition." *Change* 36, no. 2 (2004): 10-17.

Borden, Victor M.H., and John W. Young. "Measurement Validity and Accountability for Student Learning." *New Directions for Institutional Research*, 2008: 19-37.

Bosanquet, Lyn. *Transforming the Academic Library - The New Value Proposition.* University of New South Wales, 2007.

Botha, Erika, Rene Erasmus, and Martie Van Deventer. "Evaluating the Impact of a Special Library and Information Service." *Journal of Librarianship and Information Science* 41, no. 2 (2009): 108-123.

Bouchet, Marie-Laure, Tracy Hopkins, Margaret Kinnell, and Cliff McKnight. "The Impact of Information Use on Decision Making in the Pharmaceutical Industry." *Library Management* 19, no. 3 (1998): 196-206.

Boyer Commission on Educating Undergraduates in the Research University. *Reinventing Undergraduate Education: A Blueprint for America's Research Universities.* 1998. http://naples.cc.sunysb.edu/Pres/boyer.nsf/673918d46fbf653e852565ec0056ff3e/d9 55b61ffddd590a852565ec005717ae/$FILE/boyer.pdf (accessed May 10, 2010).

Boyer, Ernest L. *College: The Undergraduate Experience in America.* New York: Harper and Row, 1987.

Braunstein, Yale M. "Information as a Factor of Production: Substitutability and Productivity." *Information Society* 3, no. 3 (1985): 261-273.

Breivik, Patricia Senn. "Resources: The Fourth R." *Community College Frontiers* 5 (1977).

Brewer, Dominic J., Susan M. Gates Brewer, and Charles A. Goldman. *In Pursuit of Prestige.* New Brunswick: Transaction, 2002.

Brophy, Peter. *Measuring Library Performance: Principles and Techniques.* London: Facet, 2006.

———. "The Evaluation of Public Library Online Services: Measuring Impact." *People's Network Workshop Series.* 2002.

Budd, John M. "Faculty Publishing Productivity: An Institutional Analysis and Comparison with Library and Other Measures." *College and Research Libraries* 56 (1995): 547-554.

———. "Faculty Publishing Productivity: Comparisons Over Time." *College and Research Libraries* 67, no. 3 (2006): 230-239.

———. "Increases in Faculty Publishing Activity: An Analysis of ARL and ACRL Institutions." *College and Research Libraries* 60 (1999): 308-315.

Bundy, Alan. "Beyond Information: The Academic Library as Educational Change Agent." *7th International Bielefeld Conference.* Germany, 2004.

Burger, Shannon, and Mary Ann McFarland. "Action Research and Wikis: An Effective Collaboration." *Library Media Connection* 28, no. 2 (2009): 38-40.

Butler, Jeanne. "Addressing Six Critical Questions of Senior Administrators Using Online Tracking of Assessment and Accreditation Requirements." WEAVEonline, September 15, 2009.

Butz, H. E., and L. D. Goodstein. "Measuring Customer Value: Gaining the Strategic Advantage." *Organizational Dynamics* 24 (1996): 63-77.

Cable, Lesley G. "Cost Analysis of Reference Service to Outside Users." *Bulletin of the Medical Library Association* 68, no. 2 (1980): 247-48.

Callison, Daniel. "Evaluation Criteria for the Places of Learning." *Knowledge Quest* 35, no. 3 (2007): 14-19.

Capaldi, Elizabeth D., John V. Lombardi, and Victor Yellen. "Improving Graduation Rates." *Change*, 2006: 44-50.

Capaldi, Elizabeth D., John V. Lombardi, Craig W. Abbey, and Diane D. Craig. *The Top American Research Universities.* The Center for Measuring University Performance, 2008.

Carlson, Scott. "Lost in a Sea of Science Data." *The Chronicle of Higher Education*, 2006.

Carrigan, Dennis P. "Improving Return on Investment: A Proposal for Allocating the Book Budget." *Journal of Academic Librarianship* 18, no. 5 (1992): 292-297.

Carter, Elizabeth W. "'Doing the Best You Can with What You Have': Lessons Learned from Outcomes Assessment." *Journal of Academic Librarianship* 28, no. 1 (2002): 36-41.

Case, Mary M. "Partners in Knowledge Creation: An Expanded Role for Research Libraries in the Digital Future." *Journal of Library Administration* 48, no. 2 (2008): 141-156.

Castonguay, Courtney. "Evaluating School Library Media Centers." *PNLA Quarterly* 68, no. 4 (2004): 8-9, 34-36.

Center for Measuring University Performance. *Graduate Program Quality.* 2007. http://mup.asu.edu/gradPrgQual.html (accessed May 10, 2010).

Champlin, Connie, David V. Loertscher, and Nancy A.S. Miller. *Sharing the Evidence: Library Media Center Assessment Tools and Resources.* Salt Lake City: Hi Willow Research, 2008.

Charleston Observatory. "The Economic Downturn and Libraries: Survey Findings." *Charleston Conference.* 2009.

Chernatony, L. De, F. Harris, and F. Dall'Olmo Riley. "Added Value: Its Nature, Role, and Sustainability." *European Journal of Marketing* 34, no. 1/2 (2000).

Chung, Hye-Kyung. "Measuring the Economic Value of Special Libraries." *The Bottom Line: Managing Library Finances* 20, no. 1 (2007): 30-44.

———. "The Contingent Valuation Method in Public Libraries." *Journal of Librarianship and Information Science* 40, no. 2 (2008): 71-80.

Cluff, E. Dale, and David J. Murrah. "The Influence of Library Resources on Faculty Recruitment and Retention." *Journal of Academic Librarianship* 13, no. 1 (1987): 19-23.

Coalition for Evidence-Based Policy. *Identifying and Implementing Educational Practices Supported By Rigorous Evidence: A User Friendly Guide.* Washington, D.C.: U.S. Department of Education, Institute of Education Sciences, National Center for Education Evaluation and Regional Assistance, 2003.

Cohen, D. "What's Your Return on Knowledge?" *Harvard Business Review*, 2006.

CollegeBoard. "How Colleges Organize Themselves to Increase Student Persistence." 2009. http://professionals.collegeboard.com/profdownload/college-retention.pdf (accessed May 10, 2010).

Collier, Jackie. "School Librarians Rock! Librarians' Powerful Impact on Literacy Development: Reflections of Teacher Candidates." *Ohio Media Spectrum* 59, no. 1 (2007): 29-36.

Commission on Colleges and Universities. *Accreditation Handbook.* Bellevue, Washington, 1999.

Cook, Colleen, Fred Heath, Bruce Thompson, and Russel Thompson. "LibQUAL+: Service Quality Assessment in Research Libraries." *IFLA Journal* 27, no. 4 (2001): 264-268.

Cooper, Jeffrey M., and Marilyn C. Crouch. "Benefit Assessment Help Open Doors of One Cash-Strapped California Library." *American Libraries* 25 (1994): 232-234.

Cornell University Library. *Library Value Calculations.* 2010. http://research.library.cornell.edu/value (accessed MAY 10, 2010).

Council for Higher Education Accreditation. "2010 CHEA Award for Outstanding Institutional Practice in Student Learning Outcomes." *CHEA Chronicle* 11, no. 1 (2010): 1.

Council of Regional Accrediting Commissions. *Regional Accreditation and Student Learning: Principles for Good Practices.* 2003. http://www.msche.org/publications/Regnlsl050208135331.pdf (accessed May 10, 2010).

Council on Library and Information Resources. *No Brief Candle: Reconceiving Research Libraries for the 21st Century.* Washington, D.C.: Council on Library and Information Resources, 2008.

Counter. *Counting Online Usage of Networked Electronic Resources.* 2007. http://www.projectcounter.org/about.html (accessed May 10, 2010).

Creighton, Peggy Milam. "Impact as a 21st Century Library Media Specialist." *School Library Media Activities Monthly* 24, no. 7 (2008).

Cyrenne, Philippe, and Hugh Grant. "University Decision Making and Prestige: An Empirical Study." *Economics of Education Review* 28 (2009): 237-248.

Dahlin-Brown, Nissa. "The Perceptual Impact of U.S. News and World Report Rankings on Eight Public MBA Programs." *Journal of Marketing for Higher Education* 15, no. 2 (2005): 155-179.

Dando, Priscille M. "First Steps in Online Learning: Creating an Environment for Instructional Support and Assessment." *Knowledge Quest* 34, no. 1 (2005): 23-24.

Daniels, Sally. "From Design to Assessment: Assessment 'Does' Make a Difference!" *Knowledge Quest* 35, no. 4 (2007): 40-43.

Day, George S. "The Capabilities of Market-Driven Organizations." *Journal of Marketing* 58 (1994): 37-52.

Debono, Barbara. "Assessing the Social Impact of Public Libraries: What the Literature is Saying." *Australasian Public Libraries and Information Services* 15, no. 2 (2002): 80-95.

Deiss, Kathryn, and Mary Jane Petrowski. *ACRL 2009 Strategic Thinking Guide for Academic Librarians in the New Economy.* Chicago: Association of College and Research Libraries, 2009.

Dent, Valeda F. "Observations of School Library Impact at Two Rural Ugandan Schools." *New Library World* 107, no. 9-10 (2006): 403-421.

Dewey, Barbara. "The Embedded Librarian: Strategic Campus Collaborations." *Resource Sharing & Information Networks* 17, no. 1/2 (2005): 5-17.

Dickenson, Don. *How Academic Libraries Help Faculty Teach and Students Learn: The Colorado Academic Library Impact Study.* Library Research Service, 2006. http://www.lrs.org/documents/academic/ALIS_final.pdf (accessed May 10, 2010).

Dickinson, Gail K. "From Research to Action in School Library Media Programs." *North Carolina Libraries* 15, no. 1 (2001): 15-19.

Dominguez, Magaly Báscones. "Applying Usage Statistics to the CERN E-Journal Collection: A Step Forward." *High Energy Physics Libraries Webzine*, 2005.

Doran, Harold C., and J.R. Lockwood. "Fitting Value-Added Models in R." *Journal of Educational and Behavioral Statistics* 31 (2006): 205-230.

Dougherty, Richard M. "Assessment + Analysis = Accountability." *College and Research Libraries*, 2009: 417-418.

Dow, Ronald F. "Using Assessment Criteria to Determine Library Quality." *Journal of Academic Librarianship*, 1998: 277-281.

Dubbin, Diane, Eveiyn L. Beyer, and Becky Prueit. "Texas Library Standards Online Assessment: A Dynamic Website." *Texas Library Journal* 78, no. 2 (2002): 64-68.

Dukart, James R. "Wherefore ROI?" *AIIM E-Doc Magazine* 21, no. 1 (2007): 47-49.

Dumond, Ellen J. "Value Management: An Underlying Framework." *International Journal of Operations and Production Management* 20, no. 9 (2000): 1062-1077.

Duncan, Ross. "Best Bang for the Buck: The Economic Benefits of Sunshine Coast Libraries Queensland." *Australasian Public Libraries and Information Services* 21, no. 4 (2008): 140-153.

Dundar, Halil, and Darrell R. Lewis. "Determinants of Research Productivity in Higher Education." *Research in Higher Education* 39, no. 6 (1998): 607-631.

Durrance, Joan C., and Karen E. Fisher. *How Libraries and Librarians Help: A Guide to Identifying User-Centered Outcomes.* Chicago: American Library Association, 2005.

———. "Toward Developing Measures of the Impact of Library and Information Services." *Reference and User Services Quarterly* 42, no. 1 (2002): 43-53.

Economist, The. "A Survey of Universities: The Knowledge Factory." October 4-10, 1997: 4-8.

Edgar, William. "Corporate Library Impact, Part I: A Theoretical Approach." *Library Quarterly* 74, no. 2 (2004): 122-151.

Edwards, Valerie A. "Formative Assessment in the High School IMC." *Knowledge Quest* 35, no. 5 (2007): 50-53.

Eisenberg, Mike. "personal communication." February 2010.

Elley, W. *How in the World Do Children Read? IEA Study of Reading Literacy.* Hamburg: International Association for the Evaluation of Educational Achievement, 1992.

Ellis, Jean. *Accountability and Learning: Developing Monitoring and Evaluation in the Third Sector.* Research Report, London: Charities Evaluation Services, 2008.

Emmons, Mark, and Frances C. Wilkinson. "The Academic Library Impact on Student Persistence." *College and Research Libraries*, forthcoming.

Estabrook, Leigh S. "Interim Report." 2006.

———. *What Chief Academic Officers Want from Their Libraries: Findings from Interviews with Provosts and Chief Academic Officers.* October 2007. http://www.ala.org/ala/mgrps/divs/acrl/publications/whitepapers/Finalreport-ACRLCAOs.pdf (accessed May 10, 2010).

Everest, Katherine, and Philip Payne. "The Impact of Libraries on Learning, Teaching and Research." Report of the LIRG Seminar, Leeds, UK, 2001.

Everhart, Nancy. "Evaluation of School Library Media Centers: Demonstrating Quality." *Library Media Connection* 21, no. 6 (2003).

———. "Research into Practice." *Knowledge Quest* 29, no. 3 (2002): 36-37.

Ewell, Peter T. "Power in Numbers: The Values in Our Metrics." *Change*, 2005: 10-16.

———. "Rising to the Occasion: The Alliance for New Leadership for Student Learning and Accountability." *Assessment Update* 21, no. 1 (2009): 13-14.

———. "'Shovel-Ready' Data: The Stimulus Package and State Longitudinal Data Systems." *Assessment Update* 21, no. 5 (2009): 11-12.

———. "Well, Um, We Actually Have a National System for Tracking Student Progress." *Assessment Update* 21, no. 3 (2009): 12-13.

Ewell, Peter, and Jane Wellman. "Enhancing Student Success in Education: Summary Report of the NPEC Initiative and National Symposium on Postsecondary Student Success." 2007.

Fairweather, J.S. "The Highly Productive Faculty Member: Confronting the Mythologies of Faculty Work." In *Faculty Productivity: Facts, Fictions, and Issues*, edited by W.G. Tierney, 55-98. New York: Falmer, 1998.

Fister, Barbara. "Academic Libraries: A View from the Administration Building." *Library Journal Critical Assets* blog, May 1, 2010. http://www.libraryjournal.com/article/CA6726948.html (accessed October 18, 2010).

Flint, D. J., R. B. Woodruff, and S. Fisher Gardial. "Exploring the Phenomenon of Customers' Desired Value Change in a Business-to-Business Context." *Journal of Marketing* 66 (2002): 102-117.

Flowers, Lamont, Steven J. Osterlind, Ernest T. Pascarella, and Christopher T. Pierson. "How Much Do Students Learn in College? Cross-Sectional Estimates Using the College BASE." *Journal of Higher Education* 72, no. 5 (2001): 565-583.

Frade, Patricia A., and Allyson Washburn. "The University Library: The Center of a University Education?" *portal: Libraries and the Academy* 6, no. 3 (2006): 327-346.

Francis, John G., and Mark C. Hampton. "Resourceful Responses: The Adaptive Research University and the Drive to Market." *Journal of Higher Education* 70, no. 6 (1999): 625-641.

Franklin, Brinley. "Academic Research Library Support of Sponsored Research in the United Space." *Proceedings of the 4th Northumbria International Conference on Performance Measurement in Libraries and Information Services*. Washington, D.C., 2002.

Fraser, Bruce T., Charles R. McClure, and Emily H. Leahy. "Toward a Framework for Assessing Library and Institutional Outcomes." *portal: Libraries and the Academy* 2, no. 4 (2002): 505-528.

Gansemer-Topf, Ann M., and John H. Schuh. "Institutional Selectivity and Institutional Expenditures: Examining Organizational Factors that Contribute to Retention and Graduation." *Research in Higher Education* 47, no. 6 (2006): 613-642.

Garner, Sarah. *High-Level Colloquium on Information Literacy and Lifelong Learning*. 2005. http://archive.ifla.org/III/wsis/High-Level-Colloquium.pdf (accessed May 10, 2010).

Gater, Denise S. *A Review of Measures Used in U.S. News and World Report "America's Best Colleges".* The Lombardi Program on Measuring University Performance, 2002.

Geitgey, Gayle A., and Ann E. Tepe. "Can You Find the Evidence-Based Practice in Your School Library?" *Library Media Connection* 25, no. 6 (2007): 10-12.

Gerlich, Bella Karr. *Work in Motion/Assessment at Rest: An Attitudinal Study of Academic Reference Librarians, A Case Study at Mid-Size University.* PhD dissertation, University of Pittsburgh, 2006.

Gerlich, Bella Karr, and G. Lynn Berard. "Testing the Viability of the READ Scale (Reference Effort Assessment Data): Qualitative Statistics for Academic Reference Services." *College & Research Libraries* 71, no. 2 (2010): 116-137.

Giaquinto, Richard A. "Instructional Issues and Retention of First-Year Students." *Journal of College Student Retention* 11, no. 2 (2009): 267-285.

Gilmore, Jeffrey L., and Duc-Le To. "Evaluating Academic Productivity and Quality." In *New Directions for Institutional Research*, 35-47. 1992.

Glendale Community College. *Statistical Evaluation of Information Competency Program Student Outcomes.* Glendale Community College, 2007.

Glick, A. "Colorado Researchers will Repeat Landmark Study Showing Benefits of School Libraries." *School Library Journal* 44, no. 11 (1998): 15.

———. "Smart State Shortchanges School Libraries." *School Library Journal* 46, no. 12 (2000).

Goener, Cullen F., and Sean M. Snaith. "Predicting Graduation Rates: An Analysis of Student and Institutional Factors at Doctoral Universities." *Journal of College Student Retention* 5, no. 4 (2003/2004): 409-420.

Goetsch, Lori A. "What is Our Value and Who Values Us?" *C&RL News* 70, no. 9 (2009): 502-503.

Gonzalez, Jennifer. "Education Experts Discuss Ways to Improve College Completion Rates." *Chronicle of Higher Education*, 2010.

Gordon, Jonathan, Joe Ludlum, and J. Joseph Hoey. "Validating NSSE Against Student Outcomes: Are They Related?" *Research in Higher Education* 49, no. 1 (2008): 19-39.

Gorman, Michael. "'The Louder They Talked of Outcomes, the Faster We Counted Our Beans': Measuring the Impact of Academic Libraries." *SCONUL.* London, 2009. http://mg.csufresno.edu/papers/SCONUL_2009.pdf (accessed May 10, 2010).

Gratch-Lindauer, Bonnie. "College Student Engagement Surveys: Implications for Information Literacy." In *New Directions for Teaching and Learning*, 101-114. 2008.

———. "Comparing the Regional Accreditation Standards: Outcomes Assessment and Other Trends." *Journal of Academic Librarianship* 28 (2001): 14-25.

———. "Defining and Measuring the Library's Impact on Campuswide Outcomes." *College and Research Libraries* 59, no. 6 (1998): 546-570.

———. "Information Literacy-Related Student Behaviors." *C&RL News* 68, no. 7 (2007): 432-441.

Greer, Jeff. "Four Reasons Why the Library Should Affect Your College Choice." *U.S. News and World Report*, June 17, 2010.

Grieves, Maureen. "The Impact of Information Use on Decision Making: Studies in Five Sectors - Introduction, Summary, and Conclusions." *Library Management* 19, no. 2 (1998): 78-85.

Griffith, Amanda, and Kevin Rask. "The Influence of the U.S. News and World Report Collegiate Rankings on the Matriculation Decision of High-Ability Students: 1995-2004." *Economics of Education Review* 26, no. 2 (2004): 1-12.

Griffiths, Jose Marie, and Donald W. King. *A Manual on the Evaluation of Information Centers and Services.* Oak Ridge, Tennessee: King Research, 1990.

———. *An Information Audit of Public Service Electric and Gas Company Libraries and Information Resources.* Rockville, Maryland: King Research, 1988.

———. "Libraries: The Undiscovered National Resource." In *The Value and Impact of Information*, edited by M. Feeney and M. Grieves, 79-116. London: Bowker and Saur, 1994.

———. *Special Libraries: Increasing the Information Edge.* Washington, D.C.: Special Libraries Association, 1993.

———. *The Contribution Libraries Make to Organizational Productivity.* Rockville, Maryland: King Research, 1985.

———. "The Value of Information Centers." In *Managing Information for the Competitive Edge*, edited by Ethel Auster and Chun W. Choo, 419-437. New York: Neal-Schuman, 1996.

Griffiths, Jose Marie, Donald W. King, Christinger Tomer, Thomas Lynch, and Julie Harrington. "Taxpayer Return on Investment in Florida Public Libraries." Summary Report, 2004.

Gronroos, C. *Service Management and Marketing—A Customer Relationship Management Approach.* 2nd. New York: Wiley, 2000.

Grunig, Stephen D. "Research, Reputation, and Resources: The Effect of Research Activity on Perceptions of Undergraduate Education and Institutional Resource Acquisition." *Journal of Higher Education* 68 (1997): 17-52.

Guskin, Alan E. "Facing the Future." *Change* 28, no. 4 (1996): 26-38.

———. "Reducing Student Costs and Enhancing Student Learning." *Change* 26, no. 4 (1994): 22-30.

———. "Restructuring the Role of Faculty." *Change* 26, no. 5 (1994): 16-26.

Guskin, Alan E., and Mary B. Marcy. "Dealing with the Future NOW: Principles for Creating a Vital Campus in a Climate of Restricted Resources." *Change* 35, no. 4 (2003): 10-21.

Habley, Wesley R., and Randy McClanahan. *What Works in Student Retention?* ACT, 2004.

Halpern, Diane F. "Introduction and Overview." In *Student Outcomes Assessment*, 5-6. 1987.

Hamilton-Pennell, Christine, Keith Curry Lance, Marcia J. Rodney, and Eugene Hainer. "Dick and Jane Go to the Head of the Class." *School Library Journal* 46, no. 4 (2000): 44-47.

Hamrick, Florence A., John H. Schuh, and II., Mack C. Shelley. "Predicting Higher Education Graduation Rates From Institutional Characteristics and Resource Allocation." *Education Policy Analysis Archives* 12, no. 19 (2004).

Hand, Dorcas. "What can Teacher-Librarians do to Promote Their Work and the School Library Media Program? Keep Everyone in the Loop Constant Advocacy." *Teacher Librarian* 36, no. 2 (2008): 26-27.

Harada, Violet H. "Building Evidence Folders for Learning Through Library Media Centers." *School Library Media Activities Monthly* 23, no. 3 (2006): 25-30.

———. "From Eyeballing to Evidence: Assessing for Learning in Hawaii Library Media Centers." *School Library Media Activities Monthly* 24, no. 3 (2007): 21-25.

———. "Librarians and Teachers as Research Partners: Reshaping Practices Based on Assessment and Reflection." *School Libraries Worldwide* 11, no. 2 (2005): 49-74.

———. "Working Smarter: Being Strategic about Assessment and Accountability." *Teacher Librarian* 33, no. 1 (2005): 8-15.

Hardesty, Larry. *Do We Need Academic Libraries?* 2000. http://www.ala.org/ala/mgrps/divs/acrl/publications/whitepapers/doweneedacademic.cfm (accessed May 10, 2010).

Harper, Shaun R., and George D. Kuh. "Myths and Misconceptions about Using Qualitative Methods in Assessment." *New Directions for Institutional Research*, no. 136 (2007): 5-14.

Hart Research Associates. "Raising the Bar: Employers' Views on College Learning in the Wake of the Economic Downturn." 2010. http://www.aacu.org/leap/documents/2009_EmployerSurvey.pdf (accessed May 10, 2010).

———. "Trends and Emerging Practices in General Education." 2009.

Hawgood, John, and Richard Morley. *Project for Evaluating the Benefits from University Libraries: Final Report.* OSTI Report 5056, Durham: University of Durham, 1969.

Hawkins, Brian L., and Patricia Battin. *The Mirage of Continuity: Reconfiguring Academic Information Resources for the 21st Century.* Washington, D.C.: Council on Library and Information Resources, 1998.

Haycock, Ken. "Clear Criteria and Procedures for Evaluation." *Teacher Librarian* 29, no. 3 (2002): 35.

Haycock, Ken. "The Student Perspective." *Teacher Librarian* 31, no. 4 (2004): 40.

Hayes, Robert M., and T. Erickson. "Added Value as a Function of Purchases of Information Services." *Information Society* 1, no. 4 (1982): 307-338.

Head, Alison J., and Michael B. Eisenberg. "Lessons Learned: How College Students Seek Information in the Digital Age." Project Information Literacy Progress Reports, 2009. http://projectinfolit.org/pdfs/PIL_Fall2009_Year1Report_12_2009.pdf (accessed May 10, 2010).

Henczel, Susan. "Measuring and Evaluating the Library's Contribution to Organisational Success." *Performance Measurement and Metrics* 7, no. 1 (2006): 7-16.

Henri, James, Lyn Hay, and Dianne Oberg. "An International Study on Principal Influence and Information Services in Schools: Synergy in Themes and Methods." *School Libraries Worldwide* 8, no. 1 (2002): 49-70.

Hernon, Peter. "Quality: New Directions in the Research." *Journal of Academic Librarianship* 28, no. 4 (2002): 224-231.

Hernon, Peter, and Ellen Altman. *Assessing Service Quality: Satisfying the Expectations of Library Customers.* Chicago: American Library Association, 1998.

Hernon, Peter, Robert E. Dugan, and Candy Schwartz. *Revisiting Outcomes Assessment in Higher Education.* Westport, Connecticut: Libraries Unlimited, 2006.

Hider, Philip. "How Much are Technical Services Worth? Using the Contingent Valuation Method to Estimate the Added Value of Collection Management and Access." *LRTS* 52, no. 4 (2008): 254-262.

——. "Using the Contingent Valuation Method for Dollar Valuations of Library Services." *Library Quarterly* 78, no. 4 (2008): 437-458.

Hillenbrand, Candy. "A Place for All: Social Capital at the Mount Barker Community Library, South Australia." *Australasian Public Libraries and Information Services* 18, no. 2 (2005): 41-60.

——. "Public Libraries as Developers of Social Capital." *Australasian Public Libraries and Information Services* 18, no. 1 (2005): 4-12.

Hiller, Steve, and James Self. "From Measurement to Management: Using Data Wisely for Planning and Decision-Making." *Library Trends* 53, no. 1 (2004): 129-155.

Hiscock, Jane E. "Does Library Usage Affect Library Performance?" *Australian Academic and Research Libraries* 17, no. 4 (1986).

Hisle, W. Lee. "The Changing Role of the Library in the Academic Enterprise." *ACRL National Conference.* Minneapolis, MN, 2005.

Holt, Glen E., and Donald Elliott. "Measuring Outcomes: Applying Cost-Benefit Analysis to Middle-Sized and Smaller Public Libraries." *Library Trends* 51, no. 3 (2003): 424-440.

Horowitz, Lisa R. "Assessing Library Services: A Practical Guide for the Nonexpert." *Library Leadership and Management* 23, no. 4 (2009): 193-203.

Housewright, Ross. "Themes of Change in Corporate Libraries: Considerations for Academic Libraries." *portal: Libraries and the Academy* 9, no. 2 (2009): 253-271.

Housewright, Ross, and Roger Schonfeld. *Ithaka's 2006 Studies of Key Stakeholders in the Digital Transformation in Higher Education.* Ithaka, 2008.

Houston, Cynthia. "Getting to Proficiency and Beyond: Kentucky Library Media Centers' Progress on State Standards and the Relationship of Library Media Program Variables to Student Achievement." *LIBRES* 18, no. 1 (2008): 1-18.

Howard, John Brooks. "Modeling Cyberinfrastructure Services Through Collaborative Research." *Living the Future.* Tucson, 2008. http://drs.asu.edu/fedora/get/asulib:144270/PPS-1 (accessed May 10, 2010).

Hoyt, Jeff E. "Integrating Assessment and Budget Planning Processes: A Good or a Bad Idea?" *Assessment Update* 21, no. 5 (2009): 9-10, 16.

Huber, F., A. Herrmann, and R. E. Morgan. "Gaining Competitive Advantage through Customer Value Oriented Management." *Journal of Consumer Marketing* 18, no. 1 (2001).

Hughes-Hassell, Sandra, and Kay Bishop. "Using Focus Group Interviews to Improve Library Services for Youth." *Teacher Librarian* 32, no. 1 (2004): 8-12.

Hutchings, Pat. "The New Guys in Assessment Town." *Change*, 2009: 26-33.

Illinois Library Association. *Selected Academic Library Value Study Links.* 2010. http://www.ila.org/index.php?option=com_content&view=article&catid=35%3Aorgani zation&id=273%3Aselected-academic-libraries-value-study-links&Itemid=201 (accessed May 10, 2010).

Imholz, Susan, and Jennifer Weil Arns. "Worth Their Weight: An Assessment of the Evolving Field of Library Valuation." *Public Libraries Quarterly*, 2007.

Immroth, Barbara, and W. Bernar Lukenbill. "Promoting Collaboration Through a Human Information Behavior Study." *Texas Library Journal* 83, no. 2 (2007): 66-67.

Indiana Business Research Center. *The Economic Impact of Libraries in Indiana.* Bloomington: Indiana University, 2007.

"Information Management Under Fire: Measuring ROI for Enterprise Libraries." *Outsell* 9 (2007).

Institute for Library and Information Literacy Education. *Principal's Project.* 2010. http://www.ilile.org/initiatives/principal_project/index.html (accessed May 10, 2010).

Institute of Museum and Library Services. *Museums, Libraries, and 21st Century Skills.* Washington, D.C.: Institute of Museum and Library Services, 2009.

———. *Perspectives on Outcome Based Evaluation for Libraries and Museums.* Washington, D.C.: Institute of Museum and Library Services.

————. *The Future of Museums and Libraries: A Discussion Guide.* Washington, D.C.: Institute of Museum and Library Services, 2009.

Jacoby, JoAnn, and Nancy P. O'Brien. "Assessing the Impact of Reference Services Provided to Undergraduate Students." *College & Research Libraries* 66, no. 4 (2005): 324-340.

Jager, Karin De. "Successful Students: Does the Library Make a Difference?" *Performance Measurement and Metrics* 3 (2002).

Jaschik, Scott. "Turning Surveys into Reforms." *Inside Higher Ed*, October 2009.

Jewett, Linda. "Standards and Assessment: The Bottom Line." *CSLA Journal* 26, no. 2 (2003): 4, 7.

Johnson, Catherine A. "Do Public Libraries Contribute to Social Capital? A Preliminary Investigation into the Relationship." *Library and Information Science Research* 32 (2010): 147-155.

Johnson, Doug. "What Gets Measured Gets Done: The Importance of Evaluating Your Library Media Program." *The Book Report* 20, no. 2 (2001): 14-15.

Jones, Elizabeth A. "Expanding Professional Development Opportunities to Enhance the Assessment Process." *Assessment Update* 21, no. 3 (2009): 3-4.

————. *National Assessment of College Student Learning: Identifying College Graduates' Essential Skills in Writing, Speech and Listening, and Critical Thinking.* Washington, D.C.: National Center for Education Statistics, 1995.

Jorgensen, Shirley, Vittoria Ferraro, Catherine Fichten, and Alice Havel. "Predicting College Retention and Dropout: Sex and Disability." June 2009. http://adaptech.dawsoncollege.qc.ca/webfm_send/19 (accessed May 10, 2010).

Joubert, Douglas J., and Tamera P Lee. "Empowering Your Institution Through Assessment." *Journal of the Medical Library Association* 95, no. 1 (2007): 46-53.

Julien, Heidi, and Stuart Boon. "Assessing Instructional Outcomes in Canadian Academic Libraries." *Library and Information Science Research* 26 (2004): 121-139.

Jura Consultants. "Economic Impact Methodologies for the Museums, Libraries, and Archives Sector: What Works and What Doesn't." 2008. http://research.mla.gov.uk/evidence/documents/Economic%20Impact%20Methodologies%20June%202008%20Final%20Version.pdf (accessed May 10, 2010).

Kantor, Paul B. "The Library as an Information Utility in the University Context: Evolution and Measurement of Service." *Journal of the American Society for Information Science*, 1976: 100-112.

————. "Three Studies of the Economics of Academic Libraries." *Advances in Library Administration and Organization* 5 (1986): 221-286.

Kantor, Paul B., and Tefko Saracevic. "Quantitative Study of the Value of Research Libraries: A Foundation for the Evaluation of Digital Libraries." 1999. http://citeseerx.ist.psu.edu/viewdoc/download?doi=10.1.1.124.6382&rep=rep1&type=pdf (accessed May 10, 2010).

Kantor, Paul B., Tefko Saracevic, and J. D'Esposito-Wachtmann. *Studying the Cost and Value of Library Services.* Tech. Rep. No. APLAB/94-3/1,2,3,4, New Brunswick: Rutgers State University of New Jersey, 1995.

Kaske, Neal K., and Mary Lou Cumberpatch. *What is the Return on Investment for Your Library?* Silver Spring, Maryland, April 1, 2009. http://conferences.infotoday.com/stats/documents/default.aspx?id=1734&lnk=http%3 A%2F%2Fconferences.infotoday.com%2Fdocuments%2F32%2FE302_Kaske.ppt (accessed May 10, 2010).

Kassel, Amelia. "Practical Tips to Help You Prove Your Value." *Marketing Library Services* 16, no. 4 (2002).

Kaufman, Paula T. "Carpe Diem: Transforming Services in Academic Libraries." 2009. http://hdl.handle.net/2142/12032 (accessed October 18, 2010).

Kaufman, Paula T. "The Library as Strategic Investment." *Liber Quarterly* 18, no. 3/4 (2008): 424-436.

———. "The Library as Strategic Investment: Results of the University of Illinois 'Return on Investment' Study." *Online Information.* 2008. 29-36.

Kaufman, Paula, and Sarah Barbara Watstein. "Library Value (Return on Investment, ROI) and the Challenge of Placing a Value on Public Services." *Reference Services Review* 36, no. 3 (2008): 226-231.

Kaufman, Roger. "Toward Determining Societal Value-Added Criteria for Research and Comprehensive Universities." The Center Reports, 2001. http://mup.asu.edu/kaufman1.pdf (accessed May 10, 2010).

Keeling, Richard P. *Learning Reconsidered 2: Implementing a Campus-Wide Focus on the Student Experience.* American College Personnel Association, 2006.

Keeling, Richard P., Andrew F. Wall, Ric Underhile, and Gwendolyn J. Dungy. *Assessment Reconsidered: Institutional Effectiveness for Student Success.* International Center for Student Success and Institutional Accountability, 2008.

Kelly, Ursula, Iain McNicholl, and Donald McLellan. *Towards the Estimation of the Economic Value of the Outputs of Scottish Higher Education Institutions: An Overview of the Content of the Main Report.* University of Strathclyde, 2005.

Kerby, Debra, and Sandra Weber. "Linking Mission Objectives to an Assessment Plan." *Journal of Education for Business* 75, no. 4 (2000): 202-209.

Kerslake, Evelyn, and Margaret Kinnell. "Public Libraries, Public Interest and the Information Society: Theoretical Issues in the Social Impact of Public Libraries." *Journal of Librarianship and Information Science* 30, no. 3 (1998): 159-167.

Kertesz, Christopher J. "Massachusetts Flunks School-Library Test." *American Libraries* 31, no. 11 (2000): 17.

Keyes, Alison M. "The Value of the Special Library." *Special Libraries* 86, no. 3 (1995): 172-187.

Kim, Mikyong Minsun, Gary Rhoades, and Dudley B. Woodard Jr. "Sponsored Research Versus Graduating Students? Intervening Variables and Unanticipated Findings in Public Research Universities." *Research in Higher Education* 44, no. 1 (2003): 51-81.

King, David N. "The Contribution of Hospital Library Information Services to Clinical Care: A Study in Eight Hospitals." *Bulletin of the Medical Library Association* 75, no. 4 (1987): 291-301.

King, Donald W., Jose Marie Griffiths, Nancy K. Roderer, and Robert R. Wiederkehr. *Value of the Energy Data Base.* Rockville, Maryland: King Research, 1982.

King, Donald W., Sarah Aerni, Fern Brody, Matt Herbison, and Amy Knapp. *The Use and Outcomes of University Library Print and Electronic Collections.* 2004. The Use and Outcomes of University Library Print and Electronic Collections (accessed May 10, 2010).

Knapp, Patricia B. *Monteith College Library Experiment.* New York: Scarecrow Press, 1996.

Koenig, Michael. "The Importance of Information Services for Productivity 'Under-Recognized' and Under-Invested." *Special Libraries* 83, no. 4 (1992): 199-210.

Kostiak, Adele. "Valuing Your Public Library: The Experience of the Barrie Public Library, Ontario, Canada." *The Bottom Line: Managing Library Finances* 15, no. 4 (2002): 159-162.

Koufogiannakis, Denise, and Ellen Crumley. "Research in Librarianship: Issues to Consider." *Library Hi Tech* 24, no. 3 (2006): 324-330.

Kramer, Lloyd A., and Martha B. Kramer. "The College Library and the Drop-Out." *College and Research Libraries* 29, no. 4 (1968): 310-12.

Krashen, Stephen. "Current Research: The Positive Impact of Libraries." *CSLA Journal* 29, no. 1 (2001): 21-24.

———. "School Libraries, Public Libraries, and the NAEP Reading Scores." *School Library Media Quarterly* 23, no. 4 (1995): 235-237.

———. *The Power of Reading: Insights from the Research.* 2nd. Portsmouth, New Hampshire: Libraries Unlimited, 2004.

Kraushaar, Robert, and Barbara Beverley. "Library and Information Services for Productivity." *The Bookmark* 48 (1990): 163-169.

Krupnick, Matt. "Focus on Graduation Could be Rough for Small Private Colleges." *Contra Costa Times*, February 8, 2010.

Kuh, George D. *High-Impact Educational Practices.* Association of American Colleges and Universities, 2008.

———. "Risky Business: Promises and Pitfalls of Institutional Transparency." *Change*, 2007: 30-35.

Kuh, George D., and Robert M. Gonyea. "The Role of the Academic Library in Promoting Student Engagement in Learning." *ACRL Eleventh National Conference.*

Charlotte, North Carolina: Association of College and Research Libraries, 2003. 256-82.

Kuh, George D., Ty M Cruce, Rick Shoup, Jillian Kinzie, and Robert M. Gonyea. "Unmasking the Effects of Student Engagement on First-Year College Grades and Persistence." *Journal of Higher Education* 79, no. 5 (2008): 540-563.

Kuhlthau, Carol C. "Keeping Current: The Center for International Scholarship in School Libraries: CISSL at Rutgers." *School Library Media Activities Monthly* 21, no. 5 (2005): 49-51.

Kyrillidou, Martha. "An Overview of Performance Measures in Higher Education and Libraries." *Journal of Library Administration* 35, no. 4 (2002): 7-18.

———. "From Input to Output Measures to Quality and Outcome Measures, or, From the User in the Life of the Library to the Library in the Life of the User." *Journal of Academic Leadership* 28, no. 1 (2002): 42-46.

Laird, Thomas F. Nelson, and George D. Kuh. "Student Experiences with Information Technology and Their Relationship to Other Aspects of Student Engagement." *Research in Higher Education* 46, no. 5 (2005).

Lakos, Amos, and Shelley E. Phipps. "Creating a Culture of Assessment: A Catalyst for Organizational Change." *portal: Libraries and the Academy* 4, no. 3 (2004): 345-361.

Lance, Keith Curry. "Enough Already! Blazing New Trails for School Library Research." Library Research Service.

———. "How School Libraries Leave No Child Behind: The Impact of School Library Media Programs on Academic Achievement of U.S. Public School Students." *School Libraries in Canada* 22, no. 2 (2002): 3-6.

———. "Impact of School Library Media Programs on Academic Achievement." *Teacher Librarian* 29, no. 3 (2002): 29-34.

———. "Powering Achievement: The Impact of School Libraries and Librarians on Academic Achievement." Library Research Service.

———. "Proof of the Power: Recent Research on the Impact of School Library Media Programs on the Academic Achievement of U.S. Public School Students." ED372759, 2004.

———. "Still Making an Impact: School Library Staffing and Student Performance." *Colorado Libraries* 25, no. 3 (1999): 6-9.

———. "The Future of School Librarianship." Library Research Service.

Lance, Keith Curry, and Becky Russell. "Scientifically Based Research on School Libraries and Academic Achievement: What Is It? How Much of It Do We Have? How Can We Do It Better?" *Knowledge Quest* 32, no. 5 (2004): 13-17.

Lance, Keith Curry, and David V. Loertscher. *Powering Achievement: School Library Media Programs Make a Difference: The Evidence.* 3rd. Salt Lake City: Hi Willow Research, 2001.

————. *Powering Achievement: School Library Media Programs Make a Difference: The Evidence Mounts.* Salt Lake City, Utah: Hi Willow Research & Publishing, 2005.

Lance, Keith Curry, Marcia J Rodney, and Bill Scwharz. "The Impact of School Libraries on Academic Achievement: A Research Study Based on Responses from Administrators in Idaho." *School Library Monthly* 26, no. 9 (2010): 14-17.

Lance, Keith Curry, Marcia J. Rodney, and Christine Hamilton-Pennell. "How School Librarians Help Kids Achieve Standards: The Second Colorado Study." 2000.

Lang, Daniel W. "'World Class' or the Curse of Comparison." *Canadian Journal of Higher Education* 35, no. 3 (2005): 27-55.

Lange, Bonnie, Nancy Magee, and Steven Montgomery. "Does Collaboration Boost Student Learning? (Case Study)." *School Library Journal*, 2003: 4-9.

Lara, Juan Francisco. "Differences in Quality of Academic Effort Between Successful and Unsuccessful Community College Transfer Students." *American Educational Research Association Annual Conference.* Los Angeles, 1981.

Laudel, Grit. "The 'Quality Myth': Promoting and Hindering Conditions for Acquiring Research Funds." *Higher Education* 52 (2006): 375-403.

Leckie, Gloria J., and Jeffrey Hopkins. "The Public Place of Central Libraries: Findings from Toronto to Vancouver." *Library Quarterly* 72, no. 3 (2002): 326-372.

Lederman, Doug. "Imperfect Accountability." *Inside Higher Ed*, March 2010.

Lehner, John. "Return on Investment in Academic Libraries Research." 2009.

Leskes, Andrea, and Barbara D. Wright. *The Art & Science of Assessing General Education Outcomes: A Practical Guide.* Washington, D.C.: Association of American Colleges & Universities, 2005.

Levesque, Nancy. "Partners in Education: The Role of the Academic Library." *The Idea of Education Conference.* Oxford, 2002. 1-11.

Levin, Driscoll, and Fleeter. "Value for Money: Southwestern Ohio's Return from Investment in Public Libraries." 2006.

Levinson-Rose, Judith, and Robert J. Menges. "Improving College Teaching: A Critical Review of Research." *Review of Educational Research* 51, no. 3 (1981): 403-434.

Levitov, Deborah. "Assessment Tool: Levels of Communication, Cooperation, and Collaboration." *School Library Media Activities Monthly* 23, no. 2 (2006): 2.

Lewin, Tamar. "Study Finds Public Discontent with Colleges." *The New York Times*, February 17, 2010.

Lewis, David W. *Exploring Models for Academic Libraries.* 2007. http://acrlog.org/2007/03/12/exploring-models-for-academic-libraries/ (accessed May 10, 2010).

Li, Xin, and Zsuzsa Koltay. *Impact Measures in Research Libraries: SPEC KIT 318.* Washington, D.C.: Association of Research Libraries, 2010.

http://www.ala.org/ala/mgrps/divs/acrl/about/sections/is/projpubs/researchagendalibr
ary.cfm (accessed May 10, 2010).

Library Council of New South Wales. "Enriching Communities: The Value of Public
Libraries in New South Wales." *Australasian Public Libraries and Information
Services* 22, no. 1 (2009): 6-12.

Lincoln, Yvonna.S. & Guba, Egon G. "But is it Rigorous? Trustworthiness and
Authenticity in Naturalistic Evaluation." In *ASHE Reader Series: Assessment and
Program Evaluation,* edited by W.Y. Lee. 643-650. Boston: Pearson Custom
Publishing, 2003.

Liu, Lewis G. "The Economic Behavior of Academic Research Libraries: Toward a
Theory." *Library Trends* 51, no. 3 (2003): 277-292.

Lloyd, Anne, and Kirsty Williamson. "Towards an Understanding of Information Literacy
in Context: Implications for Research." *Journal of Librarianship and Information
Science* 40, no. 1 (2008): 3-12.

Loertscher, David V., and Ross J. Todd. *We Boost Achievement: Evidence-Based
Practice for School Library Media Specialists.* Salt Lake City: Hi Willow Research,
2003.

Loertscher, David, and Blanche Woolls. "You Need the Library to Meet Standards."
School Library Journal, 2003: 6-7.

Logan, Debra Kay "A Measure of Success." *Library Media Connection,* 2010: 7.

———. "Being Heard…Advocacy + Evidence + Students = IMPACT!" *School Library
Media Activities Monthly* 23, no. 1 (2006): 46-48.

Long, Bridget Terry. *Using Research to Improve Student Success: What More Could Be
Done?* National Postsecondary Education Cooperative, 2006.

Loomis, J., T. Brown, B. Lucero, and G. Peterson. "Improving Validity Experiments of
Contingent Valuation Methods: Results of Efforts to Reduce the Disparity of
Hypothetical and Actual Willingness to Pay." *Land Economics* 72 (1996): 450-461.

Lougee, Wendy. "The Diffuse Library Revisited: Aligning the Library as Strategic Asset."
Library Hi Tech 27, no. 4 (2009): 610-623.

Lustig, Joanne. "Briefing: What Executives Think About Information Management."
Information Management Service 11 (2008).

Luther, Judy. *University Investment in the Library: What's the Return? A Case Study at
the University of Illinois at Urbana-Champaign.* San Diego: Elsevier, 2008.

Lutz, Frank W., and Robert W. Field. "Business Valuing in Academia." *Higher Education*
36 (1998): 383-419.

Lynch, Beverly P., et al. "Attitudes of Presidents and Provosts on the University Library."
College and Research Libraries 68, no. 3 (2007): 213-227.

MacEachern, Ruth. "Measuring the Added Value of Library and Information Services:
The New Zealand Approach." *IFLA Journal* 27 (2001): 232-236.

Machlup, Fritz. "Uses, Value, and Benefits of Knowledge." *Knowledge: Creation, Diffusion, Utilization* 14, no. 4 (1993): 448-466.

Machung, Anne. "Playing the Rankings Game." *Change* 30, no. 4 (1998): 12-16.

Maki, Peggy L. "Developing an Assessment Plan to Learn about Student Learning." *Journal of Academic Librarianship* 28, no. 1 (2002): 8-13.

———. "Moving Beyond a National Habit in the Call for Accountability." *Peer Review* 11, no. 1 (2009).

Mallinckrodt, Brent, and William E. Sedlacek. "Student Retention and the Use of Campus Facilities by Race." *NASPA Journal* 24, no. 3 (1987).

Manning, Helen. "The Corporate Librarian: Great Return on Investment." In *President's Task Force on the Value of the Information Professional*, edited by James M. Matarazzo, 23-34. Washington, D.C.: Special Libraries Association, 1987.

Marcum, James W. "From Information Center to Discovery System: Next Step for Libraries?" *Journal of Academic Librarianship* 27, no. 2 (2001): 97-106.

Marginson, Simon. "Dynamics of National and Global Competition in Higher Education." *Higher Education* 52 (2006): 1-39.

Marie, Kirsten L. "From Theory to Practice: A New Teacher-Librarian Tackles Library Assessment." *Teacher Librarian* 33, no. 2 (2005): 20-25.

Marie, Kirsten L., and Janine Weston. "Survey Says: Online Survey Tools for Library Assessment." *Library Media Connection* 28, no. 2 (2009): 50-53.

Mark, Amy E., and Polly D. Boruff-Jones. "Information Literacy and Student Engagement: What the National Survey of Student Engagement Reveals About Your Campus." *College and Research Libraries*, 2003: 480-493.

Markless, Sharon, and David Streatfield. *Evaluating the Impact of Your Library.* London: Facet, 2006.

Marsh, Patricia. "What Is Known About Student Learning Outcomes and How Does It Relate to the Scholarship of Teaching and Learning?" *International Journal for the Scholarship of Teaching and Learning* 1, no. 2 (2007): 1-12.

Marshall, Joanne G. "The Impact of the Hospital Library on Clinical Decision Making: The Rochester Study." *Bulletin of the Medical Library Association* (80) 2 (1992): 169-178.

———. *The Impact of the Special Library on Corporate Decision-Making.* Washington, D.C.: Special Libraries Association, 1993.

———. "Measuring the Value and Impact of Health Library and Information Services: Past Reflections, Future Possibilities." *Health Information and Libraries Journal* 24 (2007): 4-17.

Mason, Robert M., and Peter G. Sassone. "A Lower Bound Cost Benefit Model for Information Services." *Information Processing and Management* 14, no. 2 (1978): 71-83.

Matarazzo, James M. *Closing the Corporate Library: Case Studies on the Decision-Making Process.* New York: Special Libraries Association, 1981.

Matarazzo, James M., and Laurence Prusak. "Valuing Corporate Libraries: A Senior Management Survey." *Special Libraries* 81, no. 2 (1990): 102-110.

———. *The Value of Corporate Libraries: Findings from a 1995 Survey of Senior Management.* Washington, D.C.: Special Libraries Association, 1995.

Matier, Michael W. "Retaining Faculty: A Tale of Two Campuses." *Association for Institutional Research Annual Meeting.* Baltimore, 1989.

Matthews, Joseph R. "Determining and Communicating the Value of the Special Library." *Information Outlook* 7, no. 3 (2003).

———. *Library Assessment in Higher Education.* Westport, Connecticut: Libraries Unlimited, 2007.

———. *The Bottom Line: Determining and Communicating the Value of the Special Library.* Westport, Connecticut: Libraries Unlimited, 2002.

———. *The Evaluation and Measurement of Library Services.* Westport, Connecticut: Libraries Unlimited, 2007.

———. "What's the Return When You ROI? The Benefits and Challenges of Calculating Your Library's Return on Investment." *Library Leadership and Management*, under review.

McClure, Charles R., Bruce T. Fraser, Timothy W. Nelson, and Jane B. Robbins. *Economic Benefits and Impacts From Public Libraries in the State of Florida.* Final Report, School of Information Studies, 2000.

McGregor, J. "Flexible Scheduling: How Does a Principal Facilitate Implementation?" *School Libraries Worldwide* 8, no. 1 (2002): 71-84.

McGriff, Nancy, Carl A. Harvey II, and Leslie B. Preddy. "Collecting the Data: Monitoring the Mission Statement." *School Library Media Activities Monthly* 20, no. 6 (2004): 24-29.

———. "Collecting the Data: Program Perception." *School Library Media Activities Monthly* 20, no. 10 (2004): 19-20, 45.

McRostie, Donna, and Margaret Ruwoldt. "The Devils in the Details - The Use of Statistics and Data for Strategic Decision Making and Advocacy." *World Library and Information Congress.* Milan, Italy, 2009. 1-10.

Means, Martha L. "The Research Funding Service: A Model for Expanded Library Services." *Bulletin of the Medical Library Association* 88, no. 2 (2000): 178-186.

Melo, Luiza Baptista, and Cesaltina Pires. "The Impact of the Electronic Resources in Portuguese Academic Libraries: Results of a Qualitative Survey." *Qualitative and Quantitative Methods in Libraries International Conference.* Chania, Crete, Greece, 2009. 1-9.

Mendelsohn, Jennifer. "Perspectives on Quality of Reference Service in an Academic Library: A Qualitative Study." *RQ* 36 (1997): 544-557.

Meredith, Marc. "Why do Universities Compete in the Ratings Game? An Empirical Analysis of the Effects of the 'U.S. News and World Report' College Rankings." *Research in Higher Education* 45, no. 5 (2004): 443-461.

Merisotis, Jamie P. "It's the Learning, Stupid." *Howard R. Bowen Lecture.* Claremont, California: Claremont Graduate University, 2009.

Mezick, Elizabeth M. "Return on Investment: Libraries and Student Retention." *Journal of Academic Librarianship* 33, no. 5 (2007): 561-566.

Michael, Steve O. "The Cost of Excellence: The Financial Implications of Institutional Rankings." *International Journal of Educational Management* 19, no. 5 (2005): 365-382.

Michalko, James, Constance Malpas, and Arnold Arcolio. *Research Libraries, Risk and Systemic Change.* OCLC Research, 2010.

Michigan Academic Library Council. *Academic Library Case Statement.* Michigan Academic Library Council, 2007.

Middaugh, M. F. *Understanding Faculty Productivity: Standards and Benchmarks for Colleges and Universities.* San Francisco: Jossey-Bass, 2001.

Miller, Margaret A., and Peter T. Ewell. *Measuring Up on College-Level Learning.* National Center for Public Policy and Higher Education, 2005.

Mogavero, Louis N. "Transferring Technology to Industry Through Information." In *Information and Industry: Proceedings of the North Atlantic Treaty Organization, Advisory Group for Aerospace Research and Development (AGARD), Technical Information Panel's Specialists' Meeting.* Paris, 1979.

Mondschein, Lawrence G. "SDI Use and Productivity in the Corporate Research Environment." *Special Libraries* 81, no. 4 (1990): 265-279.

Monks, J., and R. G. Ehrenberg. *The Impact of US News and World Report College Rankings on Admission Outcomes and Pricing Decisions at Selective Private Institutions.* NBER Working Paper No. 7227, Cambridge, Massachusetts: National Bureau of Economic Research, 1999.

Moore, Deborah, Steve Brewster, Cynthia Dorroh, and Michael Moreau. "Information Competency Instruction in a Two-Year College: One Size Does Not Fit All." *Reference Services Review* 30, no. 4 (2002): 300-306.

Moreillon, Judi, and Kristin Fontichiaro. "Teaching and Assessing the Dispositions: A Garden of Opportunity." *Knowledge Quest* 37, no. 2 (2008): 64-67.

Morest, Vanessa Smith. "Accountability, Accreditation, and Continuous Improvement: Building a Culture of Evidence." *New Directions for Institutional Research*, no. 143 (2009): 17-27.

Morris, Anne, John Sumsion, and Margaret Hawkins. "Economic Value of Public Libraries in the UK." *Libri* 52 (2002): 78-87.

Morris, Anne, Margaret Hawkins, and John Sumsion. "Value of Book Borrowing from Public Libraries: User Perceptions." *Journal of Librarianship and Information Science* 33 (2001): 191-198.

Muddiman, Dave, Shuraz Durrani, Martin Dutch, Rebecca Linley, John Pateman, and John Vincent. *Open to All? The Public Library and Social Exclusion.* Research Report 86, Library and Information Commission , 2000.

Mueller, Jon. "Authentic Assessment in the Classroom and the Library Media Center." *Library Media Connection* 23, no. 7 (2005): 14-18.

Museums, Libraries, and Archives Council. *Inspiring Learning.* 2008. http://www.inspiringlearningforall.gov.uk (accessed May 10, 2010).

Näslund, Dag, Annika Olsson, and Sture Karlsson. "Operationalizing the Concept of Value—An Action Research-Based Model." *The Learning Organization* 13, no. 3 (2006): 300-332.

National Academies. *Star Metrics - Phase II.* 2010. http://sites.nationalacademies.org/PGA/fdp/PGA_057159 (accessed May 10, 2010).

National Center for Education Statistics. *Academic Libraries 2006: First Look.* Washington, D.C.: U.S. Department of Education, 2006.

National Center for Public Policy and Higher Education. *Measuring Up 2000.* 2000. http://measuringup.highereducation.org/2000/ (accessed May 10, 2010).

———. *Measuring Up 2008 .* 2008. http://measuringup2008.highereducation.org/print/NCPPHEMUNationalRpt.pdf (accessed May 10, 2010).

"National Conference on Student Recruitment, Marketing, and Retention." Atlanta: Noel-Levitz, 2010. https://www.noellevitz.com/Events/National+Conference+on+Student+Recruitment+Marketing+Retention/ (accessed May 10, 2010).

National Institute for Learning Outcomes and Assessment. 2010. http://www.learningoutcomesassessment.org/ (accessed May10 2010).

National Institute for Learning Outcomes Assessment. "More Than You Think, Less Than We Need: Learning Outcomes Assessment in American Higher Education." 2009.

National States Geographic Information Council. *Economic Justification: Measuring Return-on-Investment (ROI) and Cost Benefit Analysis (CBA).* 2006. http://www.nsgic.org/hottopics/return_on_investment.pdf (accessed May 10, 2010).

National Survey of Student Engagement. "Using NSSE to Assess and Improve Undergraduate Education." 2009.

Neal, James G. "What Do Users Want? What Do Users Need? W(h)ither the Academic Research Library?" *Journal of Library Administration* 49, no. 5 (2009): 463-468.

Neelameghan, A. "Knowledge Management in Schools and Role of the School Library/Media Centre." *Information Studies* 13, no. 1 (2007): 5-22.

Nef Consulting. *Proving Value and Improving Practice: A Discussion About Social Return on Investment.* Museums Libraries Archives Council, 2009.

"New Study Reaffirms School Library, Academic Link." *American Libraries* 39, no. 4 (2008): 12.

New York Library Association. *Marist Poll.* 2004. http://www.nyla.org/index.php?page_id=801 (accessed May 10, 2010).

Nicholson, Scott. "A Conceptual Framework for the Holistic Measurement and Cumulative Evaluation of Library Services." *Journal of Documentation* 60, no. 2 (2004): 164-182.

Nimon, Maureen. "The Role of Academic Libraries in the Development of the Information Literate Student: The Interface Between Librarian, Academic, and Other Stakeholders." *Australian Academic and Research Libraries* 32, no. 1 (2001): 43-52.

Noel-Levitz. "National Conference on Student Recruitment, Marketing, and Retention." Atlanta, Georgia, 2010.

Nova Scotia Regional Libraries Funding Formula Review Committee. *Report.* Halifax, Nova Scotia: Department of Education, 1993.

Oakleaf, Megan. "Are They Learning? Are We? Learning Outcomes and the Academic Library." *Library Quarterly*, 81, no.1 (2011) Forthcoming.

———. "Dangers and Opportunities: A Conceptual Map of Information Literacy Assessment Tools." *portal: Libraries and the Academy* 8, no. 3 (2008): 233-253.

———. "Writing Information Literacy Assessment Plans: A Guide to Best Practice." *Communications in Information Literacy* 3, no. 2 (2010): 80-90.

Oakleaf, Megan, and Lisa Hinchliffe. "Assessment Cycle or Circular File: Do Academic Librarians Use Information Literacy Assessment Data?" *Library Assessment Conference.* Seattle, 2008. 159-164.

Oakleaf, Megan, and Neal Kaske. "Guiding Questions for Assessing Information Literacy in Higher Education." *portal: Libraries and the Academy*, 2009: 273-286.

OCLC. *How Libraries Stack Up 2010.* 2010. http://www.oclc.org/reports/stackup/ (accessed May 10, 2010).

O'Hanlon, Nancy. "Information Literacy in the University Curriculum." *portal: Libraries and the Academy* 7, no. 2 (2007): 169-189.

Olsen, Danny R., and Kristoffer B. Kristensen. *Harold B. Lee Library Resource Usage Study.* Provo, Utah: Brigham Young University, 2002.

Ontario Libraries and Community Information Branch. "The Economics and Job Creation Benefits of Ontario Public and First Nation Libraries." 1995.

Oppenheim, Charles, and David Stuart. "Is There a Correlation Between Investment in an Academic Library and a Higher Education Institution's Ratings in the Research Assessment Exercise?" *Aslib Proceedings* 56, no. 3 (2004): 156-165.

Organization for Economic Co-Operation and Development.
http://www.oecd.org/document/22/0,3343,en_2649_35961291_40624662_1_1_1_1,
00.html (accessed May 10, 2010).

Orr, Debbie, and Jacky Cribb. "Information Literacy - Is It Worth the Investment."
Australian Academic and Research Libraries 34, no. 1 (2003): 43-51.

Outsell. "Normative Database." December 2002.

———. *Outsell's Neighborhoods of the Information Industry: A Reference Guide.*
Burlingame, California, 2004.

Oviatt Library. "Oviatt Library Valuation Study." 2008.

Owen, Patricia L. "Using TRAILS to Assess Student Learning: A Step-by-Step Guide."
Library Media Connection 28, no. 6 (2010): 36-38.

Pasamba, Nehemias A. "Valuing Library Services." *CONSAL.* Thailand: Mission
College, 2009.

Pascarella, Ernest T. "Cognitive Growth in College." *Change* 33 no. 6 (2001): 21-27.

Pascarella, Ernest T., and Patrick T. Terenzini. *How College Affects Students: A Third
Decade of Research.* San Francisco: Jossey-Bass, 2005.

———. "Predicting Voluntary Freshman Year Persistence/Withdrawal Behavior in a
Residential University: A Path Analytic Validation of Tinto's Model." *Journal of
Educational Psychology* 75, no. 2 (1983): 215-226.

Patrick, William J., and Elizabeth C Stanley. "Assessment of Research Quality."
Research in Higher Education 37, no. 1 (2006): 23-41.

Pfeiffer, J.J. "From Performance Reporting to Performance-Based Funding: Florida's
Experiences in Workforce Development Performance Measurement." *New
Directions for Community Colleges* 104 (1998): 17-28.

Picco, M. A. Paola. "Multicultural Libraries' Services and Social Integration: The Case of
Public Libraries in Montreal Canada." *Public Library Quarterly* 27, no. 1 (2008): 41-
56.

Pike, Gary R. "Limitations of Using Students' Self-Reports of Academic Development as
Proxies for Traditional Achievement Measures." *Research in Higher Education* 37
(1996).

———. "Measuring Quality: A Comparison of U.S. News Rankings and NSSE
Benchmarks." *Research in Higher Education* 45, no. 2 (2004): 193-208.

Pike, Gary R., John C. Smart, George D. Kuh, and John C. Hayek. "Educational
Expenditures and Student Engagement: When Does Money Matter?" *Research in
Higher Education* 47, no. 7 (2006): 847-872.

Pittas, Peggy Sheffer. *Faculty Perceptions of Barriers to their Professional Performance
at Private Comprehensive Colleges and Universities.* PhD dissertation, University of
Virginia, 2001.

Poll, Roswitha. "Impact/Outcome Measures for Libraries." *Liber Quarterly* 13 (2003): 329-342.

———. "Quality Measures for Special Libraries." *World Library and Information Congress: 73rd IFLA General Conference and Council.* Oslo, 2007.

Poll, Roswitha, and Philip Payne. "Impact Measures for Library and Information Services." *Library Hi Tec* 24, no. 4 (2006): 547-562.

Porter, Stephen R., and Michael E. Whitcomb. "Non-Response in Student Surveys: The Role of Demographics, Engagement, and Personality." *Research in Higher Education* 46, no. 2 (2005): 127-152.

Portugal, Frank H. *Valuating Information Intangibles: Measuring the Bottom Line Contribution of Librarians and Information Professionals.* Washington, D.C.: Special Libraries Association, 2000.

Preer, Jean. "Where Are Libraries in Bowling Alone?" *American Libraries* 32, no. 8 (2001).

Pritchard, Sarah M. "Determining Quality in Academic Libraries." *Library Trends* 44, no. 3 (1996).

———. "Special Collections Surge to the Fore." *portal: Libraries and the Academy* 9, no. 2 (2009): 177-180.

Pung, Caroline, Ann Clarke, and Laurie Patten. "Measuring the Economic Impact of the British Library." *New Review of Academic Librarianship* 10, no. 1 (2004): 79-102.

Quinn, Brian. "Beyond Efficacy: The Exemplar Librarian as a New Approach to Reference Evaluation." *Illinois Libraries* 76 (1994): 163-73.

Radcliff, Carolyn J., Mary Lee Jensen, Joseph A. Salem Jr., Kenneth J. Burhanna, and Julie A. Gedeon. *A Practical Guide to Information Literacy Assessment for Academic Librarians.* Westport, Connecticut: Libraries Unlimited, 2007.

Rader, Hannelore B. "Building Faculty-Librarian Partnerships to Prepare Students for Information Fluency: The Time for Sharing Expertise is Now." *College and Research Libraries News* 65 (2004).

Rampell, Catherine. "Investing in Colleges." *New York Times.* July 21, 2009. http://economix.blogs.nytimes.com/2009/07/21/investing-in-colleges/ (accessed May 10, 2010).

Ratteray, Oswald M.T. "Information Literacy in Self-Study and Accreditation." *Journal of Academic Librarianship* 28, no. 6 (2002): 368-375.

Ray, Kathlin L. "The Postmodern Library in an Age of Assessment." *ACRL Tenth National Conference.* Denver, 2001. 250-254.

Reeder, Geneva. "ALA's The State of America's Libraries 2008." *Learning Media* 38, no. 3 (2008): 28-30.

———. "Where's the Evidence? Understanding the Impact of School Libraries." *Learning Media* 36, no. 1 (2008): 30.

Reid, Christine, Julie Thomson, and Jayne Wallace-Smith. "Impact of Information on Corporate Decision Making: The UK Banking Sector." *Library Management* 19, no. 2 (1998): 86-109.

Renaud, Robert. "Learning to Compete: Competition, Outsourcing, and Academic Libraries." *Journal of Academic Librarianship* 23, no. 2 (1997): 85-90.

Rhodes, Terrel L. "VALUE: Valid Assessment of Learning in Undergraduate Education." *New Directions for Institutional Research*, 2008: 59-70.

Rockman, Ilene. "Strengthening Connections between Information Literacy, General Education and Assessment Efforts." *Library Trends* 51 (2002).

Roderer, Nancy K., Donald W. King, and Sandra E. Brouard. *The Use and Value of Defense and Technical Information Center Products and Services.* Rockville, Maryland: King Research, 1983.

Rodger, Eleanor Jo. "Public Libraries: Necessities or Amenities?" *American Libraries*, 2009: 46-48.

———. "What's a Library Worth?" *American Libraries* 38, no. 8 (2007): 58-61.

Rodriguez, Derek A. "How Digital Library Services Contribute to Undergraduate Learning: An Evaluation of the 'Understanding Library Impacts' Protocol." 2009.

Rogers, Carton. "There Is Always Tomorrow? Libraries on the Edge." *Journal of Library Administration* 49, no. 5 (2009): 545-558.

Rosenblatt, S. "Developing Performance Measures for Library Collections and Services." In *The Mirage of Continuity: Reconfiguring Academic Information Resources for the 21st Century*, edited by B. L. Hawkins and P. Battin, 278-289. Washington, D.C.: Council on Library and Information Resources, 1998.

Rosenfeldt, Debra. "Libraries Building Communities Paper." *Country Public Libraries Association of NSW Conference.* 2004.

Rothstein, Samuel. *The Development of Reference Services.* Chicago: Association of College and Research Libraries, 1955.

Rubin, Rhea Joyce. *Demonstrating Results: Using Outcome Measurement in Your Library.* Chicago: American Library Association, 2006.

Rushing, Darla, and Deborah Poole. "The Role of the Library in Student Retention." In *Making the Grade: Academic Libraries and Student Success*, edited by Maurie Caitlin Kelly and Andrea Kross, 91-101. Chicago: Association of College and Research Libraries, 2002.

Sakalaki, Maria, and Smaragda Kazi. "How Much is Information Worth? Willingness to Pay for Expert and Non-Expert Informational Goods Compared to Material Goods in Lay Economic Thinking." *Journal of Information Science* 33, no. 3 (2007): 315-325.

"Sample Evaluation Checklists." *School Libraries in Canada* 23, no. 1 (2003): 30-33.

Sánchez, Angel Martínez, and Manuela Pérez Pérez. "Lean Indicators and Manufacturing Strategies." *International Journal of Operations & Production Management* 166 (2001): 1433-1451.

Saracevic, Tefko, and Paul B. Kantor. "Studying the Value of Library and Information Services. Part I. Establishing a Theoretical Framework." *Journal of the American Society for Information Science* 48, no. 6 (1997): 527-542.

Saunders, Laura. "Perspectives on Accreditation and Information Literacy as Reflected in the Literature of Library and Information Science." *Journal of Academic Librarianship* 34, no. 4 (2008): 305-313.

———. "Regional Accreditation Organizations' Treatment of Information Literacy: Definitions, Collaboration, and Assessment." *Journal of Academic Librarianship* 33, no. 3 (2007): 317-326.

———. "The Future of Information Literacy in Academic Libraries: A Delphi Study." *portal: Libraries and the Academy* 9, no. 1 (2009): 99-114.

Scharf, Meg. "Tellin' Our Story—Or Not: Assessment Results on Academic Library Web Sites." March 13, 2009.

Schloman, Barbara F., and Julie A. Gedeon. "Creating Trails: Tool for Real-Time Assessment of Information Literacy Skills." *Knowledge Quest* 35, no. 5 (2007): 44-47.

Scholastic. *School Libraries Work!* 2008. http://www2.scholastic.com/content/collateral_resources/pdf/s/slw3_2008.pdf (accessed May 10, 2010).

Schonfeld, Roger C., and Ross Housewright. *Faculty Survey 2009: Key Strategic Insights for Libraries, Publishers, and Societies.* Ithaka, 2010.

Schwartz, Charles A. "The University Library and the Problem of Knowledge." *College and Research Libraries* 68, no. 3 (2007): 238-244.

Scott, Geoff, Mahsood Shah, Leonid Grebennikov, and Harmanpreet Singh. "Improving Student Retention: A University of Western Sydney Case Study." *Journal of Institutional Research* 14, no. 1 (2008): 9-23.

Sennyey, Pongracz, Lyman Ross, and Caroline Mills. "Exploring the Future of Academic Libraries: A Definitional Approach." *Journal of Academic Librarianship* 35, no. 3 (2009): 252-259.

Shaw, Joan. "Demystifying the Evaluation Process for Parents: Rubrics for Marking Student Research Projects." *Teacher Librarian* 32, no. 2 (2004): 16-19.

Shumaker, David. *Models of Embedded Librarianship.* Special Libraries Association, 2009.

Shupe, David. "Significantly Better: The Benefits for an Academic Institution Focused on Student Learning Outcomes." *On the Horizon* 15, no. 2 (2007): 48-57.

Simmel, Leslie. "Building Your Value Story and Business Case." *C&RL News*, 2007: 88-91.

Simmons-Welburn, Janice, Georgie Donovan, and Laura Bender. "Transforming the Library: The Case for Libraries to End Incremental Measures and Solve Problems for Their Campuses Now." *Library Administration & Management* 22, no. 3 (2008): 130-134.

Small, Ruth V., and Jaime Snyder. "Research Instruments for Measuring the Impact of School Libraries on Student Achievement and Motivation." *School Libraries Worldwide* 16, no. 1 (2010): 61-72.

Smart, John C., Kenneth A. Feldman, and Corinna A. Ethington. *Holland's Theory and Patterns of College Success.* National Postsecondary Education Cooperative, 2006.

Smith, Christine, Vivienne Winterman, and Angela Abell. "The Impact of Information on Corporate Decision Making in the Insurance Sector." *Library Management* 19, no. 3 (1998): 154-173.

Smith, Don Noel. "Challenges to the Credible Assessment of Learning." *Assessment Update* 21, no. 5 (2009): 6-8.

Smith, E. G. *Texas School Libraries: Standards Resources, Services, and Students' Performance.* Texas: Texas State Library and Archives Commission, 2001.

Smith, Erin T. "Assessing Collection Usefulness: An Investigation of Library Ownership of the Resources Graduate Students Use." *College and Research Libraries* 64 (2003): 344-355.

Smith, Kenneth R. "New Roles and Responsibilities for the University Library: Advancing Student Learning Through Outcomes Assessment." *Journal of Library Administration* 35, no. 4 (2007): 29-36.

Smith, Sonya S. "Who Wants to Know? Some Ideas for Sharing Assessment Data with School Administrators and Others." *Learning Media* 35, no. 1 (2007): 22.

Smith-Doerr, Laurel. "Stuck in the Middle: Doctoral Education Ranking and Career Outcomes for Life Scientists." *Bulletin of Science, Technology, and Society* 26, no. 3 (2006): 243-255.

Snelson, Pamela. "Communicating the Value of Academic Libraries." *C&RL News* 67, no. 8 (2006): 490-492.

Snyder, Maureen M., and Janet Roche. "Road Map for Improvement: Evaluating Your Library Media Program." *Knowledge Quest* 37, no. 2 (2008): 22-27.

Stalker, John C., and Marjorie E. Murfin. "Quality Reference Service: A Preliminary Case Study." *Journal of Academic Librarianship* 22 (1996): 423-29.

Steadman, David G. "Accreditation is Not School Accountability." *NASC Report* 13, no. 2 (2001).

Stoffle, Carla J., Alan E. Guskin, and Joseph A. Boisse. "Teaching, Research, and Service: The Academic Library's Role." In *New Directions for Teaching and Learning*, 3-14. San Francisco: Jossey-Bass, 1984.

Strand, Jill. "Strike Up the Brand: How to Market Your Value to the Rest of the World." *Information Outlook*, 2004: 11-15.

Stratus Consulting. "Business Case for Information Services: EPA's Regional Libraries and Centers." 2004.

Streatfield, David, and Sharon Markless. "Evaluating the Impact of Information Literacy in Higher Education: Progress and Prospects." *Libri* 58 (2008): 102-109.

———. "What is Impact Assessment and Why is it Important?" *Performance Measurement and Metrics* 10, no. 2 (2009): 134-141.

Strouse, Roger. "Corporate Information Centers in the Year of Accountability." *Online* 25, no. 4 (2001).

———. "Demonstrating Value and Return on Investment: The Ongoing Imperative." *Information Outlook* 7, no. 3 (2003).

Student Development Theory Chart. 2010. http://www.freewebs.com/studentaffairs/collegeimpact.htm (accessed May 10, 2010).

Sumsion, John, Margaret Hawkins, and Anne Morris. "The Economic Value of Book Borrowing from Public Libraries: An Optimisation Model." *Journal of Documentation* 58, no. 6 (2002): 662-682.

Surrey Public Library Administration. *Surrey Public Library Economic Impact Study.* Surrey, British Columbia: Surrey Public Library, 1994.

Sykes, Jan. "Measuring Our Value So We Can Market It." 2001. http://www.sla.org/content/Shop/Information/infoonline/2001/mar01/sldc.cfm (accessed May 10, 2010).

Tenofsky, Deborah. "Teaching to the Whole Student: Building Best Practices for Collaboration Between Libraries and Student Services." *Research Strategies* 20 (2005): 284-299.

Tenopir, Carol. "Investment in the Library: What's the Return?" *American Library Association Midwinter Conference.* Boston, 2010.

———. "Measuring the Value and Return on Investment of Academic Libraries." *ICAL.* 2009. 9-12.

Tenopir, Carol, Amy Love, Joseph Park, Lei Wu, Bruce Kingma, and Donald W. King. "Return on Investment in Academic Libraries: An International Study of the Value of Research Libraries to the Grants Process." White Paper, 2009.

Tenopir, Carol, and Donald W. King. "Perceptions of Value and Value Beyond Perceptions: Measuring the Quality and Value of Journal Article Readings." *Serials* 20, no. 3 (2007): 199-207.

Teodorescu, Daniel. "Correlates of Faculty Publication Productivity: A Cross-National Analysis." *Higher Education* 39 (2000): 201-222.

Tepe, Ann E., and Gail A. Geitgey. "Student Learning through Ohio School Libraries: A Proposal Submitted to The State Library of Ohio." 2002.

Texas Library Association. "A Pocket Guide to 21st Century Libraries." Austin: Texas Library Association.

Thompson, Bruce, Colleen Cook, and Martha Kyrillidou. "Concurrent Validity of LibQUAL+ Scores: What do LibQUAL+ Scores Measure?" *Journal of Academic Librarianship* 31, no. 6 (2005): 517-522.

Tinto, Vincent, and Brian Pusser. *Moving from Theory to Action: Building a Model of Institutional Action for Student Success.* National Postsecondary Education Cooperative, 2006.

Todd, Ross J. "Collaboration: From Myth to Reality: Let's Get Down to Business. Just Do It!" *School Library Media Activities Monthly* 24, no. 7 (2008).

———. "Evidence Based Practice and School Libraries: From Advocacy to Action." In *School Reform and the School Library Media Specialist*, edited by Violet H. Harada and Sandra Hughes-Hassell, 57-78. Westport, Connecticut: Libraries Unlimited, 2007.

———. "Hearing the Voices of Those We Help: Finding the Natural, Multidimensional Perspectives on the Value of School Libraries." *School Library Media Research* 10 (2007).

———. "A Question of Evidence." *Knowledge Quest* 37, no. 2 (2008): 16-21.

———. "School Administrators' Support for School Libraries: The Impact on Student Academic Achievement." *Learning Media* 35, no. 1 (2007): 13-16.

———. "The Evidence-Based Manifesto." *School Library Journal* 54, no. 4 (2008): 38-43.

Todd, Ross J., Carol C. Kuhlthau, and Jannica E. Heinstrom. "School Library Impact Measure: A Toolkit and Handbook for Tracking and Assessing Student Learning Outcomes of Guided Inquiry Through the School Library." Center for International Scholarship in School Libraries, 2005.

Toutkoushian, Robert K., and John C. Smart. "Do Institutional Characteristics Affect Student Gains from College?" *Review of Higher Education* 25, no. 1 (2001): 39-61.

Town, Stephen. "The SCONUL Value and Impact Measurement Programme (VAMP): A Progress Report." *Focus* 38 (2006). 114-116

———. "Value and Impact Workshop." *American Library Association Annual Conference.* Washington, D.C.: Association of Research Libraries, 2010.

U.S. Department of Education. *A Test of Leadership: Charting the Future of U.S. Higher Education.* Report of the Commission Appointed by Secretary of Education Margaret Spellings, Washington, D.C.: U.S. Department of Education, 2006.

Ulaga, W., and S. Chacour. "Measuring Customer Perceived Value in Business Markets." *Industrial Marketing Management* 30 (2001): 525-540.

Upcraft, M. Lee, and John H. Schuh. "Assessment vs. Research: Why We Should Care About the Difference." *About Campus*, 2002: 16-20.

Urquhart, Christine. "How Do I Measure the Impact of My Service?" In *Evidence-Based Practice for Information Professionals*, edited by Andrew Booth and A. Brice, 210-222. London: Facet, 2004.

Urquhart, Christine, and John Hepworth. *The Value of Information Services to Clinicians.* London: British Library Research and Development Department, 1995.

Urquhart, D. J. "Economic Analysis of Information Services." *Journal of Documentation* 32, no. 2 (1976): 123-125.

Valenza, Joyce Kasman. "Are We Passing Our Own Test?" *School Library Journal* 50, no. 3 (2004): 8.

Vandeventer, Lori. "Getting Better Every Day: High School Students Use Continuous Improvement Tools." *Indiana Libraries* 26, no. 4 (2007): 23-25.

Veenstra, R. J., and E. H. Gluck. "A Clinical Librarian Program in the Intensive Care Unit." *Critical Care Medicine* 20 (1992): 1038-1042.

Volkwein, J. Fredericks, and Kyle V. Sweitzer. "Institutional Prestige and Reputation Among Research Universities and Liberal Arts Colleges." *Research in Higher Education* 47, no. 2 (2006): 129-148.

Voluntary System of Accountability. *College Portrait.* 2010. http://www.voluntarysystem.org/index.cfm (accessed May 10, 2010).

Vondracek, Ruth. "Comfort and Convenience? Why Students Choose Alternatives to the Library." *portal: Libraries and the Academy* 7, no. 3 (2007): 277-293.

Wagner, K. C., and G. D. Byrd. "Evaluating the Effectiveness of Clinical Medical Librarian Programs: A Systematic Review of the Literature." *Journal of the Medical Library Association* 92 (2004): 14-33.

Walsh, Andrew. "Information Literacy Assessment: Where Do We Start?" *Journal of Librarianship and Information Science* 41, no. 1 (2009): 19-28.

Walter, Scott. "Engelond: A Model for Faculty-Librarian Collaboration in the Information Age." *Information Technology and Libraries* 19, no. 1 (2000): 34-41.

Warner, Dorothy Anne. *A Disciplinary Blueprint for the Assessment of Information Literacy.* Westport, Connecticut: Libraries Unlimited, 2008.

Webster, Duane, and Betty Sue Flowers. "Community Forum: Research Libraries in the Digital Age." *Journal of Library Administration* 49, no. 3 (2009): 303-310.

Webster, Thomas J. "A Principal Component Analysis of the 'U.S. News and World Report' Tier Rankings of Colleges and Universities." *Economics of Education Review* 20 (2001): 235-244.

Weightman, Alison L., and Jane Williamson. "The Value and Impact of Information Provided Through Library Services for Patient Care: A Systematic Review." *Health Information and Libraries Journal* 22 (2005): 4-25.

Weil, Ben H. "Benefits from Research Use of the Published Literature at the Exxon Research Center." In *Special Librarianship: A New Reader*, edited by Eugene B. Jackson, 586-594. Metuchen, New Jersey: Scarecrow, 1980.

Weiner, Sharon. "The Contribution of the Library to the Reputation of a University." *Journal of Academic Librarianship* 35, no. 1 (2009): 3-13.

Weiss, Laura B. "Canada Links Libraries with Achievement." *School Library Journal* 52, no. 5 (2006): 19.

Whelan, Debra Lau. "13,000 Kids Can't Be Wrong." *School Library Journal*, 2004.

———. "Up, Up, and Away: How a Group of Researchers is Reinventing School Libraries." *School Library Journal*, 2010: 32-36.

White, Herbert S. "Cost-Effectiveness and Cost-Benefit Determinations in Special Libraries." *Special Libraries* 70, no. 4 (1979): 163-169.

Whitehall, Tom. "Value in Library and Information Management: A Review." *Library Management* 16, no. 4 (1995): 3-11.

Whitmire, Ethelene. "Academic Library Performance Measures and Undergraduates' Library Use and Educational Outcomes." *Library and Information Science Research* 24 (2002): 107-128.

———. "The Relationship Between Undergraduates' Background Characteristics and College Experiences and Their Academic Library Use." *College and Research Libraries* 62, no. 6 (2001): 528-540.

Wiegand, W. A. "The Rich Potential of Public School Library History: Research Needs and Opportunities for Historians of Education and Librarianship." *Librarians and the Cultural Record* 42, no. 1 (2007): 57-74.

Wiggins, Grant P. *Educative Assessment: Designing Assessments to Inform and Improve Student Performance.* San Francisco: Jossey-Bass, 1998.

Wilson, Concepcion S., and Carol Tenopir. "Local Citation Analysis, Publishing and Reading Patterns: Using Multiple Methods to Evaluate Faculty Use of an Academic Library's Research Collection." *Journal of the American Society for Information Science and Technology* 59, no. 9 (2008): 1393-1408.

Wilson, Despina Dapias, Theresa Del Tufo, and Anne E.C. Norman. *The Measure of Library Excellence: Linking the Malcolm Baldrige Criteria and Balanced Scorecard Methods to Assess Service Quality.* Jefferson, North Carolina: McFarland and Company, 2008.

Wilson, Richard M S, Joan Stenson, and Charles Oppenheim. *Valuation of Information Assets.* Research Report, Loughborough University, 2000.

Wimmer, Ulla. "What do Higher Education Management and Administration Expect of Library Benchmarking?" *Performance Measurement and Metrics* 10, no. 2 (2009): 116-121.

Winning, M. A., and C. A. Beverley. "Clinical Librarianship: A Systematic Review of the Literature." *Health and Information Libraries Journal* 20 (2003): 10-21.

Winterman, Vivienne, Christine Smith, and Angela Abell. "Impact of Information on Decision Making in Government Departments." *Library Management* 19, no. 2 (1998): 110-132.

Wisconsin Technology Council. *The Economic Value of Academic Research and Development in Wisconsin.* Wisconsin Technology Council, 2009.

http://www.wisconsinangelnetwork.com/documents/academic_r&d_report.pdf (accessed May 10, 2010).

Wolff, R. A. "Using the Accreditation Process to Transform the Mission of the Library." In *Information Technology and the Remaking of the University Library*, edited by Beverly P. Lynch, 77-91. San Francisco: Jossey-Bass, 1995.

Woodruff, R. B. "Customer Value: The Next Source for Competitive Advantage." *Journal of Academy of Marketing Science* 25, no. 2 (1997): 139-153.

Worrell, Diane. "The Learning Organization: Management Theory for the Information Age or New Age Fad?" *Journal of Academic Librarianship*, 1995: 351-357.

York, Sherry. "Elbowing in on the Evaluation Process." *Library Media Connection* 22, no. 5 (2004): 38-40.

Zeithaml, Valarie A. "Consumer Perceptions of Price, Quality, and Value: A Means-End Model of Synthesis Evidence." *Journal of Marketing* 52 (1988): 2-22.

Zhang, Liang. "Do Measures of College Quality Matter? The Effect of College Quality on Graduates' Earnings." *Review of Higher Education* 28, no. 4 (2005): 571-596.

Zhong, Ying, and Johanna Alexander. "Academic Success: How Library Services Make a Difference." *ACRL 13th National Conference Proceedings*. Chicago, Illinois: American Library Association, 2007.

ACKNOWLEDGEMENTS

The author would like to thank Patricia Owen, Leah Sopchak, Anna Dahlstein, and Tamika Barnes for their contributions to this work, particularly in the area of school, public, and special libraries respectively. Extra appreciation goes to Patricia Owen who edited the work repeatedly. Finally, the author appreciates the assistance of George Kuh, Bruce Kingma, Martha Kyrillidou, Debra Gilchrist, Joe Matthews, Steve Hiller, and the ACRL Board for reading early drafts, as well as all the other fantastic librarians who helped along the way.

Outcomes
- ☐ Define library outcomes in the context of institutional mission.
- ☐ Map library outcomes to institutional, department, and student affairs outcomes as well as accreditation guidelines.

Data Management
- ☐ Create a library assessment plan.
- ☐ Conduct an institutional impact audit (Oakleaf, Are They Learning? 2011).
- ☐ Conduct an existing data audit.
- ☐ Develop or purchase an assessment management system.
- ☐ Populate the assessment management system with outcomes and available data.
- ☐ Develop systems to track individual user behavior (after removing personally identifiable information from data to protect user privacy).
- ☐ Organize and present assessment results in ways that resonate with stakeholders (MacEachern 2001).

Student Enrollment
- ☐ Collect data demonstrating the library's role in recruiting prospective students and matriculating admitted students.

Student Retention and Graduation Rates
- ☐ Collect data demonstrating the library's role in retaining students until graduation.
- ☐ Pair institutional retention and graduation data with academic library data (e.g., NCES IPEDS data, National Student Clearinghouse data, Academic Library Survey data).

Student Success
- ☐ Collect data demonstrating the library's role in helping students do well in internships, secure job placements, earn salaries, gain acceptance to graduate/professional schools, or obtain marketable skills.

Student Achievement
- ☐ Collect data demonstrating the library's role in contributing to student GPA or professional/educational test scores.
- ☐ Conduct test audits; identify test items that measure information literacy skills.

Student Learning
- ☐ Collect data demonstrating the library's role in producing student learning.
- ☐ Conduct "help" studies targeting various user groups.
- ☐ Review course and co-curricular content to analyze the integration of library services and resources into student learning environments.

☐ Use products like MINES for Libraries to determine what library services and resources enable students to do.

☐ Participate in higher education assessment initiatives like the AAC&U VALUE rubric assessment project.

☐ Assess student learning using authentic, integrated, performance assessments—with results recorded and organized in assessment management systems.

Student Experience, Attitude, and Perception of Quality

☐ Collect data demonstrating the library's role in improving student experiences, attitudes, and perceptions of quality.

☐ Integrate library services and resources into high-impact practices.

☐ Augment national engagement surveys with information literacy or library questions.

☐ Augment senior and alumni surveys with information literacy or library questions (MacEachern 2001).

Faculty Research Productivity

☐ Collect data demonstrating the library's role in supporting faculty research productivity.

☐ Investigate the library's role in assisting faculty to gain tenure and higher education professionals to attain promotion.

☐ Use products like MINES for Libraries to determine what library services and resources enable faculty to do.

Faculty Grants

☐ Collect data demonstrating the library's role in developing faculty grant proposals.

☐ Conduct citation analysis of institutional grant proposals focusing on the role of the library in providing cited resources.

Faculty Teaching

☐ Collect data demonstrating the library's role in enriching faculty teaching.

☐ Document integration of library services and resources into faculty teaching (e.g., guest lectures, online tutorials, and LibGuides) and collaborations with faculty on curriculum, assignment, and assessment design.

Institutional Reputation or Prestige

☐ Collect data demonstrating the library's role in augmenting institutional reputation or prestige.

☐ Document how library services and resources help recruit faculty, earn awards, impact institutional rank, and support institutional engagement in service to their communities.

Library and Institutional Leaders
- ☐ Establish a culture of assessment (Lakos and Phipps 2004); use evidence-based decision making (Hiller and Self 2004).
- ☐ Communicate clear expectations regarding assessment (Keeling, et al. 2008, 94).
- ☐ Integrate assessment into planning, budget, and reward structures.
- ☐ Communicate how the library and information literacy fits into broader strategic initiatives (Saunders, Future of Information Literacy 2009, 110).
- ☐ Dedicate assessment personnel.
- ☐ Provide resources for assessment efforts and professional development.
- ☐ Create regular collaborative opportunities for employees from different units (Keeling, et al. 2008, 94).
- ☐ Communicate assessment results to stakeholders.

Higher Education Conversations
- ☐ Participate in Tuning USA, NILOA, VSA, VFA, U-CAN, and AHELO initiatives.
- ☐ Attend and present at higher education assessment conferences; publish in higher education assessment journals.
- ☐ Provide liaison librarian services to key institutional decision makers.
- ☐ Engage in institutional accreditation processes.
- ☐ Work to infuse information literacy into accreditation guidelines.
- ☐ Encourage academic library journals to become indexed in databases that include higher education literature and vice versa.
- ☐ Encourage academic library conferences to include presentations and proceedings in library literature databases.

Financial Perspective
- ☐ Collect evidence to demonstrate excellent management of financial resources.
- ☐ Demonstrate financial value of services and resources (e.g., special collections).
- ☐ Capture library value data that can be expressed in financial terms (e.g., grant funding or faculty time saved).

Professional Development
- ☐ Inventory librarian assessment skills (Oakleaf, Are They Learning? 2011).
- ☐ Encourage attendance at ACRL Assessment Immersion or the ARL Library Assessment Conference.
- ☐ Engage in professional development (e.g., invite consultants, participate in webinars, and establish assessment resource collections).
- ☐ Replicate research on library value included in this report.
- ☐ Investigate areas of library value included the Research Agenda.

Brophy, Peter. *Measuring Library Performance: Principles and Techniques.* London: Facet, 2006.

Dugan, Robert E., Peter Hernon, and Danuta A. Nitecki. *Viewing Library Metrics from Different Perspectives: Inputs, Outputs, and Outcomes.* Santa Barbara, California.: Libraries Unlimited, 2009.

Hernon, Peter, Robert E. Dugan, and Candy Schwartz. *Revisiting Outcomes Assessment in Higher Education.* Westport, Connecticut: Libraries Unlimited, 2006.

Keeling, Richard P., Andrew F. Wall, Ric Underhile, and Gwendolyn J. Dungy. *Assessment Reconsidered: Institutional Effectiveness for Student Success.* International Center for Student Success and Institutional Accountability, 2008.

Markless, Sharon, and David Streatfield. *Evaluating the Impact of Your Library.* London: Facet, 2006.

Matthews, Joseph R. *The Evaluation and Measurement of Library Services.* Westport, Connecticut: Libraries Unlimited, 2007.

Matthews, Joseph R. *Library Assessment in Higher Education.* Westport, Connecticut: Libraries Unlimited, 2007.

Oakleaf, Megan. "Are They Learning? Are We? Learning Outcomes and the Academic Library." *Library Quarterly* 81, no. 1 (2011). Forthcoming.

Oakleaf, Megan. "Writing Information Literacy Assessment Plans: A Guide to Best Practice." *Communications in Information Literacy* 3, no. 2 (2010): 80-90.

Radcliff, Carolyn J., Mary Lee Jensen, Joseph A. Salem Jr., Kenneth J. Burhanna, and Julie A. Gedeon. *A Practical Guide to Information Literacy Assessment for Academic Librarians.* Westport, Connecticut: Libraries Unlimited, 2007.

Rubin, Rhea Joyce. *Demonstrating Results: Using Outcome Measurement in Your Library.* Chicago: American Library Association, 2006.

ABOUT ACRL

The Association of College and Research Libraries (ACRL) is the largest division of the American Library Association (ALA), representing more than 12,000 academic and research librarians and interested individuals. ACRL is the only individual membership organization in North America that develops programs, products and services to meet the unique needs of academic and research librarians. Its initiatives enable the higher education community to understand the role that academic libraries play in the teaching, learning, and research environments.

ACRL is the source for standards and guidelines on academic libraries, producing standards and guidelines to help libraries, academic institutions, and accrediting agencies understand the components of an excellent library. The association stands at the forefront of issues such as information literacy, scholarly communication, and the value of academic libraries and actively advocates for libraries in the legislative process.

ACRL's sections, chapters, discussion groups, and interest groups provide a wealth of opportunities for members to network and share ideas. The association's publications and professional development programs keep academic and research library community up-to-date on trends and issues facing the profession and higher education.

The ACRL awards program honors the best and brightest stars of academic librarianship. More than twenty awards recognize and honor the professional contributions and achievements of ACRL members.

ACRL is on the Web at http://www.acrl.org/, Twitter at @ala_acrl, and Facebook at http://www.facebook.com/ala.acrl.